I0831441

THE ALEXIAD

VOLUME ONE OF TWO

The Alexiad
Komnene, Anna 1083 – 1153
Translated by Elizabeth Dawes
Published by Kegan Paul, Trench,
Trübner & Co., in 1928
Dawes, Elizabeth 1864 – 1954

Text set in 18 point Helvetica.
Chapter headings set in Helvetica Neue.

ISBN: 978-1-83412-410-0 Volume One
ISBN: 978-1-83412-411-7 Volume Two

THE ALEXIAD

VOLUME ONE OF TWO

ANNA KOMNENE

Translated by
Elizabeth A. S. Dawes

GRAND TYPE CLASSICS

CONTENTS

VOLUME ONE

VOLUME TWO

INTRODUCTION

THE "ALEXIAD" of Anna Comnena has long been used as a source of information by historians of the Byzantine Empire and by writers on the First Crusade, and numerous extracts from it have been quoted and translated, yet a complete English translation of it has not been published before.

It was to supply what appeared to me a regrettable omission that I attempted to fill the gap and, as I proceeded with the work, I became more and more interested, for the book gives a picture of wonderful mental and physical energy in the person of its hero, the Emperor Alexius, and helps us to realize the enormous difficulties which confronted a Byzantine Emperor at this period.

Readers of Sir Walter Scott's Count Robert of Paris may also be glad to have a full translation of a work to which he so often alludes.

The present translation is not a free adaptation of the original but is as literal as a translation can well be; hence there is much repetition of words and phrases, for I have striven to reproduce Anna's style as far as possible.

The text on which I have based my version is that of Aug. Reifferscheid in the Teubner edition of 1884.

The proper names (with the exception of those which have acquired a definite English form) I have in most cases transliterated exactly and then added in a footnote the spelling of them as found in Bury's edition of Gibbon, e.g. Apelchasem = Abul-kassim.

I have dispensed with an historical introduction in view of the fact that the

Oxford University Press is shortly publishing a book by Mrs. Georgina Buckler, Ph.D., entitled Anna Comnena : a Study, which deals exhaustively with the chief points of interest raised by the Alexiad.

In conclusion, I wish to acknowledge my deep indebtedness to Professor F. H. Marshall, for he looked over my work in manuscript, and gave me many valuable suggestions and kind help in the elucidation of difficulties. And I must also express my grateful thanks to my sister, Mary C. Dawes, M.A., for her patient help in the revision and in the perusal of the proof-sheets.

– Elizabeth A. S. Dawes.

PREFACE

1. TIME IN ITS IRRESISTIBLE and ceaseless flow carries along on its flood all created things, and drowns them in the depths of obscurity, no matter if they be quite unworthy of mention, or most noteworthy and important, and thus, as the tragedian says, "he brings from the darkness all things to the birth, and all things born envelops in the night."[1]

But the tale of history forms a very strong bulwark against the stream of time, and to some extent checks its irresistible flow,

1 Sophocles Ajax, 646

and, of all things done in it, as many as history has taken over, it secures and binds together, and does not allow them to slip away into the abyss of oblivion.

Now, I recognized this fact. I, Anna, the daughter of two royal personages, Alexius and Irene, born and bred in the purple. I was not ignorant of letters, for I carried my study of Greek to the highest pitch, and was also not unpractised in rhetoric; I perused the works of Aristotle and the dialogues of Plato carefully, and enriched my mind by the "quaternion" of learning. (I must let this out and it is not bragging to state what nature and my zeal for learning have given me, and the gifts which God apportioned to me at birth and time has contributed).

However, to resume - I intend in this writing of mine to recount the deeds done by my father so they should certainly not be lost in silence, or swept away, as it were, on the current of time into the sea of forgetfulness, and I shall recount not only his achievements as Emperor, But also the services he rendered to various Emperors before he himself received the sceptre.

2. These deeds I am going to relate, not in order to shew off my proficiency in letters, but that matters of such importance should not be left unattested for future generations. For even the greatest of deeds, if not haply preserved in written words and handed down to remembrance, become extinguished in the obscurity of silence.

Now, my father, as the actual facts prove, knew both how to command and how to obey the rulers within reasonable limits. And though I have chosen to narrate his doings, yet I fear that the tongues of suspicion and detraction will whisper that writing my father's history is only self laudation and that the historical facts and any praise I bestow on them, are mere falsehoods and empty panegyric. Again, on the other hand, if he himself were to supply the materials, and facts themselves force me to censure some of his actions, not because of him, but from the very nature of the deed, I dread the scoffers who will cast Noah's son. Ham, in my teeth, for they look at everything askew, and owing to their malice and envy, do not discern dearly what is right, but will "blame the blameless "as Homer says. But he who undertakes the "role" of an historian must sink his personal likes and dislikes, and often award the highest praise to his enemies when their actions demand it, and often, too, blame his nearest relations if their errors require it. He must never shirk either blaming his friends or praising his enemies. I should counsel both parties, those attacked by us and our partisans alike, to take comfort from the fact that I have sought the evidence of the actual deeds themselves, and the testimony of those who have seen the actions, and the men and their actions–the fathers of some of the men now living, and the grandfathers of others were actual eye-witnesses.

3. The reason which finally determined me to write my father's history was the following. My lawful husband was the Caesar Nicephorus, a scion of the clan of the Bryennii, a man who far outshone his contemporaries by his surpassing beauty, his superior intelligence, and his accurate speech. To look at him, or to listen to him, was a pure delight. But I must not let my tale wander from its path, so for the present let us keep to the main story. My husband, as I said, was most remarkable in every way; he accompanied my brother John, the Emperor, on several other expeditions against the barbarians ... as well as on the one against . . . who held the city of Antioch. As Nicephorus could not abide neglecting his literary work, he wrote several excellent monographs even during times of stress and trouble. But his task of predilection was that enjoyed by the Queen, to wit, a compilation of the history of the reign of Alexius, Emperor of the Romans, and my

father, and to set out the doings of his reign in books whenever opportunity granted him a short respite from strife and warfare, and the chance of turning his mind to his history, and literary studies. Moreover, he approached this subject from an earlier period (for in this detail too he obeyed the will of our mistress), and starting from Diogenes,[2] Emperor of the Romans, he worked down to the man about whom he had himself purposed to write.

At the accession of Diogenes my father had just entered upon his brilliant youth and before this was not even a full-grown boy, and had done nothing worthy of recording, unless, forsooth, the deeds of his childhood were made the theme of a panegyric.

Such then was the Caesar's intention as his own writing shews; but his hopes were not fulfilled, and he did not complete his history. He brought it down to the

2 Romanus IV Diogenes

Emperor Nicephorus (III) Botaniates, and opportunity forbade his carrying it further, thus causing loss to the events he meant to describe, and depriving his readers of a great pleasure. For this reason, I myself undertook to chronicle my father's doings, that the coming generations should not overlook deeds of such importance.

Now, the harmonious structure and great charm of the Caesar's writings are well-known to all who have chanced to take a look at his books. However, as I have already mentioned, when he had got as far as my father's reign, and sketched out a draft of it, and brought it back to us half-finished from abroad, he also, alas! brought back with him a fatal disease. This was induced, maybe, by the endless discomfort of a soldier's life, or by his over-many expeditions, or again, from his overwhelming anxiety about us, for worrying was innate in him, and his troubles were incessant. In addition to these causes, the varieties and severities of climate experienced, all contributed to mix the fatal draught for him. For he started hence on an expedition against the Syrians and Cilicians when seriously out of health; from Syria he went on ill to the Cilicians, from them to the Pamphylians, from the Pamphylians to the Lydians, and Lydia sent him on to Bithynia, who finally returned him to us and to the Queen of cities suffering from an internal tumour caused by his incessant sufferings. Yet, ill as he was, he was anxious to tell the tragic story of his adventures, but was unable to do so, partly because of his disease, and partly because we forbade it through fear that the effort of talking might cause the tumour to burst.

4. Having written so far, dizziness overwhelms my soul, and tears blind my eyes. Oh! what a counsellor the Roman Empire has lost! Oh, for his accurate understanding of affairs, all of which he had gained from experience! And his knowledge of literature, and his varied acquaintance

with both native and foreign learning! Think, too, of the grace of his figure and beauty of face, which would have befitted not only a king, as the saying goes, but even a more powerful, nay, a divine person!

To turn to myself–I have been conversant with dangers ever since my birth "in the purple," so to say; and fortune has certainly not been kind to me, unless you were to count it a smile of kind fortune to have given me "emperors" as parents, and allowing me to be born "in the purple room," for all the rest of my life has been one long series of storms and revolutions. Orpheus, indeed, could move stones, trees, and all inanimate nature, by his singing; Timotheus, too, the flute-player, by piping an "orthian" tune to Alexander, incited the Macedonian thereby to snatch up his arms and sword; lout the tale of my woes would not cause a movement in place, nor rouse men to arms and war, but they would move the hearer to tears, and compel sympathy from animate, and even inanimate, nature. Verily, my grief for my Caesar and his unexpected death have touched my inmost soul, and the wound has pierced to the profoundest depths of my being. All previous misfortunes compared with this insatiable calamity I count literally as a single small drop compared with this Atlantic Ocean, this turbulent Adriatic Sea of trouble: they were, methinks, but preludes to this, mere smoke and heat to forewarn me of this fiery furnace and indescribable blaze; the small daily sparks foretold this terrible conflagration. Oh! thou fire which, though unfed, dost reduce my heart to ashes! Thou burnest and art ever kept alight in secret, yet dost not consume. Though thou scorchest my heart thou givest me the outward semblance of being unburnt, though thy fingers of fire have gripped me even to the marrow of my bones, and to the dividing of my soul! However, I see that I have let my feelings carry me away from my subject, but the mention of my Caesar and my grief for him have instilled devastating sorrow into me.

Now I will wipe away my tears and recover myself from my sorrow and continue my task, and thus in the words of the tragedian; "I shall have double cause for tears, as a woman who in misfortune remembers former misfortune."[3] To have as my object the publication of the life of so great and virtuous a King will be a reminder of his wondrous achievements, and these force me to shed warm tears, and the whole world will weep with me. For to recall him, and make his reign known, will be a subject of lamentation to me, but will also serve to remind others of the loss they have sustained.

Now I must begin my father's history at some definite point, and the best point will be that from which my narrative can be absolutely clear and based on fact.

---

3 Euripides, Hecuba 518

BOOK ONE

From Alexius' Youth to the Last Months of Botaniates' Reign

CHAPTER ONE

THE EMPEROR ALEXIUS, who was also my father, had been of great service to the Roman Empire even before he reached the throne, for he started campaigning as early as during the reign of Romanus Diogenes. Amongst his contemporaries he shewed himself remarkable, and a great lover of danger. In his fourteenth year he was anxious to join the Emperor Diogenes on the extremely arduous campaign he was conducting against the Persians, and by this very longing he declared his animosity against the barbarians, and shewed that, if he ever should come to blows with them, he would make his sword drunk with their blood; of such a warlike temper was the boy . However, on that occasion the Emperor Diogenes did not allow him to accompany him, as a heavy sorrow had befallen Alexius' mother, for she was then mourning the death of her firstborn son, Manuel, a man who had done great and admirable deeds for his country. In order that she might not be quite inconsolable, for she did not yet know where she had buried the elder of her sons, and if she sent the younger to the war, she would be afraid of something untoward happening to the lad, and might not even know in what part of the world he fell, for these reasons he compelled the boy Alexius to return to his mother. So on that occasion he was indeed parted from his fellow-soldiers, though sorely against his will, but the future opened out to him countless opportunities for valiant deeds; for under the Emperor Michael Ducas, after the deposition of the Emperor Diogenes, he shewed of what mettle he was made in his war against Ursel[4].

Now this man was a Frank by birth who had been enrolled in the Roman Army, reached a high pitch of prosperity, and after gathering a band, or rather quite a considerable army, of men from his own country, and also of other races, he immediately became a formidable tyrant. For when the hegemony of the Romans had received several checks, and the luck of the Turks was in the ascendancy,

---

4 Roussel of Bailleul, a Norman mercenary who proclaimed his independence in 1073

and the Romans had been driven back like dust shaken from their feet, at that moment this man too attacked the Empire. Apart from his tyrannical nature, what more especially incited him to openly establishing his tyranny just then was the depressed state of the imperial affairs, and he laid waste nearly all the Eastern provinces.

Although many were entrusted with the war against him, men of high reputation for bravery and of very great knowledge of war and fighting, yet he openly baffled even their long experience. For sometimes he would take the offensive himself and rout his opponents by his meteor-like attacks, and at others he obtained help from the Turks, and was quite irresistible in his onrushes, so that he actually overpowered some of the most powerful chieftains, and utterly confounded their phalanxes. I At that time, my father Alexius was under his brother, and openly served as lieutenant under this man, who was invested with the command of all the armies, both of the East and the West.

Then, just when the affairs of the Romans were in this critical condition, with this barbarian rushing upon everything like a thunderbolt, my brilliant father Alexius was thought of as the one man able to resist him, and appointed absolute commander by the Emperor Michael. Accordingly he summoned up all his shrewdness and the experience he had gained as general and soldier, and that too, by the way, he had not had much time to gather. (But thanks to his exceeding love of industry and ever alert intellect, the picked men among the Romans considered him to have reached the acme of military experience, and regarded him as that famous Roman Aemilius, or Scipio, or Hannibal the Carthaginian, for he was quite young, and had still "the first down on his cheeks" as the saying goes). This youngman captured Ursel as he rushed with might against the Romans and restored the affairs of the East within the space of a few days; for he was quick at discovering what was expedient, and still quicker in executing it. The manner of his capturing Ursel is told at length by the Caesar in the second book of his history of his own times; but I will relate it too in as far as it concerns my history.

CHAPTER TWO

THE BARBARIAN TUTACH[5] had just then come down with a considerable army from the depths of the East to ravage the Roman territory. Ursel was often hard pressed by the general, and losing one fortress after another in spite of his large army and his men being excellently and generously equipped, because in ingenuity he was far surpassed by my father Alexius, and he therefore determined to seek refuge for a

5 or "Tutush"

time with Tutach.

Finally, in absolute despair, he arranged a meeting with Tutach, offered him friendship, and earnestly solicited him to form an alliance. However, the general Alexius met this by a counter-stratagem, and was the quicker in winning over the barbarian, and attracting him to his side by words and gifts and every means and device. For he was inventive beyond ordinary men, and could find a way out of the most impossible situations. Certainly the most effective of his methods for conciliating Tutach was, speaking broadly, a kind of offering the right hand of friendship; his words were these; "The two, your Sultan and my Emperor, are friends! This barbarian Ursel is lifting his hand against both, and he is a most dangerous foe to both, for he keeps on attacking the latter, and is always stealing away a bit here and there from the Roman Empire, and, on the other hand, he is robbing Persia of parts of Persia which might have been preserved to her. In all this he uses great art, for at present he is overshadowing me by your help, and then later, at a propitious moment, he will leave me when he thinks himself secure, and turn round again and attack you. So if you will listen to me, you should, when Ursel next comes to you, seize him with superior numbers and send him captive to us. If you do this," he continued, "you will gain three things: firstly, such a sum of money as no one ever gained before; secondly, you will win in addition the goodwill of the Emperor; and as a result you will quickly reach the acme of prosperity; and thirdly, your Sultan will be greatly pleased at the removal of so formidable a foe, who practised violence against Romans and Turks alike." This was the tenor of the despatch sent to the aforementioned Tutach by my father, at that time Commander-in-Chief of the Roman Army. Together with it he also sent some members of the noblest families as hostages; and at an agreed moment and for a sum of money, he persuaded Tutach's barbarian followers to seize Ursel; and this they did quickly, and after his capture he was forwarded to the General at Amaseia.

But in the meantime the money was slow to come in, for Alexius himself had no fund wherewith to pay it off, and the sums due from the Emperor did not arrive, consequently, it did not only "journey at slow speed,"[6] as the tragedian says, but it did not come at all! Tutach's followers meanwhile were insistent in their demands for the money promised or for the surrender of the man they had sold and said that he should be allowed to return to the place where he had been seized; and my father had no means of paying the purchase-price. After spending a whole night in the greatest perplexity, he decided to borrow the sum from the inhabitants of Amaseia.

---

6 Eurpides

At the break of day, though it was a hard task, he summoned them all, especially the most influential and the richest men, and fixing his eyes on them chiefly, he said; "You all know how this barbarian has treated all the cities of the Armenian theme, how many villages he has sacked, upon how many persons he has inflicted intolerable atrocities, and how much money he has stolen from you. But now the moment has come for freeing yourselves from his ill-treatment if you wish. Accordingly we must not let him slip, for you see, I suppose, that, by the will of God above all and by our own energy, this barbarian is now our prisoner. But Tutach, his captor, is asking us for payment, and we are utterly penniless, for we are in a foreign country, have been fighting against the barbarian for a considerable time, and have spent all our income. If the Emperor had not been so far off, or the barbarian had granted us respite, I should have endeavoured to have the money fetched from the capital; but since, as you yourselves know, nothing of this is practicable, it is you who must contribute this money, and whatever you subscribe, shall be repaid you from the Emperor at my hands." No sooner had he said this than he was hooted and his words excited a terrible uproar, for the Amaseians were moved to rebellion. Certain evilly-disposed and daring fellows who were clever agitators stirred up this tumult.

A great confusion thereupon arose, for one part insisted that Ursel should be kept prisoner, and stirred up the multitude to lay hold of him, while the other party made a great noise (as is ever the case with a mixed rabble), and wished to seize Ursel, and free him from his chains. The General, seeing so large a mob raging, recognized that his affairs were indeed in a parlous state, yet he was in no wise cast down, but taking courage, quieted the multitude with his hand. After a long time and with difficulty he silenced them, and addressing the mob, he said: “I marvel, men of Amaseia, that you are so utterly blind to the machinations of these men who deceive you, and purchase their own safety with your blood, and continually cause you some hurt. For of what benefit is Ursel’s tyranny to you, unless you count murders and mutilations and the maiming of limbs as such? Now these men, the authors of your calamities, have kept their own fortunes intact by paying court to the barbarian on the one hand, and on the other they have received a glut of gifts from the Emperor by representing to him that they had not surrendered you and the town to the barbarian; and that too though they have never yet taken any account of you. For this reason they wish to support Ursel’s tyranny, so that by fawning upon him with good wishes they may preserve their own skins intact, and also demand honours and emoluments from the Emperor. Should, however, any revolt occur, they will again keep themselves out of the business, and kindle the Emperor's wrath against you. But if you will follow my advice, you will bid these stirrers-up of sedition now go hang. Return quietly to your respective homes, reflect on my proposition, and thus you will recognize who is counselling you to your best advantage."

CHAPTER THREE

ON HEARING THESE WORDS, they changed their minds as quickly as "heads become tails," and went home. But the General, well aware that a crowd is wont to change its mind in a twinkling, especially if urged on by malicious men, feared that during the night they might come upon him with fell intent, fetch out Ursel from prison, release him from his bonds, and let him go. As his forces were insufficient to resist such an attack, he devised the following Palamedian plan:[7] he pretended to have Ursel apparently blinded. Ursel was laid flat on the ground, the executioner applied the iron, while the victim howled and groaned like a lion roaring; but all this was only a feint of depriving him of his sight, for he who apparently was being blinded had been ordered to shout and shriek, and he who seemingly was gouging out the eyes, to stare harshly at his prisoner on the ground, and do everything savagely, and yet only to act the blinding. And so Ursel was blinded, yet not blinded, and the rabble clapped their hands, and the blinding of Ursel was buzzed about everywhere. This bit of play-acting persuaded the whole multitude, natives and foreigners alike, to swarm in like bees to pay their contributions, For the whole point of Alexius' device was that those who

---

7 Palamedes had outwitted Odysseus

were disinclined to give money, and plotted to rescue Ursel from Alexius' my father's hands, should be foiled in their expectations, as he had now made their plot futile; and, in consequence, failing in their plan of the previous day, would adopt his plan, making him their friend, and averting the Emperor's wrath. Thus the; admirable commander, having got Ursel into his power, kept him like a lion in a cage, with bandages still over his eyes as symbol of his supposed blinding. Even so, he was not satisfied with what had been accomplished, nor did he relax over the rest of the business, as if he had gained sufficient glory, but he annexed several more cities and fortresses and placed under the protection of the Emperor those which had I fared badly during Ursel's regime. Then he turned his horse's head, and rode straight to the Royal City. But when he had reached his grandfather's city he allowed himself and the whole army a short rest from their many labours, and after that he manifested as marvellous a deed as Heracles did in the rescue of Admetus' wife, Alcestis.

For a certain Docianus nephew of the former Emperor, Isaac Comnenus and, cousin of this Alexius (a man too of good standing, both by birth and worth), seeing Ursel bearing the marks of blinding, and led by the hand, heaved a deep sigh, burst into tears over him and denounced the General's cruelty. Yea, he heaped blame upon him, and upbraided him for taking the sight of such a noble fellow and a downright hero, whom he ought to have left unpunished. To this Alexius answered; at the time, "My dear friend, wait a bit, and you shall hear the reasons for his blinding"; and in a little he took him; and Ursel into a small room, uncovered the latter's face and shewed him Ursel's eyes gleaming fierily. At this sight, Docianus was struck .dumb with amazement, and did not know what to make of this miracle. He repeatedly applied his hands to Ursel's eyes in case what he had seen was only a dream perchance, or a magic portent, or some other new invention of the kind; but when he grasped, the kindness his cousin had shewn to the man and the artfulness combined with the kindness he was overjoyed, and embraced and kissed him repeatedly, changing his wonder into joy. And the Emperor Michael, and his suite, and indeed everybody, felt just the same about it.

CHAPTER FOUR

AFTERWARDS, the Emperor Nicephorus (Botaniates) who had now obtained the throne, sent him away again - to the West this time, against Nicephorus Bryennius, who was upseting the whole of the West by putting the crown on his own head, and proclaiming himself Emperor of the Romans. For scarcesly had Michael Ducas been deposed, and adopted the high-priestly alb and humeral in place of the imperial diadem and cloak, than Botaniates took his place on the imperial throne, married the princess Maria (as I will relate more circumstantially further on), and undertook the management of the Kingdom. But Nicephorus Bryennius, on the other hand, who had been appointed Duke of Dyrrachium in the time of the Emperor Michael, had designs on the throne even before Nicephorus became Emperor, and meditated a revolt against Michael. The "why" and "wherefore" of this I need not relate, as his revolt has previously been recounted in the Caesar's history. And yet it is absolutely necessary for me to narrate briefly how he used Dyrrachium as a jumping-off place for over-running all the Western provinces, how he brought them under his sway, and also the manner of his capture. But anyone who wishes for details of this revolt we refer to the Caesar. Bryennius was a very clever warrior, as well as of most illustrious descent, conspicuous by height of stature, and beauty of face, and preeminent among his fellows by the weightiness of his judgment, and the strength of his arms. He was, indeed, a man fit for kingship, and his persuasive powers, and his skill in conversation, were such as to draw all to him even at first sight; consequently, by unanimous consent both of soldiers and civilians, he was accorded the first place and deemed worthy to rule over both the Eastern and Western dominions. On his approaching any town, it would receive him with suppliant hands, and send him on to the next with acclaim. Not only Botaniates was disturbed by this news, but it also created a ferment in the home-army, and reduced the whole kingdom to despair; and, consequently, it was decided to dispatch my father, Alexius Comnenus, lately elected "Domestic of the Schools," against Bryennius with all available forces. In these regions the fortunes of the Roman Empire had sunk to their lowest ebb. For the armies of the East were dispersed in all directions, because the Turks had overspread, and gained command of, nearly all the countries between the Euxine Sea[8] and the Hellespont, and the Aegean and Syrian Seas, and the various bays, especially those which wash Pamphylia, Cilicia, and empty themselves into the Egyptian Sea. Such was the position of the Eastern armies, whilst in the West, so many legions had flocked to Bryennius' standard that the Roman Empire was left with quite a small and inadequate army. There still remained to her a few "Immortals" who had only recently grasped spear and sword, and a few soldiers from Coma, and a Celtic regiment, that had shrunk to a small number of men. These were given to Alexius, my father, and at the same time allied troops were called for from the Turks, and the Emperor's Council

8 Black Sea

ordered Alexius to start and engage in battle with Bryennius, for he relied not so much on the army accompanying him as on the man's ingenuity and cleverness in military matters. Alexius did not wait for the allies as he heard that the enemy was pushing on fast, but armed himself and his army, marched out from the Royal City, and passing through Thrace, pitched his camp without palisades or trenches near the river Halmyrus. For learning that Bryennius was bivouacking in the plains of the Cedoctus, he determined to interpose a considerable distance between his own and the enemy's armies. For he was not able to face Bryennius, for fear that the state of his forces might be detected, and the enemy have an opportunity of observing of what numbers his army consisted. Because he was on the point of fighting with inexperienced against experienced warriors, and with few against many, he abandoned the idea of making a bold and open attack, and intended to win a victory by stealth.

CHAPTER FIVE

SINCE OUR STORY has now placed these two in opposition, Bryennius and. my father, Alexius Comnenus, both brave men (for neither was a whit behind the other in courage, nor did the experience of the one surpass that of the other), it is worth our while to place them in their lines and hostile array, and thence to view the fortune of war. (They certainly were both handsome and brave men, and were their bravery and experience weighed, the balance would stand level; but we must try to understand how fortune inclined it to one side. Bryennius, in addition to his confidence in his forces, was protected by their experience and orderliness, whereas Alexius, on the other hand, centred but few, and those very meagre, hopes on his army, but as counter-defence, could rely on the strength of his scientific knowledge and his strategic device.

Now when they were aware of each other, and the right moment for battle had come, Bryennius, on being informed that Alexius Comnenus had cut off his approaches and was encamped near Calaura, drew up his troops in the following order and marched against him. He posted the main army on the right and left wings, and gave the command of the right to his brother John; the men in this wing numbered 5,000, and were Italians, and those belonging to the detachment of the famous Maniaces, as well as some horse-soldiers from Thessaly, and a detachment, of no mean birth, of the "Hetaireia." The other, the left wing, was led by Catacalon Tarchaniotes, and was composed of fully-armed Macedonians and Thracians, numbering in all about 3,000. Bryennius himself held the centre of the phalanx, consisting of Macedonians and Thracians, and the picked men of the whole nobility. All the Thessalians were on horseback[9], and what with their iron cuirasses and helmets on their heads gleaming brightly, the horses pricking up their ears, and the shields clashing together, such a brilliant light falling from their persons and their helmets caused terror. Bryennius too, circling amidst them like an Ares or Giant, overtopping all the others head and shoulders by an ell, was a sheer wonder, and object of dread to the onlookers. Outside this regular army at about two stades' distance were some allied Scythians, distinguished by barbaric weapons. And the order given was that when the enemy came in sight and the trumpet sounded the attack, the Scythians should at once fall upon them from the rear, and distress the enemy by thick and

9 or "they were all mounted on Thessalian horses"

continuous showers of darts, whilst the rest should form in very close order, and attack with all their might. That was how one general disposed his men. My father, Alexius Comnenus, on his side, after examining the lie of the land, placed half his men in some hollows, and the rest front to front with Bryennius. When both sections, both the hidden and the invisible, were in battle array, he aroused the bravery of them individually by winged words, and enjoined upon the division lying in ambush to attack suddenly, and dash with the greatest possible force and violence against the right wing of the enemy, as soon as they perceived they were to the rear of them. The so-called "Immortals" and some of the Celtic troops he reserved for himself, and took command of them in person. He appointed Catacalon leader of the troops from Coma and the Turkish forces, and bade him pay special attention to the Scythians and to counter their incursions.

Such then were the dispositions of the armies. Now, when Bryennius' army had come near the hollows, then, immediately on my father, Alexius, giving the signal, the men in ambush Jumped out on them with wild yells and war cries. And by the suddenness of their onslaught, each striking and killing those whom he chanced to meet, they threw the enemy into a panic, and compelled them to flight. But John Bryennius, the own brother of the general, mindful hereupon of his "impetuous strength" and courage, turned his horse with his curb, and cutting down at a blow the "Immortal" coming at him, stayed the discomfited phalanx, rallied the men, and drove the enemy off. The "Immortals," in their turn, began to flee headlong in some disorder, and many were cut down by the soldiers who were ever behind them.

Then, my father, hurling himself into the midst of the foe, by his valiant struggles did indeed discomfit just that part in which he happened to be, for he struck anyone who approached him, and laid him low at a blow, but he also hoped that some of his soldiers were following with him and protecting him, and so he kept on fighting desperately. But when he saw that his phalanx was utterly broken, and fleeing in all directions he collected the more courageous souls (who were six in all), and advised them to draw their swords, rush at Bryennius remorselessly, when they got near him, and then, if need be, to die with him. However, a certain Theodotus, a private, who had been my father's servant from childhood, dissuaded him from this plan, characterizing such an attempt as mere foolhardiness. So Alexius turned in the opposite direction, and decided to retire to a short distance from Bryennius' army; then he collected the men personally known to him from the dispersed soldiery, re-organized them, and returned to the work. But before my father could withdraw secretly from the mêlée, the Scythians with many yells and shouts began to harass the men from Coma under Catacalon; and as they had little difficulty in beating these too, and driving them to flight, they turned their minds to looting, and went off on their own devices, for such is the Scythian nation. Before they have even entirely routed their adversary, or consolidated their gain, they spoil their victory by looting. For all the slaves and camp followers who formed the rear of Bryennius' army had pressed forward into the ranks from fear of being killed by the Scythians; and as this crowd was continually augmented by others who had escaped from the hands of the Scythians, no small confusion arose in the ranks, and the standards became commingled. In the meanwhile, my father Alexius, as we said before, was cut off and moving about within Bryennius' army, when he saw one of the royal grooms leading a horse of Bryennius', decked with a purple cloth, and gilt bosses; and moreover, the men holding the large swords which customarily accompany the Emperor were running close beside it. On seeing this he covered his face with his vizor which depended from the rim of his helmet, and rushing with violence against these men with his six soldiers (whom the story has already mentioned), he not only knocked down the groom, but also seized the royal horse, and together with it carried off the swords and then escaped: unnoticed from the army. Arrived in a safe spot he started off the gilt-bedight horse, and the swords which are usually carried either side of the Emperor, and a herald with a very loud voice, bidding him run through the whole army crying out "Bryennius has fallen! This action brought back to the battle from all quarters many of the scattered soldiers belonging to the army of the Great Domestic of the Schools (to wit, my father), and others it encouraged to carry on. They stood still, where each happened to be, and having turned their eyes behind them were astonished at the unexpected sight. And you might have witnessed a strange sight in their case! for the heads of the horses were pointing forwards, whilst their own faces were turned backwards, and they neither moved forwards, nor did they wish to turn their bridles, but were quite aghast, and at their wits' ends to understand what had occurred. As for the Scythians, they were dreaming of going home, and had no intention of further pursuit. As they were now far away from both armies, they wandered vaguely about where they were with their booty. The proclamation that Bryennius had been taken, and overwhelmed, put courage into the whilom cowards and fugitives, and the announcement gained credibility from the fact that the horse was shewn everywhere with its royal accoutrements, and the large swords all but cried aloud that Bryennius, who should be protected by them, had become the possession of the enemy.

CHAPTER SIX

THEN FORTUNE, too, contributed the following incident to Alexius' success. A detachment of the Turkish allies happened upon Alexius, the Great Domestic, and on hearing that he had restored the battle, and asking where the enemy was, they accompanied him, my father, to a little hill, and when my father pointed out the army, they looked down upon it from an observation tower, as it were. And this was the appearance of Bryennius' army; the men were all mixed up anyhow, the lines had not yet been re-formed, and, as if they had already carried off the victory, they were acting carelessly and thought themselves out of danger. And they had slackened off chiefly because after the initial rout of our men, my father's contingent of Franks had gone over to Bryennius. For when the Franks dismounted from their horses and offered their right hands to Bryennius, according to their ancestral custom in giving pledges, men came running up towards them from all sides to see what was happening. For like a trumpet-blast the rumour had resounded throughout the army that the Franks had joined them and deserted their Commander-in-Chief, Alexius. The officers with my father, and the newly-arrived Turks, duly noted this state of confusion, and as a result they divided their forces into three parties and ordered two to remain in ambush somewhere on the spot, and the third they commanded to advance against the foe. The whole of this plan was due to Alexius.

The Turks did not attack all together, drawn up regularly into phalanx, but separately and in small groups, standing some distance apart from each other; then he ordered each squadron to attack, charging the enemy with their horses, and to let loose heavy showers of darts. Following upon the Turks came my father Alexius, the author of this strategy, with as many of his scattered men as the occasion warranted. Next, one of the “Immortals” with Alexius, a hot-headed, venturesome fellow, spurred on his horse, and out-riding the others, dashed at full gallop straight at Bryennius, and thrust his spear with great violence against the latter’s breast. Bryennius for his part whipped out his sword quickly from its sheath, and before the spear could be driven home, he cut it in two, and struck his adversary on the collar bone, and bringing down the blow with the whole power of his arm, cut away the man’s whole arm, breastplate included.

The Turks, too, one group following up another, overshadowed the army with their showers of darts. Bryennius’ men were naturally taken aback by the sudden attack, yet they collected themselves, formed themselves into line, and sustained the shock of the battle, mutually exhorting each other to play the man. The Turks, however, and my father, held their ground for a short time against the enemy, and then planned to retire in regular order to a little distance, in order to lure on the enemy, and draw them by guile to the ambuscade. When they had reached the first ambush, they wheeled round, and met the enemy face to face. Forthwith, at a given signal, those in ambush rode through them like swarms of wasps, from various directions, and with their loud war-cries, and shouts, and incessant shooting, not only filled the ears of Bryennius' men with a terrible din, but also utterly obscured their sight by showering arrows upon them from all sides. Hereupon, as the army of Bryennius could no longer put up any resistance (for by now all, both men and horses, were sorely wounded), they turned their standard to retreat, and offered their backs as a target to their foes. But Bryennius himself, although very weary from fighting, shewed his courage and mettle. For at one minute, he would turn to right or left to strike a pursuer, and at the next, carefully and cleverly arrange the details of the retreat. He was assisted by his brother on the one side, and his son on the other, and by their heroic defence on that occasion they seemed to the enemy miraculous.

As Bryennius' horse was now very weary, and unable either to flee or pursue (in fact, it was pretty well at death's door from continuous coursing), he halted it, and, like some brave athlete, stood ready for the grip, and called a challenge to two highborn Turks. One of these struck at him with his spear, but was not quick enough to give him a heavy blow before receiving a heavier one himself from Bryennius' right hand. For Bryennius with his sword succeeded in cutting off the man's hand, which rolled to the ground, spear and all. The second man leapt off his own horse, and like a panther, darted on to that of Bryennius, and planted himself on its flank, and clung tightly to it, and tried to get on its back. Bryennius kept twisting round like an animal in his endeavours to stab him with his sword. However, he did not succeed, for the Turk behind his back escaped all the blows by bending aside. Therefore, when his right hand was exhausted from only encountering emptiness, and the athlete's strength gave out, he surrendered there and then to the whole body of the enemy. So the soldiers-seized him. and with a feeling of haying won great glory , led him away to Alexius Comnenus, who happened to be standing not, far from the spot where Bryennius was captured, and was busy drawing up his own men, and the Turks, into line, and inciting them to battle. News of Bryennius' capture had already been brought by heralds, and then the man himself was placed before the General, and a terrifying object he certainly was, both when fighting, and when captured. And now, having secured Bryennius in this manner, Alexius Comnenus sent him away as the prize of his spear .to the. Emperor Botaniates, without doing any injury whatsoever to his eyes. For it was not the nature of Alexius to proceed to extremities against his opponents after their capture as he considered that being captured was in itself sufficient punishment, but after their capture he treated them with clemency, friendliness and generosity. This clemency he now displayed towards Bryennius, for after his capture he accompanied him a fair distance, and when they reached the place called ... he said to him (for he was anxious to relieve the man's despondency and restore hope in him); "Let us get off our horses and sit down and rest awhile." But Bryennius, in fear of his life resembled a maniac, and was by no means in need of rest, for how should a man be who has lost all hope of life? And yet he immediately complied with the General's wish, for a slave readily submits to every command, more especially if he is a prisoner of war. When the two leaders had dismounted, Alexius at once lay down on some green grass, as if on a couch, while Bryennius sat further off, and rested his head on the roots of a tall oak. My father slept, but "gentle sleep," as it is called in sweet poetry, did not visit the other.

But lying there he raised his eyes and saw the sword hanging from the branches, and as he did not see anybody about just then, he shook off his despondency, conceived a daring plan and plotted to kill my father. And the thought would quickly have been translated into action, had not some divine power from oh high prevented him, which appeased the fierce emotions of his mind, and forced him to look kindly at the General. I have often heard the latter tell this tale.

Whoever likes may learn from this how God was guarding the Comnenus like a precious object, for a greater dignity, intending by means of him to restore the fortune of the Romans. If later on undesirable things happened to Bryennius, the blame must be laid on certain of the Emperor's courtiers; my father was blameless. Such then was the end of Bryennius' rebellion.

CHAPTER SEVEN

BUT ALEXIUS, the Great Domestic, who was also my father, was not destined to rest in quiet, but to proceed from one struggle to another. On his return, Borilus, a barbarian, and confidant of Botaniates, went out from the city to meet my father, the Great Domestic, and taking over Bryennius from him he did to him that which he did. He also brought an order from the Emperor to my father to proceed against Basilacius, who in his turn had now assumed the diadem, and exactly as Bryennius had done, was making the West seethe with unrest. Now, this man Basilacius, was one of the most conspicuous for bravery, courage, daring, and bodily strength, and as he possessed, moreover, a domineering spirit, he took to himself all the most exalted offices, and as for honours, he plotted for some and demanded others. And after Bryennius' overthrow, this man became, as it were, his successor, and arrogated to himself the whole business of the tyranny. Starting from Epidamnus (the metropolis of Illyria), he pushed on to the chief city of Thessaly, having subdued all the country on his way, and voted and acclaimed himself Emperor, and Bryennius' roving army following him whithersoever he wished. Besides other admirable qualities, this man had that fine physique, strength of arm, and dignified appearance by which rustics and soldiers are most attracted. For they do not look through to the soul, nor have a keen eye for virtue, but they stop at the outward excellencies of the body, and admire daring, and strength, speed in running, and size, and consider these as fit qualifications for the purple robe and diadem.

Now he had these qualities in no mean measure, as well as a manly, invincible soul; in short, this Basilacius was kingly both in mind and appearance. He had a voice like thunder, of a nature to strike fear into a whole army, and his shout was enough to quell the courage of the boldest. Further, his eloquence was irresistible, whether he tried to excite the soldiers to battle or check them in flight.

With all these natural advantages and an unconquerable army under his command, the man started on his campaign, and seized the city of the Thessalians, as we have said. My father, Alexius Comnenus, made his counter-preparations as if for a battle with the mighty Typho, or the hundred-handed Giant, and girt himself for the fray with an antagonist worthy of his steel, by summoning all his strategic knowledge and courageous spirit. And before he had shaken off the dust of his late contest, or washed the gore from his sword and hands, he marched out, his spirit all aflame, like a grim lion against this long-tusked boar, Basilacius. Soon he reached the river Bardarius[10] (for that is its local name), which comes down from the mountains near Mysia, and after flowing through many intervening districts, and dividing the country round Beroea and Thessalonica into East and West, it empties itself into our so-called South sea.

What happens in every large river is this; when a considerable embankment has been raised by the deposit they bring down, then they flow to a lower level, and forsaking as it were their first bed, leave

10 River Vardar

it quite dry and bereft of water, and fill the new bed they now traverse with rushing streams. Between two such channels of the Bardarius, one the old gully, the other the newly-formed passage, lay a piece of ground, and when that clever strategist, Alexius, my father, saw it, he pitched his camp there, since the two channels were not more than three stades distant from one another. The running river he considered, would be a bulwark on the one side, and the old river-bed, which had become a deep ravine from the river's strong current, he utilized as a natural trench. The men were immediately put under orders to rest by day, and strengthen themselves with sleep, and to give their horses a good feed; for as soon as night fell, they would have to watch, and expect a surprise attack by the enemy. My father made these arrangements, I believe, because he foresaw danger from the enemy that evening. He quite expected them to attack him, for either his long experience made him guess this, or he had other reasons for his conjecture. This presentiment had come to him suddenly, nor did he only foresee and then neglect the necessary precautions. No, but he left the camp with his forces and their weapons, horses, and everything needful for battle, and left it with lights shining everywhere and entrusted the camp, with the supplies of food and other equipment he carried with him, to his body-servant "Little John," a former monk. He himself drew off to a good distance with his troops ready armed, and sat down to await the course of events. This was cunningly planned so that Basilacius, when he saw camp fires burning on all sides, and my father's tent illuminated with lamps, should imagine that he was resting inside, and that it would, consequently, be an easy matter to capture him and get him into his power.

CHAPTER EIGHT

AS WE HAVE ALREADY hinted, this presentiment of my father's was not unfounded. For Basilacius came down suddenly upon the army he thought to find with cavalry and infantry (10,000 men in all); there he found the men's quarters lighted up everywhere, and when he saw the General's tent gleaming, he rushed into it with a tremendous, hair-raising shout. But as the man he expected to find was nowhere to be seen, and no soldier or officer turned up anywhere, only a few insignificant camp servants, he shouted still more loudly, and cried out, "Where in the world is the Stammerer?" thus in his words too jeering at the Great Domestic. For, except in one respect, this Alexius, my father, had a very clear utterance, and no one was a better natural orator than he in his arguments and demonstrations, but only over the letter "r" his tongue lisped slightly, and stammered a little, although his enunciation of all the other letters was quite unimpeded. Shouting such insults, Basilacius continued his search, and turned over everything, boxes, couches, furniture, and even my father's bed, to see whether perchance he was hidden anywhere. And he frequently looked at "Little John," the monk so called. Alexius' mother had carefully arranged that he should have one of the better-born monks to share his tent in all his campaigns, and her kindly son had yielded to his mother's wish, not only whilst a child, but even after he had joined the ranks of youths; nay, indeed, until he took to himself a wife. Basilacius searched through the whole tent, and, as Aristophanes would say, did not stop "groping about in darkness,"[11] while asking Little John a stream of questions about the Domestic. On John's asserting that Alexius had gone out with his whole army some time ago, he recognized that he had been grossly tricked, and in utter despair, and with much noise and shouting, he yelled out: "Fellow soldiers, we have been deceived, the enemy is outside." Hardly had he said this, as they were going out of the camp, than my father, Alexius Comnenus, was on them, for he had hurriedly galloped on ahead of the army with a few attendants. He noticed a man trying to bring the heavy infantry into battle-array - and, by the way, the majority of Basilacius' soldiers had betaken themselves to looting and plunder (this too was an old device of my father's), and before they could be reassembled and drawn up in line, the Great Domestic loomed before them as a sudden danger.

11 Clouds 192

He, as I have said, saw someone drawing up the phalanxes, and judging either from his size, or from the brilliance of his armour (for his armour gleamed in the light of the stars) that he must be Basilacius, dashed swiftly up to him, and struck at his hand, and the hand, with the sword it held, fell to the ground - an incident which greatly upset the phalanx. But after all it was not Basilacius himself, but a very brave man of his suite who was not a tittle inferior in courage to Basilacius. Then Alexius with a heavy hand began a wild attack on them; he shot with arrows, inflicted wounds with his spear, uttered war-cries, confounded them in the darkness. He used the place, the time, everything, as a means to victory, and availed himself of them with unperturbed mind and unshaken judgment, and though men of both armies were fleeing in various directions, he discerned, in every case, whether he were friend or foe. Then, too, a certain Cappadocian, called Goules, a faithful servant of my father's, a hard-hitter, of ungovernable fury in battle, saw Basilacius, and making sure that it was he, struck him on his helmet. But he suffered the fate of Menelaus, when fighting against Paris; for his sword "shattered into 3 or 4 pieces,"[12] fell from his hand, and only the hilt remained in his grip. The General seeing this straightway mocked at him for not holding his sword tight, and called him a coward, but when the soldier shewed him the hilt of his sword which he still grasped, he became less abusive. Another man, a Macedonian, Peter by name, but nicknamed Tornicius, fell among the enemy and slew a number. The phalanx followed its leader though in ignorance of what was being done; for as the struggle was carried on in the dark, not all were able to grasp the course of events. Comnenus would attack that part of the phalanx which was still intact, and strike

12 Iliad 3:363

down all adversaries, and in a moment be back with his own men, urging them to break up that portion of Basilacius' phalanx which still held its ground, and sending messages to the rear to bid them not to be so slow, but to follow him, and overtake him more quickly. During this time, a Frank, belonging to the Domestic's troops, and, to make a long story short, a brave soldier, instinct with the spirit of Ares, noticed my father coming out from the enemy's centre, bare sword in hand, all smoking with blood, and took him for one of the enemy. In a trice he fell upon him, knocked him on the chest with his spear, and was within an ace of hurling the General off his horse, had the General not seated himself more firmly, and addressed the soldier by name, and threatened to cut off his head with his sword. However, the Frank, by pleading his want of recognition, and the confusion consequent upon a night-battle, was allowed to remain among the living!

CHAPTER NINE

SUCH THEN WERE the deeds of the Domestic and a few followers during that night. As soon as dawn smiled upon the earth, and the sun peeped over the horizon, Basilacius' officers endeavoured with all their might to drive together their men who had abandoned the battle and been busy about the spoil. The Great Domestic also re-formed his own lines, and then marched straight against Basilacius. Some of the Domestic's troops saw stragglers from Basilacius' army in the distance, so rode down upon them, routed them, and brought some back to him alive. Basilacius' brother, Manuel, mounted a hillock, and from there encouraged his army by shouting loudly, "To-day the day and the victory are to Basilacius!" A certain Basileios, nicknamed Curticius, an intimate friend of Nicephorus Bryennius (whose story we have told), and very active in war, ran from Comnenus' battle-line up towards this hillock. Basilacius Manuel drew his sword, and at full speed galloped down upon him; but Curticius, instead of taking his sword, snatched the staff hanging from his saddle-cloth, struck Manuel on the head with it, knocked him off his horse, and dragging him bound behind him, brought him to my father as if he were a bit of the spoils. In the meantime, when the remnants of Basilacius' army saw Comnenus advance with his own divisions, they resisted him for a little, and then took to flight. And so Basilacius fled, and Alexius Comnenus pursued him. When they reached Thessalonica, the Thessalonians at once received Basilacius, but straightway barred the gates before the General. But not even then did Alexius relax, nor did he take off his breastplate, or lay aside his helmet, or ungird his shield from his shoulders, or cast aside his sword, but he encamped, and threatened to besiege the city forthwith, and then sack it . As he wished, however, to save Basilacius, he sent his monk-companion, "Little John" (a man renowned for his integrity) to him with a proposal for peace, and promised that Basilacius should suffer no ill-treatment if he gave securities and surrendered himself and the city. Basilacius, however, was inflexible, but the Thessalonians, through fear of their city being taken and destroyed, granted Comnenus ingress. But Basilacius, when he saw what was being done by the multitude, betook himself to the Acropolis and leapt from one spot to another. Even in these extremities his fighting spirit did not forsake him, although the Domestic gave his word that he should not be barbarously treated; but in difficulties and dangers Basilacius ever shewed himself a man indeed. He would not abate his courage and brave attitude in the slightest, until at last the inhabitants and custodians of the Acropolis drove him out of it against his will, took him by force, and handed him over to the Great Domestic. Alexius at once sent news of his capture to the Emperor but stayed on himself a little longer in Thessalonica to arrange things there, and then returned to Constantinople in triumph. Between Philippi and Amphipolis he met messengers from the Emperor who handed him written orders about Basilacius. They took the latter in charge, led him to a village called Chlempina, and near the spring in it put out his eyes: hence the spring is to this day called “the Spring of Basilacius.” This was the third “Labour” accomplished, by the great Alexius before he became Emperor, and he might rightly be styled a second Heracles. For you would not be wide of the mark in calling this fellow Basilacius the Erymanthian boar, and my most noble father Alexius, a modern Heracles. Such, then, were the successes and achievements of Alexius before he ascended the throne, and as reward for them all he received from the

Emperor the rank of "Sebastos," and was proclaimed "Sebastos" in public assembly.

CHAPTER TEN

IT SEEMS TO ME that if a body is sickly, the sickliness is often aggravated by external causes, but that occasionally, too, the causes of our illnesses spring up of themselves, although we are apt to blame the inequalities of the climate, indiscretion in diet, or perhaps, too, the humours of our animal juices, as the cause of our fevers. Similarly, like these physical ailments, I fancy the weakness of the Romans at that time was partly the cause of these deadly plagues: I mean the various men before mentioned, the Ursels, the Basilacii, and all the crowd of pretenders, but partly, too, it was Fate that introduced other aspirants to the throne from abroad, and foisted them on the Empire like an irremediable sore and incurable disease. To this latter class belonged that braggart Robert, so famed for his tyrannical disposition. Normandy indeed begot him, but he was nursed and reared by consummate Wickedness. The Roman Empire really brought this formidable foe upon herself by affording a pretext for all the wars he waged against us in proposing a marriage with a foreign, barbaric race, quite unsuitable to us; or rather it was the carelessness of the reigning Emperor, Michael, who united our family with the Ducas. Let no one be angry with me if I sometimes censure one of my blood-relations (for I am allied by blood to the Ducas on my mother's side), for I have determined to write the truth before all things, and, as far as this man is concerned, I have voiced the general censures. For this same Emperor, Michael Ducas, betrothed his own son, Constantine, to this barbarian's daughter, and from that arose all the hostilities. Now, we shall give an account of this prince Constantine in due course; also of his nuptial contract, in other words this barbaric alliance, and also of his appearance, and beauty, and size, and physical and mental characteristics. At that point I shall also briefly deplore my own misfortunes after I have told the tale of this alliance, and the defeat of the whole barbarian force, and the death of these pretenders from Normandy, who had been reared against the Roman Empire by Michael's want of prudence. But first I must retrace my steps a little, and speak of this man Robert[13], and give details of his descent and career, and relate to what a pitch of power the turn of affairs had brought him, or to put it more reverentially, bow far Providence had allowed him to rise by shewing indulgence to his mischievous desires and machinations.

---

13 Robert Guiscard, Duke of Apulia and Calabria, son of Tancred

This Robert was Norman by descent, of insignificant origin in temper tyrannical, in mind most cunning, brave in action, very clever in attacking the wealth and substance of magnates, most obstinate in achievement, for he did not allow any obstacle to prevent his executing his desire. His stature was so lofty that he surpassed even the tallest, his complexion was ruddy, his hair flaxen, his shoulders were broad, his eyes all but emitted sparks of fire, and in frame he was well-built where nature required breadth, and was neatly and gracefully formed where less width was necessary. So from tip to toe this man was well-proportioned, as I have repeatedly heard many say. Now, Homer says of Achilles that when he shouted, his voice gave his hearers the impression of a multitude in an uproar, but this man's cry is is said to have put thousands to flight. Thus equipped by fortune, physique and character, he was naturally indomitable, and subordinate to nobody in the world.

Powerful natures are ever like this, people say, even though they be of somewhat obscure descent.

CHAPTER ELEVEN

SUCH THEN WAS THE man, and as he would not endure any control, he departed from Normandy with only five followers on horseback, and thirty on foot all told. After leaving his native land, he roamed amid the mountain-ridges, caves, and hills of Lombardy, as the chief of a robber-band, and by attacks on travellers acquired horses, and also other possessions and weapons. Thus the prelude of this man's life was marked by much bloodshed and many murders. While lingering in those parts of Lombardy, he came under the notice of Gulielmus Mascabeles, who was then ruler over the greater part of the territory adjacent to Lombardy, and as he drew a rich annual income from these lands, he furnished himself with a good body of troops and became a powerful prince. He informed himself of the manner of man, physical and mentally, that Robert was, and then with a wonderful lack of foresight, attached him to himself, and betrothed one of his daughters to him. The marriage was completed, and though Gulielmus admired Robert for his strength and experience in warfare, yet his affairs did not prosper as he had hoped. He had even given him a city as a kind of wedding-gift, and lavished various other marks of kindness upon him. However, Robert grew disaffected, and meditated-rebellion. At first he played the friend and gradually increased his forces until he had trebled his cavalry and doubled his infantry. And thereafter the cloak of friendliness slipped off, and little by little his evil disposition was laid bare. Daily he would give, or pick up, some pretext for a quarrel, and continuously adopted courses of a kind that are wont to engender disputes, and then fighting and wars. Since the aforesaid Gulielmus Mascabeles far surpassed him in wealth and influence, Robert renounced all idea of meeting him openly in battle, and concocted a wicked plot instead. For, while professing friendship and feigning repentance, he was secretly preparing a terrible scheme, which was hard to detect, in order to capture all Mascabeles' towns, and make himself master of all his possessions. As a start he opened negotiations for peace, and sent an embassy to ask Gulielmus to come in person to a conference. Gulielmus welcomed peace with Robert, because he was extremely fond of his daughter, and fixed a meeting for the morrow; and Robert indicated the place where they would meet for discussion, and arranging a truce with each other. In this place were two peaked hills rising from the plain to equal height, and standing diametrically opposite each other; the intervening ground was swampy, and over-grown with all manner of trees and bushes. On this ground that crafty Robert planted an ambuscade of four very brave armed men, and adjured them to keep careful watch all round, and as soon as they saw him at grips with Gulielmus, to run up against the latter without an instant's delay. After these preliminary preparations, Robert, the arch-schemer, forsook the hill which he had designated beforehand for the conference with Mascabeles, and appropriated, so to say, the second hill, and taking fifteen horsemen and about fifty-six foot-soldiers up with him, posted them there, and then disclosed his whole plot to the more important among them. He also commanded one to hold his armour ready for him to put on quickly, namely, his helmet, shield, and short sword; to the four men in ambush he had given injunctions to rush very quickly to his aid directly they saw Mascabeles at grips with him. On the appointed day Gulielmus was coming to the hill to the spot which Robert had indicated to him beforehand, with the intention of completing a treaty; when Robert saw him drawing near, he met him on horseback, and embraced and welcomed him right heartily. So they both halted on the slope, a little distance from the summit of the hill, talking of what they meant to do. The crafty Robert wasted the time by talking of one subject after another, and then said to Gulielmus: "Why in the world should we tire ourselves by sitting on horseback? Why not dismount, and sit on the ground, and talk freely of the necessary matters?" Mascabeles foolishly obeyed, all unaware of the guile, and the danger into which he was being led, and when he saw Robert get on his horse, he dismounted too, and resting his elbow on the ground, started the discussion afresh. Robert now professed fealty to Mascabeles for the future, and called him his faithful benefactor and lord. Hereupon, Mascabeles' men, seeing that the leaders had dismounted, and apparently started an argument afresh, dismounted too; or rather some did, and tied their reins to the branches, and lay down and rested in the shade cast by the horses and the trees, while the others rode home. For they were all tired from the warmth and want of food and drink (for it was the summer season when the sun casts its rays vertically, and the heat had become unbearable). So much then for these; but Robert, the sly fox, had arranged all this beforehand, and now suddenly throws himself on Mascabeles, drops his kindly expression for a furious one, and attacks him with murderous intent. And gripping, he was gripped in return, and dragged, and was dragged, and together they went rolling down the hill. When the four men waiting in ambush saw this, they jumped out of the marsh, ran at Gulielmus, bound him, and then ran back as if to join Robert's horsemen stationed on the other hill, but they were already galloping down the slope towards them, and behind came Gulielmus' men in hot pursuit. Robert for his part jumped on his horse, quickly donned his helmet, seized his spear, and brandished it fiercely and sheltering himself behind his shield, turned round, and struck one of Gulielmus' men such a blow with his spear that he yielded up his life on the spot. In the meantime, he held back the rush of his father-in-law's cavalry, and checked the relief they were bringing (because when they saw Robert's horsemen coming down upon them from above with the position all in their favour, they immediately turned their backs). After Robert had in this wise stopped the onrush of Gulielmus' horsemen, Mascabeles was taken bound and a prisoner of war to the very fortress which he had given as wedding-gift to Robert at the time he betrothed his daughter to him. And so it came about that the city had its own master as "prisoner "within it, and hence probably it got its name of "prison-house." And it will not be amiss if I enlarge on Robert's cruelty. For when he had once got Mascabeles in his power, he first had all his teeth pulled out, and demanded for each of them a stupendous weight of money, and enquired where this money was stored. He did not leave off drawing them until he had taken all, for both teeth and money gave out simultaneously, and then Robert cast his eyes upon Gulielmus' eyes, and grudging him his sight, deprived him of his eyes.

CHAPTER TWELVE

HAVING THUS BECOME MASTER of all Mascabeles' possessions, he after that grew daily in power, and becoming ever more despotic, piled cities upon cities,. and money upon money. In a short time he had risen to ducal eminence, and was nominated Duke of all Lombardy, and from that moment everybody's envy was excited against him. But Robert, being a man with his wits very much about him, now used flattery against his adversaries and now gifts, and so quelled uprisings among the populace, and by his ingenuity repressed the envy of the nobility against him, and thus, by these means, and by occasional recourse to arms, he annexed the whole realm of Lombardy, and the neighbouring country. But this Robert was for ever aspiring at further increase of power, and because he had visions of the Roman Empire, he alleged as pretext his connection with the Emperor Michael, as I have said, and fanned up the war against the Romans. For we have already stated that the Emperor Michael for some inexplicable reason betrothed this despot's daughter (Helen by name) to his son, Constantine. Now that I am mentioning this youth again, I am convulsed in spirit, and confounded in reason: however, I will cut short my story about him, and reserve it for the right time.

Yet one thing I cannot forbear saying, even though it is out of place here, and that is that the youth was a living statue, a "chef d'oeuvre," so to say, of God's hands. If any one merely looked at him, he would say that he was a descendant of the Golden Age fabled by the Greeks; so indescribably beautiful was he. And when I call to mind this boy after so many years I am filled with sorrow; yet I restrain my tears, and husband them for "more fitting places,"[14] for I do not wish to confuse this history by mingling monodies on my sufferings with historical narration. To resume, this youth (whom we have mentioned here and elsewhere), my predecessor, born before I had seen the light of day, a clean, undefiled boy, had become a suitor for Helen, Robert's daughter, and the written contracts had been drawn up for the marriage, though they were not executed, only promised, as the youth was

14 Demosthenes 234,14

still of immature age; and the contracts were annulled directly the Emperor Nicephorus Botaniates ascended the throne. But I have wandered from the point, and will now return to the point whence I wandered! That man Robert, who from a most inconspicuous beginning had grown most conspicuous, and amassed great power, now desired eagerly to become Roman Emperor, and with this object, sought plausible-pretexts for ill-will and war against the Romans. And there are two different tales about this. One story which is bruited about, and reached our ears too, is that a certain monk, named Raictor, impersonated the Emperor Michael, and had gone over to Robert, and poured out his tale of woe to him, his marriage-connection. Michael had seized the Roman sceptre after Diogenes, and adorned the throne for a short time, then he was deprived of his throne by the rebel Botaniates, and embraced the monastic life, and was later invested with the alb and mitre and add, if you like, the humeral of an archbishop. The Caesar John, his paternal uncle, had advised this for he knew the lightheadedness of the reigning Emperor, and feared the worst for Michael. It was this Michael whom the aforementioned monk, Raictor, impersonated, or if I may call him so, "Rectes," which implies what he was, the most audacious "fabricator" of all time. He approached Robert on the plea of being his marriage-kinsman, and recited to him the tragic tale of his wrongs, how he had been driven from the imperial throne, and reduced to his present state, which Robert could see for himself, and for all these reasons, he invoked the barbarian's aid. For Helen, Robert's beautiful daughter, and his own daughter-in-law, had been left destitute, he said, and openly bereft of her betrothed, as his son Constantine, and his wife, the Princess Mary, although very unwillingly, had been compelled by force to join Botaniates' party.

By these words he inflamed the barbarian's mind, and armed him with a motive for a war against the Romans. A story of this sort reached my ears, and I must own I am not surprised that some persons of most ignoble birth impersonate those of noble and honourable race. But on other authority a far more plausible story re-echoes in my mind, and this story avers that no monk impersonated Michael, and that no such event stirred Robert to war against the Romans, but that the versatile barbarian himself easily invented the whole thing. The story runs thus, the arch-villain Robert who was hatching war against the Romans, and had been making his preparations for some time, was kept in check by the nobles of highest rank in his suite, and also by his own wife, Gaïta, on the ground that the war would be unjust and waged against Christians; indeed he was prevented several times when he was anxious to start. But he was determined to procure a specious pretext for war, and therefore sent some men to Cotrone and entrusted them with the secret of his plot, and gave them the following directions. If they could find any monk willing to cross from there to Italy to worship at the shrine of the chief apostles, the patron saints of Rome, and if he did not betray his low origin too openly in his appearance, they were to welcome him and make a friend of him, and bring him back with them. When they discovered the aforementioned Raictor, a versatile fellow without his equal for knavery, they signified the fact to Robert who was waiting at Salernum[15], by a letter to this effect: "Your kinsman Michael, who has been expelled from his kingdom has arrived here to solicit your assistance." For Robert had ordered them to write the letter to him in those words. Directly he received the letter, he read it privately to his wife, and then in an assembly of all the Counts he

15 Salerno

showed it to them too, and swore they could no longer keep him back, as he had now got hold of a really just excuse for war. As they all immediately fell in with Robert's desire, he brought the man over, and entered into association with him. Thereupon he worked up the whole drama, and put it in its proper stage-setting, pretending that that monk was the Emperor Michael, that he had been deprived of his throne, and despoiled of his wife and son and all his possessions by the usurper Botaniates, and that against all law and justice he had been clothed in a monk's garb instead of a fillet and crown, and "Now," he concluded, "he has come as suppliant to us." Robert used to harangue the people like this, and professed that because of their kinship he must restore the kingdom to him. Daily he shewed honour to the monk, as if he were the Emperor Michael, giving him the best place at table, a higher seat, and excessive respect. In various ingenious ways also Robert caught the ear of the public; one day he would commiserate himself on the sad fate of his daughter; on another he did not like, out of consideration for his marriage-kinsman, to speak of the evil days on which the latter had fallen; and on yet another he incited and stirred up the ignorant masses round him to war by artfully promising them heaps of gold which he said he would give them from the Imperial treasury. Thus he led all by the nose, and drew all, rich and poor alike, out of Lombardy, or rather he dragged the whole of Lombardy with him, and occupied Salernum, the mother city of Amalfi. Here he made good settlements for his other daughters, and then began his preparations for the war. He had two daughters with him, whilst the third, ill-fated from the day of her betrothal, was confined in the imperial city; for her young betrothed, being still immature, shrank from this alliance at the very outset, as children do from bogeys. Of the two others, he pledged one to Raymond, son of the Count Barcinon, and the second he married to Eubulus[16], another very illustrious Count. In these alliances, as in all else, Robert did not fail to have an eye to his own advantage; but from all sources he had piled up and welded together influence for himself, from his race, his rule, his rights of kin, in a word, from innumerable devices of which nobody else would even think.

CHAPTER THIRTEEN

MEANWHILE, an event occurred which is worth relating, as it, too, contributed to this man's reputation and good fortune. For I hold that the fact that all the rulers of the West were prevented from attacking him, tended very materially to the barbarian's successful progress. Fate worked for him

16 Ebal

on all sides, raised him to kingly power, and accomplished everything helpful to him. Now it happened that the Pope of Rome[17] had a difference with Henry, King of Germany[18], and, therefore, wished to draw Robert into an alliance, as the latter had already become very notable and attained to great dominion. (The Pope is a very high dignitary, and is protected by troops of various nationalities.) The dispute between the King and the Pope was this: the latter accused Henry of not bestowing livings as free gifts, but selling them for money, and occasionally entrusting archbishoprics to unworthy recipients, and he also brought further charges of a similar nature against him. The King of Germany on his side indicted the Pope of usurpation, as he had seized the apostolic chair without his consent. Moreover, he had the effrontery to utter reckless threats against the Pope, saying that if he did not resign his self-

17 Gregory VII

18 Henry IV

elected office, he should be expelled from it with contumely. When these words reached the Pope's ears, he vented his rage upon Henry's ambassadors; first he tortured them inhumanly, then clipped their hair with scissors, and sheared their beards with a razor, and finally committed a most indecent outrage upon them, which transcended even the insolence of barbarians, and so sent them away. My womanly and princely dignity forbids my naming the outrage inflicted (in them, for it was not only unworthy a high priest, but of anyone who bears the name of a Christian. I abhor this barbarian's idea, and more still the deed, and I should have defiled both my pen and my paper had I described it explicitly. But as a display of barbaric insolence, and a proof that time in its flow produces men with shameless morals, ripe for any wickedness, this alone will suffice, if I say, that I could not bear to disclose or relate even the tiniest word about what he did. And this was the work of a high priest. Oh, justice! The deed of the supreme high priest! nay, of one who claimed to be the president of the whole world, as indeed the Latins assert and believe, but this, too, is a bit of their boasting. For when the imperial seat was transferred from Rome hither to our native Queen of Cities, and the senate, and the whole administration, there was also transferred the arch-hieratical primacy. And the Emperors from the very beginning have given the supreme right to the episcopacy of Constantinople, and the Council of Chalcedon emphatically raised the Bishop of Constantinople to the highest position, and placed all the dioceses of the inhabited world under his jurisdiction. There can be no doubt that the insult done to the ambassadors was aimed at the king who sent them; not only because he scourged them, but also because he was the first to invent this new kind of outrage. For by his actions, the Pope suggested, I think, that the power of the King was despicable, and by this horrible outrage on his ambassadors that he, a demi-god, as it were, was treating with a demi-ass! The Pope consequently, by wreaking his insolence on the ambassadors, and sending them back to the King in the state I have mentioned, provoked a very great war. To prevent the King's becoming too insupportable by an alliance with Robert, he anticipated him in sending offers of peace to Robert, though before this he had not been friendly towards him. Hearing that Duke Robert had occupied Salernum, he started from Rome, and came to Beneventum, and after some intercommunication through ambassadors, they also had a personal interview in the following way. The Pope set out from Beneventum with his household troops, and Robert from Salernum with an army, and when the armies were at a convenient distance, each left his own men and advanced alone. The two then met, gave and took pledges and oaths, and then returned. The oaths were that the Pope would invest Robert with the dignity of king, and give him help against the Romans if the need should arise, whilst the Duke swore a counter-oath to assist the Pope whenever the latter called upon him. But truly these oaths taken by both of them were worthless. For the Pope was furiously incensed against the King, and in a hurry to begin war against him, whereas Duke Robert had his eyes fixed on the Roman Empire, and was gnashing his teeth, and whetting his anger like a wild boar. So these oaths amounted to no more; than words. And the pledges these barbarians gave to each other one day, they violated the next. After the meeting, Robert turned his bridle and hurried to Salernum. And that Pope (whom I can only call "abominable" when I recall his inhuman outrages on the ambassadors), the Pope clad in spiritual grace and evangelic peace, started out for civil war with all his energy and might; yes, he, the man of peace, and the disciple of the Man of Peace! For he immediately summoned the Saxons and their Counts Lantulphus[19], and Velcus[20], and besides other enticements held out to them, he promised to make them kings of all the West, and thus won them over to his side. You see how ever-ready a hand the Pope had for laying hands on the heads of kings, unheeding St. Paul's advice "Lay hands hastily on no man,"[21] for he bound the kingly fillet on the Duke of Lombardy's head, and crowned these two Saxons. When either side (to wit, Henry, King of Germany, and the Pope) had brought up their armies, and set them in battle array, directly the horn had sounded the attack, the lines dashed together, and there was fanned up by either side a great and long-continued battle. So many deeds of valour were done by both parties, and such was the endurance shewn by men already wounded by spear and

19 Ludolf

20 Welf

21 I Tim 22

arrow, that in a short time the whole plain was submerged in a sea of blood which flowed from the dying, and the survivors fought on, as if sailing on the abundant gore. In some places the soldiers got entangled by the dead bodies, and fell over, and were drowned in the river of blood. For if, as it is said, more than 30,000 men fell in that battle, what a stream of blood was poured forth, and how large a portion of the earth was defiled with gore! Both sides were, if I may so put it, of equal stature in the battle as long as Lantulphus directed the combat. But when he received a mortal wound, and straightway gave up the ghost, the Pope's lines gave way, and turned their backs to the enemy, and in their flight many were killed or wounded.

Henry rushed wildly after them, being all the more heartened in the pursuit because he had learnt that Lantulphus had fallen and become the prize of the enemy. By and by he desisted from the chase, and bade his army take a rest. Later on he got his army ready again, and hastened to Rome to besiege it. Hereupon, the Pope recalled the agreement and pledges Robert had given him, and sent an embassy to ask his help. At the same time. Henry, too, when he was starting on his march against the ancient city of Rome sent to ask his alliance. But Robert thought both of them silly for making such a request, and sent a verbal answer of some kind to the King, but to the Pope he indited a letter. His letter ran as follows; "Duke Robert to the great High-priest and his Overlord in God. I heard a talk of the attack made upon thee by thy enemies, but did not attach much real importance to the rumour as I knew that none would dare to raise his hand against thee. For what man in his senses would assail so great a father? As for me, I would have thee know that I am arming myself for a most serious war against a most formidable nation. For my campaign is against the Romans, who have filled every land and sea with their trophies. But to thee I acknowledge fidelity from the depths of my soul, and when need arises, I will prove it." And thus he dismissed the ambassadors of both those who had sought his help, the one with this letter, and the other with plausible excuses.

CHAPTER FOURTEEN

BUT WE MUST NOT omit what he did in Lombardy before he arrived in Valona with his army. He was at all times a man of tyrannical and very sharp temper, and now he imitated the madness of Herod. Not being satisfied with the soldiers who had followed his fortune from the beginning, and were experienced in war, he recruited and equipped a new army, without any distinction of age. But he collected all, under age and over age, from all over Lombardy and Apulia, and pressed them into his service. There you could see children and boys, and pitiable old men, who had never, even in their dreams, seen a weapon; but were now clad in breastplates, carrying shields and drawing their bows most unskilfully and clumsily, and usually falling on their faces when ordered to march. These requisitions were naturally the cause of unending trouble throughout the country of Lombardy; everywhere were heard the lamentations of men and the weeping of women who shared the misfortunes of their kinsfolk. One would be mourning for her husband, who was over-age for service; another for her untried son; a third for her brother, who was a farmer or engaged in business. This behaviour of Robert's was as I have said, a counterpart of Herod's madness, or even worse, for the latter only vented, his rage on., babes, whilst Robert did so against boys and old men. Yet, in spite of his recruits being absolutely unpractised, Robert drilled them daily, and brought them into good discipline.

He did all this in Salernum, before he came to Hydruntum[22]. To that town he had sent on a very efficient army, to wait for him until he had settled everything in Lombardy, and given fitting answers to the ambassadors. He dispatched a further note to the Pope, however, saying that he had enjoined upon Roger, his son (whom he had appointed ruler of the whole of Apulia, in conjunction with his brother Boritylas), to waste no time in going with a formidable troop to the help of the Roman See against King Henry as soon as the Pope summoned him. But Bohemond, his younger son, he sent ahead with a powerful army to our territory to leap upon the country round Valona (or Aulon). Now, Bohemond took after his father in all things, in audacity, bodily strength, bravery, and untamable temper; for he was of exactly the

22 Otranto

same stamp as his father, and a living model of the latter's character. Immediately on arrival, he fell like a thunderbolt, with threats and irresistible dash upon Canina, Hiericho, and Valona, and seized them, and as he fought his way on, he would ever devastate and set fire to the surrounding districts. He was, in very truth, like the pungent smoke which precedes a fire, and a prelude of attack before the actual attack. These two, father and son, might rightly be termed "the caterpillar and the locust "; for whatever escaped Robert, that his son Bohemond took to him and devoured. However, do not let us cross to Valona with Robert yet, but examine first what he did on the opposite continent.

CHAPTER FIFTEEN

LEAVING SALERNUM, he came to Hydruntum, and there spent a few days waiting for his wife, Gaita (for she too accompanied her husband, and when dressed in full armour the woman was a fearsome sight). After he had embraced her on arrival, he set off again with his whole army, and took possession of Brindisi, the seaport which has the best harbour in the whole of Iapygia. After swooping down on this town he stayed there, eagerly awaiting the gathering together of his whole army, and of all his ships, transports and long ships of war alike; for he intended to sail for the opposite coast from this port. At the same time, he was also eagerly watching for an answer from the reigning monarch, Botaniates, who had seized the sceptre from the Emperor Michael Ducas; for while still at Salernum, Robert had sent one of the nobles in his cortege, Raoul by name, as ambassador to him. He had charged him with certain remonstrances to Botaniates, and apparently specious reasons for the impending war. These were that Botaniates had separated his daughter from her betrothed. Prince Constantine (to whom she was affianced, as I have stated above), and taken the crown from Constantine; therefore, he himself was getting ready for war because Botaniates had committed an injustice. And, moreover, he had sent some presents and letters promising his friendship to the Great Domestic and Commander of the Armies of the West (and this was my father, Alexius). Whilst awaiting these answers he kept quiet at Brindisi; but before the troops had all been collected there, or the greater part of the ships launched, Raoul returned from Byzantium. He brought no answer to Robert's denunciations, and this fanned the flames of the barbarian's anger afresh. But he was even more incensed by Raoul's laying before him arguments to dissuade him from the war against the Romans. The first was that the monk in his train was a deceiver, and cheat, and only impersonating the Emperor Michael, and that the whole story about him was a pure fabrication. For he told how he had seen Michael in the royal city after his deposition from the throne clad in a grey habit, and living in a monastery, as he had made it his special business to see the deposed king with his own eyes. Secondly, he gave news of the events which had occurred during his return journey - namely, that my father had grasped the sceptre (as I will recount later), driven Botaniates out of the kingdom, sent for Ducas' son, Constantine, the most distinguished of all men living, and had again given him a share in the government. Raoul had heard, this on his way, and brought it forward in the hope of persuading Robert to relinquish his military preparations. "For with what justice," he said, "can we go to war with Alexius, when it was Botaniates who was the author of the wrong done you, and who deprived your daughter Helen of the Roman throne? Wrongs done to us by one set of men should not make us wage war upon others who have never offended against justice. And if your war has no just basis, then all will be lost, ships, equipment, men, in fine, all your military preparations." These words exasperated Robert still further; he went quite mad, and nearly did Raoul personal violence. On the other hand, that fictitious Ducas, and pseudo-emperor Michael (whom we have called "Raictor"), waxed most indignant and angry, and did not know how to contain his wrath when it was so clearly proved that he was not the Emperor Ducas, but merely a fictitious king. The tyrant Robert had yet another cause for his fury against Raoul, for Raoul's brother Roger had deserted to the Romans, and had given them detailed information of the military preparations that were being made against them, so he burned to do Raoul some harm, and threatened him with instant death. Raoul, however, who was not at all slow to take flight, escaped to Bohemond, as being the nearest refuge. Raictor vented the most abominable threats against Raoul's brother, the deserter. With loud cries, and beatings of his thigh with his right hand, he implored Robert, saying, "One thing only I beg of you - if ever I recover the crown, and am restored to the throne, hand over Roger to me, and then, if I do not condemn him to the most miserable death, and crucify him in the middle of the city, then may God do so to me, and more also!" But as I write I have to laugh at the thought of these men's folly and infatuation, and especially at their mutual boastfulness. Robert, for his part, had as ostensible reason this pretender, whom he had used as a decoy, and presentment of the Emperor, his marriage-kinsman. He showed him in all the cities he visited, and roused all he could possibly persuade to rebellion, purposing, if the haphazards of war ended in success for himself, to knock the monk on the head, and cast him out with scorn; for when the hunt is over, the decoy, too, is thrown to the dogs. Raictor, on his side, nourished himself on vain hopes that some day he would attain great power; for such things often happen quite unexpectedly. In that case he would lay hold of the sceptre with firm hand, taking it for granted that the Roman people, and the army, would never call the barbarian Robert to the throne. In the meantime, he would use Robert as an instrument for the completion of the whole fabric of his intrigue. When I think of all this, a smile rises to my lips as I wield my pen by the light of my lamp.

CHAPTER SIXTEEN

ROBERT NOW COLLECTED ALL his forces at Brindisi, both ships and soldiers; the ships numbered 150 and the soldiers, when all ranks were counted together, came to 30,000; and each ship could transport 200 men with their armour and horses. The soldiers were fully equipped in this way, because the enemies they would meet on landing would probably be fully-armed horsemen. Robert intended crossing to Epidamnus, which we must call "Dyrrachium[23]," according to the present fashion. He had, indeed, thought of crossing from Hydruntum to Nicopolis, and seizing Naupactus and the adjacent country, and all the fortresses round about it. But as the stretch of sea between these two towns was far wider than between Brindisi and Dyrrachium, he chose the latter in preference to the former, not only because he preferred the quicker passage, but also to secure a calm one for the fleet. For the season was stormy, and as the sun was turning to the southern hemisphere, and approaching Capricorn, the days were growing shorter. Therefore, to prevent the fleet's setting out from Hydruntum at daybreak and sailing all night, and perhaps meeting heavy seas, he determined to

23 Durrazzo

proceed from Brindisi to Dyrrachium with all sails set. As the Adriatic Sea contracts here, the length of the passage was curtailed. He did not after all leave even his son Roger behind, as he had first planned when he appointed him Count of Apulia, but changed his mind for some inexplicable reason, and took him with him too. During his crossing to Dyrrachium, the force which he had detached gained possession of the very strongly fortified town of Corfu, and certain other of our forts. After receiving hostages from Lombardy, and Apulia, and raising taxes and contributions in money from the whole country, Robert hoped to land at Dyrrachium. Duke of all Illyricum at that time was George Monomachatus, who had been appointed by the Emperor Botaniates. Once, indeed, he had refused this mission, and he was by no means easily persuaded to take up this branch of service, but he finally went because two of the Emperor's barbarian servants (Borilus and Germanus, Scythians by extraction) bore a grudge against him. These men were ever inventing scandalous charges against him, and denouncing him to the Emperor, for they strung together whatever tales entered their heads, and inflamed his anger against him to such a pitch that, turning to the Queen Maria, he actually said, "I suspect this Monomachatus of being an enemy to the Roman Empire."

John, one of the Alani, and a devoted friend of Monomachatus, heard this, and as he was aware of the Scythians' spiteful and frequent accusations against him, he went to Monomachatus, and repeated to him both the Emperor's words and those of the Scythians, and advised him to consult his own interests. Thereupon, Monomachatus, a prudent man, approached the Emperor, and after appeasing him with skilful flattery, eagerly accepted the post at Dyrrachium. So, having taken leave of the Emperor previous to his departure for Epidamnus, and receiving his orders about the Duchy in writing (and those Scythians, Borilus and Germanus, did their best to expedite the matter), he quitted the royal city on the morrow for his destination, Epidamnus and the country of Illyricum. But he met my father Alexius near the so-called Pege; here a church has been built in honour of my mistress, the Virgin-mother of our Lord, which is famous among the churches of Byzantium. They saw each other there, and Monomachatus at once began an impassioned speech to the Great Domestic. He told him that he was being exiled because of their mutual friendship, and because of the envy of the Scythians, Borilus and Germanus. This covetous couple, he said, had turned the wheel, so to say, of their universal maliciousness against him in full revolution; and were now banishing him from his friends, and this beloved city, for seemingly good reasons. Thus he told his tale of woe in detail, and all the false information given about him to the Emperor, and all he had endured at the hands of these servants; and the Domestic of the West deigned to console him as much as possible, and verily he was well-fitted to relieve a soul bowed down with troubles. And saying finally that assuredly God would avenge these insults, and with a reminder to him never to forget their friendship, they parted, the one bound for Dyrrachium, and the other to enter the imperial city. When Monomachatus reached Dyrrachium he heard two pieces of news; firstly, the tyrant Robert's military preparations, and, secondly, the revolt of Alexius; so he carefully weighed what his own conduct should be. Ostensibly he displayed hostility to both, but he had really a deeper plan than that of open warfare. For the Great Domestic had informed him by letter of the late occurrences, namely, that he had been threatened with the loss of his eyes, and that, in consequence of this threat, and of the tyrannous act that was being practised, he had taken measures against his enemies. He called upon Monomachatus to rise in rebellion also on behalf of his friend, and to collect money wherever he could, and send it to him. “For,” he wrote, “we are in need of money, and without money, nothing of what should be done, can be done.” However, Monomachatus did not send money, but spoke kindly to the ambassadors, and instead of money, entrusted them with a letter conceived in this strain - he still preserved his old friendship for Alexius, and promised to retain it in the future; and, with regard to the money he ordered, he (Monomachatus) longed to send him as much as he wanted. “But,” he wrote, “a point of justice restrains me. For I received this appointment from the Emperor Botaniates, and I swore the oath of fealty to him. Therefore, I should not appear, even in your eyes, a loyal subject as far as Emperors are concerned, were I at once to comply with your request. But if divine providence allots the imperial throne to you, then as I have been your friend from the beginning, so after this event I shall be your most faithful servant." This excuse Monomachatus made to my father, and tried to conciliate him (I mean my father) and Botaniates, simultaneously, but he also sent a much plainer message to the barbarian Robert, and then broke forth into open rebellion, and for this I must condemn him severely. But perhaps this kind of unstable conduct, ever changing with the changes in the government, is but natural; and all such men are prejudicial to the public weal, but steer a safe course for themselves, for they study nothing but their own personal interests, and even so they generally fail.

Behold, my steed has run off the high road of my history, but although he is out of hand, I must bring him back to our former road. Robert, indeed, had ever been wildly impatient to cross into our country, and was ever dreaming of Dyrrachium, but now, on receipt of Monomachatus' message, his ardour burst all restraint, and he pushed on the naval expedition with all his might and main, and hurried up the soldiers, and whipped up their courage by stimulating addresses. Monomachatus, having set things in trim in this direction, now began constructing a second place of refuge for himself in another place; For he won over Bodinus and Michaelas, the Ex-archs of Dalmatia by his letters, and influenced their decisions by opportune gifts; thus opening secretly, as it were, various doors for himself. For he reasoned that if he were to fail with Robert and Alexius, and be rejected by both of them, then he would turn deserter, and go straight to Bodinus and Michaelas in Dalmatia. For, supposing that Robert and Alexius declared themselves his enemies, he placed his remaining hopes on Michaelas and Bodinus, and arranged to flee to them, should the feelings of Robert and Alexius be plainly adverse to him. But here we will let these matters rest. It is high time I should turn to my father reign, and relate how and why he became ruler. I do not intend to narrate his life before he became ruler, but all his successes and failures as Emperor; if we shall occasionally find him unsuccessful in the course of the long stretch we are to traverse, I should not spare him for being my father if anything, he did struck me as not well done; nor shall I gloss over his successes to avoid the under-current of suspicion that it is a daughter writing about her father, for in either case I should be wronging truth. This then is my aim, as I have repeatedly stated already, and the subject I have chosen is the Emperor, my father. We will leave Robert in the spot to which our history has brought him, and now consider the Emperor's doings. We shall reserve the wars and battles against Robert for a later book.

BOOK TWO

The Revolt of the Comneni

CHAPTER ONE

WE MUST REFER THE reader who wishes to know the place and lineage from which Alexius sprang, to my Caesar's history, and thence he can also extract information about the Emperor Nicephorus Botaniates.

Now Manuel was the elder brother of Isaac

and Alexius and in fact, the first-begotten of all the children descended through John Comnenus from my paternal grandfather. He was general in sole command over the whole of Asia to which the former emperor, Romanus Diogenes, had appointed him, whereas the principality of Antioch had elected Isaac by lot as their Duke; these two had fought in many wars and battles, and many trophies too they had erected over their opponents. And after these my father Alexius was promoted to be General-in-Chief, and dispatched against Ursel by Michael Ducas, the reigning emperor.

Later on the Emperor Nicephorus also observed his expertness in warfare and heard how, while serving under his brother Isaac in the East, he had taken part in many contests an“d proved himself valiant beyond his years, and when he considered the manner in which Alexius had worsted Ursel, he made just as conspicuous a favourite of him as he did of Isaac. He took the two brothers to his heart and looked upon them with joy, sometimes even inviting them to share his table. This enkindled the envy of others against them and most especially that of the two aforementioned Slavonic barbarians, Borilus and Germanus. For seeing the Emperor's goodwill towards the brothers and that the latter remained unharmed by the darts that malice hurled at them, they were consumed with wrath. As the Emperor saw that Alexius although his beard was as yet scarce grown was held in high repute by all, he appointed him absolute General of the West and honoured him with the rank of Proedros. Of all the trophies which he set up throughout the West also and of the various rebels he conquered and brought as captives to the Emperor sufficient has been said already. But these doings did not please those two slaves but rather fanned the flames of their envy; They went about growling and purposing evil against them in their hearts, and told the King many tales in confidence and others in public or suborned others to tell him, for their desire was, no matter by what means, to get these brothers out of the way. In this distressing situation the Comneni judged it prudent to cultivate the officers of the women's apartments and through them to win in still greater measure the Queen's affection. For the brothers were charming men and able with their varied wiles to soften even a heart of stone. Isaac could do this the more easily as the Queen some time before had chosen him to marry her own cousin; he was a perfect gentleman both in word and deed and most like my own father. But since his own affairs had prospered so well, he took much thought for his brother Alexius, and as the latter had formerly helped him with all his power in arranging his marriage, so he in his turn now desired to see Alexius stand high in the Queen's favour. It is said that the friends Orestes and Pylades had such a deep love for each other that in time of battle either would be quite indifferent to his own foes but would ward off those who attacked his friend, and either would offer his own breast to receive the darts thrown at the other. Exactly the same phenomenon could be witnessed in the case of these two. For either brother tried to anticipate the other's dangers; and whatever prizes and honours one gained, in short the good fortune of the one, the other considered his own, and vice versa, such close affection bound them to each other. By the help of heaven, Isaac's interests had been thus secured; and after no long interval the officials of the women's apartments lent a willing ear to Isaac's suggestion that the queen should adopt Alexius. The Queen listened to them; and the two brothers came to the palace on an appointed day, and then she adopted Alexius according to the ritual prescribed from of old for such cases. Thus for the future the Great Domestic of the Western armies was relieved of a great anxiety. Thenceforth they both visited the palace very often and after paying their respects to the Emperor and staying with him a little they went in to the Queen. All this still further inflamed the envy of others against them, as the Comneni were often assured, and consequently they lived in fear of being caught in their enemies' snares. As they had no protector, they cast about for a means by which, with God's help, they might ensure safety for themselves. After revolving many plans with their mother and examining various schemes at various times they discovered one path which as far as man can judge, might lead to safety. This was to approach the Queen when some plausible reason offered, and tell her their secret. Yet they kept their plan under water and did not reveal their whole design to anyone, but like fishermen they were careful not to frighten away their prey. They intended, indeed, to run away but had been afraid to tell the Queen this, lest she might disclose their intentions to the emperor prematurely in her anxiety for the two parties, to wit, her husband and the brothers. After having settled on this plan, they turned their attention elsewhere for they were adepts in making full use of any opportunities that might occur.

CHAPTER TWO

THE EMPEROR WAS NOW too old to have expectations of a son and as he dreaded the inevitable stroke of death, he began to consider the question of his successor. At that time there was at court a certain Synadenus of Eastern origin and illustrious descent, fair of face, of profound intellect, courageous in battle, verging on young manhood, and above all akin to the emperor by race. In preference to all others the Emperor thought of leaving him as successor to the Empire, giving him the kingdom as his ancestral portion, so to speak, and in this he was ill-advised. For he would have ensured perfect safety and also regarded justice by bequeathing the imperial power to the Queen's son, Constantine; as the portion rightly accruing to him, as it were, through his grandfather and father, and this would have increased the Queen's confidence in him and gained her goodwill. However, the old man failed to see that he was arranging matters in a way which was not only unjust but also disastrous, and was begetting troubles for himself. The Queen heard whispers of this and was very sad as she foresaw danger to her son; but though she was despondent she did not openly voice her grief to anyone. This did not escape the notice of the Comneni and they determined, if they could find the opportunity they-sought to approach the Queen. Their mother furnished Isaac with a pretext for a conversation with the Queen, and his brother Alexius went with him. When they were admitted to the Queen Isaac said; "Lady, we do not behold you in the same health as heretofore, but you seem worried and obsessed by unbearable thoughts and without the courage to reveal your secret to anybody." However, she would not speak out for some time, but sighing deeply replied: "It is not right to question those who live away from home, for that in itself is sufficient source of grief to them. But as for myself, alas! what sorrows have come upon me, one after the other, and how many more methinks are in store for me shortly." The brothers stood aloof and added no more words, but with eyes cast down and both hands covered, stood a minute plunged in thought and then made their usual obeisance and departed home in deep distress. The next day they came again to talk to her, and seeing that she looked at them more cheerfully than the day before, they both went close up to her and said: "You are our mistress and we are your most devoted slaves, ready to die, if need be, for our Queen. And do not let any consideration unnerve you and lead you to indecision." Upon these words they gave the Queen an oath and after freeing themselves from all suspicion they easily guessed her secret, for they were sharp-witted, shrewd, and expert in divining from a few words a man's deeply hidden and hitherto unexpressed opinion. Straightway they associated themselves still more closely with the Queen and making their goodwill clear to her by many proofs they promised they would bravely assist her in any undertaking to which she summoned them. "Rejoice with them that rejoice and weep with them that weep,",[24] that is indeed the apostolic injunction, and this

24 Rom 12:15

they willingly observed. They asked the Queen to count them as her countrymen and intimates as they were sprung from the same stock as she was; and one thing more they urged - that she should not hesitate to divulge it to them immediately if either she, or the Emperor, got wind of a plot being formed against them by their rivals, and thus save them from unconsciously falling into their enemies' snares. This favour they asked and begged her be of good cheer, saying that with God's help they would gladly bring adequate help and as far as depended on them, her son Constantine should not be ousted from the empire. And they insisted too in ratifying their agreement by oaths, for there was no time to lose because of their jealous opponents. So the brothers were relieved of a great anxiety and recovered" their spirits and from now on showed a cheerful countenance" in their conversations with the Emperor. They were both, but Alexius more especially, practised in concealing a secret intention and a deeply laid plan by external pretences. But as the burning envy of others was now growing into a mighty fire, and nothing of what was said against them to the Emperor was any longer concealed from them owing to the agreement (with the Queen), they recognized that those two all-influential slaves were scheming to get them out of the way; consequently they no longer went together to the palace as had been their custom, but singly, on alternate days. This was a wise and Palamedean precaution to prevent their both perhaps falling into the barbarians' snares at the same time, for if only one were caught by the intrigues of those all-powerful Scythians, the other could escape. Such then was their precaution. However, matters turned out for the brothers very differently from what they had feared, for they anticipated their rivals in the race for power, as my story, starting from this point, will show very clearly.

CHAPTER THREE

ABOUT THIS TIME THE city of Cyzicus was taken by the Turks; directly the Emperor learnt of the capture of the city, he sent for Alexius Comnenus. Now it chanced that on that day Isaac had come, and when he saw his brother entering the palace contrary to their agreement, he went up to him and asked the reason for his coming. Alexius immediately told him the reason, saying: "Because the Emperor has sent for me." So they went in together and made the customary obeisance, and as it was nearly the hour for lunch the Emperor told them to stay for a little and then commanded them to sit down at table with him. And they were separated, for one sat on the right side of the table, and the other on the left, opposite each other. In a few minutes they looked intently at the attendants standing about and saw they were whispering with gloomy countenances. Then they feared lest the two slaves were meditating a sudden attack on them and that danger was nigh at hand, so they looked stealthily at each other and knew not what to do. Long before this they had won over all those in attendance on the Emperor by soft words, and paying court to them with divers forms of greetings; and by shaking hands with him they had even coaxed the head-cook into looking at them with a friendly eye. To this head-cook there came now one of Isaac Comnenus' servants and said: "Tell my master of the fall of Cyzicus! for a letter has come from there with this news." Then the cook carried in the meat to the table and at the same time informed Isaac in a low voice of what he had heard from the servant. Isaac in turn by moving his lips slightly, notified the message to Alexius; and Alexius, who had very keen intuition and was quicker than fire, at once grasped what he had said, and they both recovered from the anxiety which had held them. And pulling themselves together they considered how they might answer readily if anyone asked them about it and also give the right advice to the Emperor if he consulted them. While they were busy with these reflections the Emperor looked at them, taking for granted they did not know about Cyzicus, and told them of its capture. Then they roused the Emperor's depressed spirits (for they were ready to minister to his soul which was agitated by the sack of his cities) and heartened him up with fair hopes by assuring him that the city could be recovered easily. "The one thing needful," they said, "is that your Majesty should be safe; and as for the captors of the city they shall render sevenfold into your bosom that which they have taken." Then indeed the Emperor was delighted with them and dismissing them from the feast, spent the rest of the day free from care. Henceforward the Comneni made it their business to visit the palace and pay court to the men about the emperor even more assiduously; for they did not wish to give their adversaries the slightest handle, nor to afford them any pretext whatever for hatred, but on the contrary to win all over to liking them and being on their side both in thought and speech. They also exerted themselves to win over the Empress Maria more completely and to convince her that they only lived and breathed for her. Isaac for his part with the excuse of his marriage to her cousin, used his freedom of access to the utmost, whilst Alexius, my father, alleging his nearness of kin but still more his adoption, as a brilliant reason, visited the Queen, without arousing anybody's suspicion and threw a veil over the envy of his ill-wishers. But he was well aware of the fierce resentment of those barbarian slaves and also of the Emperor's extreme lightheaded-ness. So they naturally took thought how not to fall from his good favour, as, in that case, they might become a prey to their enemies. For light-headed dispositions are ever unstable and like the Euripus, they drift, as it were, on ever-changing currents.

CHAPTER FOUR

WHEN THEE SLAVES SAW that matters were not progressing along the lines hey wished and that the destruction of such men was not an easy job as the Emperor's goodwill towards them augmented daily, they broached many plans and as often rejected them and finally settled on another course. And what was it? - it was to-send for them one night without the ruler's knowledge and to put them out of the way by trumping up some false charge and boring out their eyes. The Comneni heard of this As they recognized that danger was very near they decided after much internal conflict that their only hope of safety lay in rebellion and that they were driven to by dire necessity. For what sense was there in waiting for the red-hot iron to be applied which would quench the light of their eyes for ever? Therefore they kept this decision deep down in their minds. Soon after this Alexius (who was at that time Domestic of the Western Empire) was ordered to call up to the city a certain division of the army to be prepared for marching against the Hagarenes who had sacked the city of Cyzicus. Seizing this reasonable opportunity, he summoned by letter those officers in the army who were well disposed to himself and their respective troops. These were all mobilized and hurried up to the metropolis. In the meantime somebody at the suggestion of that fellow, Borilus, one of the slaves, asked the Emperor whether it was by his wish that the Great Domestic was introducing all the forces into the city. The Emperor at once sent for Alexius and asked him whether this report was true; to which Alexius immediately answered that part of the army was coming in by his, the Emperor's, orders, and as for the whole of it being assembled there from all parts he parried the question plausibly. "The army you see," he said, "has been scattered in all directions, and now the various regiments which have received the signal are coming up from their different stations. And those who see them streaming in from various quarters of the Roman dominions, think the whole army is being assembled as if by agreement and are misled by mere appearance." Although Borilus had many objections to make to this speech, yet even so Alexius prevailed and was acquitted by the votes of all. Germanus who was simpler-minded, did not run down Alexius much. As the Emperor's soul was not perturbed even by these allegations against the Domestic, the slaves seized the opportunity and set about preparing and ambush for the Comneni. Now slaves are anyhow by nature hostile to their masters, but when they cannot injure their masters, they turn their power against their fellow-servants, and become quite insupportable. Of this type of character and spirit Alexius had experience in the case of these slaves I am speaking of. For they did not bear resentment against the Comneni from love of the Emperor, but Borilus even aimed at the throne, some said, and as Germanus was his partner in the plot, he helped him prepare the ambush carefully. And they discussed their plans together and imagined that the affair would turn out to their satisfaction; and now they began to speak openly of that which hitherto they had only mentioned below their breath. And thus a certain man overheard their talk, an Alanian by descent, "magister" in rank, who had long been attached to the emperor and counted among his intimates. Consequently the Magister stole out during the middle watch of the night and ran to the Comneni to report everything to the Great Domestic. Some have it that the Empress was not altogether ignorant of the Magister's visit to the Comneni. Alexius took him into his mother and brother; and after giving ear to his abominable news, they judged it necessary to execute the plan they had kept secret so long, and with God's help to compass their own safety. When, after the morrow, the Domestic had heard that the army had occupied Tzouroulus (this is a little town lying Thrace-wards) he went in the first watch of the night to Pacurianus and related everything to him - this man was "small indeed in stature, but a mighty warrior,"[25] as the poet says, and descended from a noble Armenian family. To him Alexius related the slaves' anger and envy, and their long manoeuvres against them and their immediate intention of blinding them. "But," he continued, "we cannot suffer these things as if we were

25 Iliad 5:801

captives, but we will die, if need be, after fighting bravely; for this is the prerogative of high-souled men." Pacurianus listened to it all and seeing that such circumstances admitted of no delay, but that some drastic step must be taken at once, said, "If when tomorrow's dawn breaks, you leave this city I will follow you and fight willingly on your side. But if you put it off to the next day, then be assured that without the slightest delay I shall go straight to the Emperor and denounce you and your followers." To which Alexius replied, "as I see that you really care for my safety, which is undoubtedly the work of God, I shall not reject your counsel, only let us mutually secure ourselves by oath." Thereupon they exchanged assurances with oaths to the effect that if Providence raised Alexius to the Imperial throne, he should raise Pacurianus to the rank of Domestic which he himself held in the meantime.

Taking leave of Pacurianus he hurried thence to another man, also "full of warlike frenzy," namely Hubertopoulus, told him of his own intentions and put before him the reason why he had decided to escape, and invited him to join him. Hubertopoulus immediately agreed, and added, "You will always find me courageous, but more especially so when I am braving danger on your behalf." The reason above all others why these men were devoted to Alexius was that he outshone others in courage and intelligence; but they also loved him because he was exceptionally generous and very ready to give, although he had not a great abundance of money. For he was not of those who plunder and open their mouths wide for riches. True liberality is not as a rule judged by the quantity of money supplied, but is weighed by the spirit of the giver. In some cases a man of few possessions who pays in proportion to his income, may justly be termed "liberal," whereas another who has much wealth and hides it in a hole in the earth, or does not give to the needy in proportion to his wealth, would rightly be styled “a second Croesus,” or “a Midas mad for gold,” or “niggardly and penurious “or a “cummin-splitter”! That Alexius was graced with all the virtues, the men I have mentioned had known for a long time already, and for these reasons they eagerly desired his elevation to the throne. After exchanging oaths with this officer too, Alexius set off home at a run and told his people everything. It was the night of Quinquagesima Sunday (or the “Cheese-eating” Sunday) when my father made these arrangements; and on the following day at early dawn he had already left the city with his partisans. Hence it was that the populace, who approved of Alexius' spirit and shrewdness, wove a little song to him about these occurrences, composed in their own popular dialect, and it very cleverly strikes up the prelude of the affair and accentuates his prescience of the plot against him and his consequent actions. In its original words the song ran thus;

“To sabbaton tes turines chareis Alexie enoeses to kai ten deuteron to proi hupa kalos gerakin mou”

The meaning of that popular song is roughly this, “On the Saturday named after cheese, bravo to you for your shrewd-ness, Alexius! But on the Monday after the Sunday you flew away like a high-flying hawk, out of the nets of the barbarians.”

CHAPTER FIVE

ANNA DALASSENA, the mother of the Comneni, had lately managed to affiance the grandson of Botaniates to the daughter of Manuel, her eldest son; and now through fear of his tutor hearing of the scheme and divulging it to the emperor she formed a very good plan. It was this, she ordered her whole household to assemble that evening for the purpose, presumably, of making her devotions in the churches of God - for it was her habit to visit the sanctuaries frequently. This was done. All were present according to custom and they brought out the horses from the stables and pretended to be carefully spreading such saddle-cloths on them as befitted the women.

Botaniates' grandson and his tutor were asleep meanwhile, for a separate house had been appointed to them. About the first watch the Comneni who were now quite ready to arm themselves and ride away from the imperial city, locked the gates and gave their mother the keys, and they also noiselessly closed the gates of the house in which her niece's betrothed, Botaniates, was sleeping, though they did not bring the two leaves quite close together and fasten them perfectly for fear they should creak and this noise wake the boy. In these doings the greater part of the night had passed.

Before the first cock-crow they opened the gates, and taking their mothers, sisters, wives and children with them, they all walked together to the Forum of Constantine; on arrival there the Comneni took leave of the women and hastened off very quickly to the palace of Blachernae, whilst the latter ran to the Church of the Divine Wisdom. In the meantime Botaniates' tutor had awakened and guessing what had happened, went after them, torch in hand, and caught them up shortly before they reached the precincts of The 40 Saints[26]. On catching sight of him, Dalassena, the mother of those two noble sons, said to him," Somebody has denounced us to the emperor, I hear. I will therefore make a round of the churches, and use their help as much as I can; and at dawn of day I shall go from them to the palace. So do you go there now and directly the porters open the gates, apprise them of our coming." And he straightway went off to do as he was bid. Then the women arrived

26 The Church of the Forty Martyrs

at the precincts of Bishop Nicholas (which has retained its name of "The Sanctuary" to this day), this stands near the large church and was founded long ago for the protection of those being taken for crimes, as being a part of the large precinct, and was purposely constructed by our ancestors so that if anyone who had been convicted of a crime managed to take refuge there, he was released from the penalty of the law. For the old Emperors and Caesars shewed great consideration for their subjects. But the watchman of this church did not unbolt the doors for the women quickly, but asked, "Who they were and whence they came," whereupon one of the women's attendants said, "They are women from the East, who have spent all their means, and are hastening to pay their acts of devotion so as to be free to return home." Then the man immediately unbolted the doors and gave them admission. At the morrow's assembly of the Senate, the Emperor, who had learnt of the brothers' doings, spoke as was to be expected and inveighed severely against the Domestic. And afterwards he sent two men, Straboromanus and Euphemianus by name, to fetch the women to the palace. But Dalassena said to them: "Give the Emperor this message; ' My sons are the faithful servants of your imperial Majesty and have willingly served you at all times, sparing neither their lives nor their bodies, and have always been the first to risk everything for your empire. But the jealousy felt by others who could not endure your Majesty's kindness and solicitude for them, caused them to stand in great and hourly peril; and when finally their enemies decided to blind them, they got wind of it, and as they could not endure such undeserved peril they left the city, not as rebels but as your trusty servants, firstly, in order to escape this imminent danger and secondly, to inform your Majesty of the plotting against them and to implore help from your Majesty.'"

But the messengers urgently pressed her to come with them, until the woman grew indignant and said, "Allow me to enter God's church and pay my devotions to Him. For it is ridiculous to come as far as the entrance and not go in and implore the mediation of Our Immaculate Mistress, the Mother of God, both for the cause of God and the life of the Emperor." Then the ambassadors respecting her reasonable request, allowed her to enter. She advanced slowly as a woman worn out with age or grief would, or rather she simulated fatigue, and when she had almost reached the very entrance of the Sanctuary, she made two genuflexions and at the third collapsed on the ground, and clinging to the Royal Doors cried out: "Unless my hands are cut off, I shall not leave these holy precincts, until I receive the Emperor's cross as pledge of my safety." Hereupon Straboromanus pulled out the cross he carried in his bosom and gave it to her, but she replied, "I am not asking for assurance from you, but from the Emperor himself I demand the security I have mentioned. And I will certainly not accept a cross sent to me if it is of minute size, but it must be of respectable size." (This she required in order that the pledge given to her might be clearly seen; for if the promise were made over a small cross, most of the onlookers would probably not have observed its ratification.) "It is that man's verdict and mercy I require. Begone, take him my message!" And next her daughter-in-law, the wife of Isaac (who had managed to slip into the church at the time of the opening of the gates for the early hymn) drew aside the veil covering her face and said to them, "Well, she for her part may go, if she likes; but we will not leave this church without assurances, even though death lay before us." Then the man seeing the stubbornness of the women and realizing that they were growing bolder towards them than at first, and fearing some tumult might arise, went away and told the whole tale to the emperor. And he, being kindly by nature and touched by the woman's words, sent her the cross she asked for and gave her full immunity. And when she had come out of the church he ordered her with her daughters and daughters-in-law to be confined in the convent of the Petrii which is situated close to the Sidera.[27] The emperor also had her marriage-relation, the wife of the emperor John (who held the rank of Protovestiaria), fetched from the sanctuary in Blachemae, which had been founded in honour of our mistress, the Mother of God, and consigned her as well to the convent of the Petrii, and gave orders that their stores of wine and corn and all their private possessions should be preserved intact. Every morning then, the two women went to the guards and enquired whether they had any news of their sons; and the soldiers dealt fairly frankly with them and

27 ie., the Gate Sidera

told all they had heard. But the "Mistress of the Wardrobe," a woman generous in hand and mind, desired to conciliate their guards and so told them to take as much of their eatables as they liked for their own use, for the women were allowed to have all they required brought in without let or hindrance. From that time on the guards became more ready with their news and consequently not a detail of all the Comneni were doing was concealed from the women.

CHAPTER SIX

SO MUCH THEN FOR the women. Now the rebels on their part when they had reached the gate in the circular walls of Blachernae, burst its lock and thus had free access to the royal stables. And some of the horses there they left after first slitting their hind-legs from the thigh downwards with the sword, and of the rest they chose those which seemed to them in the best condition, and thence betook themselves with all speed to the monastery, somewhere near the city, called Cosmidium. And here, if I may insert something to make my tale run more clearly, they found the aforementioned Mistress of the Wardrobe, before the Emperor sent to fetch her, as I have told. They took their leave of this woman when they were ready to ride away and they persuaded George Palaeologus to take sides with them and compelled him to depart with them. For before this they had not divulged their plans to him because of a natural suspicion; for the father of this George was extremely devoted to the Emperor, and therefore revealing their project of rebellion to him would have been rather dangerous. And at first indeed, Palaeologus did not show himself at all amenable, but opposed many objections and reproved them for their breach of faith to the emperor and for the fact that, as the proverb has it, they became turncoats. But when the Mistress of the Wardrobe, Palaeologus mother-in-law, insisted firmly on his joining them under threat of dire punishment, he began to yield and his next concern was for the safety of the women, namely his wife Anna and his mother-in-law Maria, for the latter was descended from one of the first families of Bulgaria and was so attractive by reason of the beauty and grace of limbs and features that she was considered the most beautiful of all the women then living. Thus George and Alexius were not free from anxiety about her, and both felt that the women must be removed from that place, but while Alexius' party advised their being conveyed to some fortress, Palaeologus suggested the sanctuary of our Lady in Blachernae - and George's opinion prevailed. So they went off at once with these women and placed them under the care of the Holy Mother of the all-embracing Word. On their return to the place whence they started, they consulted on their best course of action, and Palaeologus and, "You two must get away from here; and I will soon overtake, you, and bring my property, with me?" For as it happened he had all his movable property stored there. Without further delay therefore the Comneni started on their journey; and, after loading his property on the monies' beasts of burden, Palaeologus rode after them. And he came up with them at Tzouroulus (a Thracian village) where by a lucky chance they all joined the army which had occupied it by command of the Domestic. Then thinking it right to send news of their doings to John Ducas, the ex-emperor, who was at that time living on his own property in the country of Morobundus, they dispatched a messenger to inform him of their rebellion. The man carrying the message happened to arrive at early dawn and was standing outside the gates of the farm asking for the Emperor. And his grandchild John, still quite a child, not even a boy yet, and consequently always with the Emperor, saw the man and at once ran in, woke up his grandfather who was still asleep, and told him of the rebellion. But the latter astounded by the words, gave the child a box on the ears, and advising him not to talk nonsense, sent him off. In a little while, however, he came back again, bringing the same news, and in addition the message addressed to his grandfather by the Comneni. Now this message had an excellent touch of wit in it which hinted at Alexius' doings for it said; "We on our side have prepared a right good meal, not wanting in rich condiments, but if you on your side wish to share this banquet, you must come with all speed to partake of it." Then the Emperor sat up and propping himself on his right elbow bade them bring in the messenger, and when this man had finished his tale about the Comneni, he at once exclaimed; "Woe is me!" and clapped his hands over his eyes. And after grasping his beard for a time, as a man will when revolving matters of deep import in his mind, he settled on this one point, namely, that he too would yield to their wish. Therefore he immediately summoned his grooms and mounting his horse, rode off to join the Comneni. On the way he chanced upon a Byzantine who was carrying a heavy purse of gold and travelling to the capital, so in the words of Homer he asked him, “Who and whence art thou?” On learning that he had collected a large sum from certain taxes and was conveying it to the treasury, he urged him to halt for the night with him, promising that at daybreak he should go off where he liked. At the other’s refusing and getting angry, the Emperor insisted all the more and finally persuaded him - for he was marvellously glib of speech and quick in thought, and persuasion sat on his tongue as if he were a second Aeschines or Demosthenes. So he took him with him and turned in at an inn, where he detained him by looking after him kindly in all ways, making him share his table and seeing that he could rest comfortably. But at dawn just when the sun was climbing up the eastern horizon, the Byzantine spread the cloths on the horses and was for hurrying off to ride at full speed to Byzantium. The Emperor seeing this called: “Stop and travel with us,” but the other not knowing where he was going and being moreover quite in the dark about the reason which made him the object of so much solicitude, became vexed and suspicious again of the Emperor and his friendly ways. But the Emperor insisted and began pulling at him, and as the other still did not yield, he changed his manner and spoke more roughly and threatened him if he would not do as he was ordered. As the other still did not obey he ordered all the stranger’s possessions to be packed with his own on his beasts and started on his journey, giving the other permission to go where he liked. Then the man abandoned his intention of going to the Palace from fear of being imprisoned if the Treasury-officials saw him come with empty hands; again he was not anxious to return home because of the unsettled and confused state of the country resultant upon the rebellion of the Comneni which had emerged, and so against his will he followed the Emperor.

And next the following incident took place. As he was starting, the Emperor fell in with some Turks who had just crossed the river Eurus.[28] So drawing reign, he enquired whence and whither they were going, and straightway promised them much money and all kinds of rewards if they would accompany him to the Comneni - and so they consented. Later he demanded an oath from their leaders as he wished to confirm their agreement by it, and this they immediately gave after their fashion and assured him that they would most readily fight on the side of the Comneni.

28 R. Hebrus

After this he started taking the Turks with him as well to the Comneni. The latter saw him from afar and were overjoyed at his strange booty, and they both, but especially my father Alexius, could scarcely contain themselves for delight. Alexius went to meet him and embraced and kissed him. And what followed? At the Emperor's suggestion and suasion they set forth on the road leading to the capital. And all the men from the country-towns flocked to Alexius as volunteers and proclaimed him Emperor - the only exception were the men of Orestias who had an old grudge against him for having captured Bryennius, and therefore they adhered to the part of Botaniates. When they had reached the Athyras, they rested there for one day and then pushed on and reached Schiza (which is also a village in Thrace) and formed an entrenched camp there.

CHAPTER SEVEN

THE WHOLE WORLD, agog with excitement, was eagerly looking forward to what would happen and each longed to see the man who was expected to be proclaimed Emperor. The majority certainly wished Alexius to gain that honour, but neither were Isaac's partisans idle, but as far as possible, they solicited everybody. And thus matters were apparently at a deadlock, for half the population desired to see the elder, and the other half desired to see the younger, brother raised to be pilot of the imperial dignity. Amongst the men present at that time were several of Alexius' kinsmen, for instance, the above-mentioned Emowor-John Ducas, a man clever in council and swift in action (whom I also saw once for a short time) and Michael and John, his grandsons, as well as the husband of their sister, George Palaeologus. These helped each other and worked hard to convert all people's opinions to their own, and letting out every reef, as they say, skilfully used every possible expedient for getting Alexius proclaimed. Consequently they won people over to agree with them, with the result that the number of Isaac's partisans gradually diminished. For wherever the Emperor John was, not a single person was able to resist him, as he was unrivalled in the dignity of his principles, the size of his body, and his king-like appearance. What did the Ducases not do? What did they not say? What good thing did they not promise both to the leaders and the whole army, if Alexius were raised to the Imperial eminence? For example they would say, "He will requite you with very great gifts and the highest honours in accordance with each man's merit, not in a haphazard way, as the ignorant and inexperienced among leaders do, for he has borne the title of “Military Commander” for a long time now and “Great Domestic of the West”; he has shared your salt, in war he has fought nobly at your side, be it in ambush or in close combat, never did he grudge his body, limbs, or even his life to ensure your safety; he has often traversed mountains and plains with you, and learnt the hardships of warfare; finally, he knows you all both as a body and individually, and being himself dear to Ares, he above all longs for brave soldiers.” In this manner spake the Ducases, but Alexius deemed Isaac worthy of much honour and in all things” preferred him, either owing to the charm of brotherhood, or rather, and this must be mentioned, for another reason. For, as the whole army was veering to his side and advocating his claims while it did not favour Isaac even in the slightest, Alexius saw that strength and power and the realization of his hopes would come from that quarter, and so he supported his brother in his intrigues for the throne, knowing that nothing untoward to himself would result from so doing, provided he for his part were raised up by force, as it were, by the whole army to the pinnacle of earthly honours and he flattered his brother in words only and made a pretence forsooth of yielding the power to him. After some time had been spent in this manner, the whole soldiery were assembled near the General's tent in a great state of excitement and each anxious for the accomplishment of his wish. Then Isaac rose and taking the red buskin tried to put it on to his brother's foot; but the latter refused several times until Isaac cried, "Let me do it, for through you God wishes to restore the dignity of our family." He also reminded Alexius of the prophecy once addressed, to him by a man who- appeared, to them somewhere near Carpianum as they were returning home from the palace. For they had reached that spot when a man suddenly met them, perhaps belonging to a race higher than mortal, but in any case gifted with very clear insight into the future. From his appearance he seemed to be a priest, with his bare head, grey hair and shaggy beard; he took hold of Alexius' leg and being on foot himself, he dragged down Alexius, who was on horseback, by the ear and recited to him this line of David's psalm: "In thy majesty ride on prosperously, because of truth and meekness and righteousness," and address him by the title Emperor Alexius! "With these words which sounded like a prophecy he vanished. And Alexius could not capture him though he looked round carefully in all directions in order, if possible, to catch sight of him, and then pursued him at full speed if perchance he might catch, him and ask more in detail who he was and whence he came. But what had been seen had completely vanished. On their return home Isaac was very inquisitive about this vision and asked Alexius to disclose the secret: and as he insisted strongly, Alexius at first made a feint of refusing but finally repeated what had been said to him in secret. Now in discussing this openly with his brother he treated the words and incident as a fraud and deception, but in his private meditations upon this man in priestly garb who had appeared to him, he likened him to the theologian, the Son of Thunder.[29] Therefore when Isaac saw what the old man had prophesied was being fulfilled in deed and expressed in words, he insisted more vehemently and by force put the red buskin on his brother's foot, especially because he saw the fervid longing of all the soldiers for Alexius. After this act the Ducases led the acclamations for they favoured this man for many reasons and especially because their relation, Iresn, my mother had been legally married to my father, And simultaneously all those akin to them by blood did likewise

29 St. John the Theologian

with a will, and the rest of the army took up the shout and sent their voices almost to the heavens. And then was witnessed a curious phenomenon - for those who before had held opposite opinions and preferred death to failure in their desire, became in one moment of the same opinion, and that too, so decidedly, that nobody could have even suspected there had been a variance of opinion between them.

CHAPTER EIGHT

WHILE THESE EVENTS WERE taking place, a rumour spread that Melissenus had already reached the promontory of Damalis with a fair-sized army, had assumed the purple and was being acclaimed as emperor. For some time the Comneni would not believe this report, but Melissenus on learning of their doings, at once dispatched ambassadors to them, who on arrival handed over his letters to the Comneni, which ran somewhat as follows: God has brought me safely as far as Damalis together with the army under my command. I have heard of your experiences, and the measures you have taken for your own safety after being delivered by the mercy of God from the malice of those slaves and their cruel plots against you. Now, as concerns relationship, I am already allied to you by ties of kin, thanks be to God! and as concerns purpose, I yield to none of your blood-relations in my unalterable affection for you (let God. the Judge of all, be my witness!). It is right that we should consult together and ensure for ourselves a firm and stable position so that we may not be upset by every wind that blows, but arrange the affairs of the empire well and thus stand on a sure foundation. This we shall certainly accomplish if, after you have captured the city by the help of God, you two administer the affairs of the

West and allow the kingdom of Asia to be allotted to me. I too must wear the diadem and be clad in purple, and, as is the custom with royalties, my name must be joined in proclamations with the name of that one of you who is chosen Emperor, so that acclamations may be made for us conjointly. In this wise, even though the countries and the business have been divided, yet our mind would be one and the same, and while we so continue the Empire would be administered by us both in perfect peace." The ambassadors did not then and there receive a full answer to the letter they had presented; the next day the Comneni sent for them, and in lengthy speech pointed out to them the impracticability of Melissenus' proposals; they further promised to let them know their decision on the matter shortly through George, called Manganes, to whose care they had entrusted the ambassadors. In spite of this business they did not by any means neglect the siege, but as often as possible made skirmishing attacks upon the walls. On the following day they called the ambassadors and announced their decision to them. This was that Melissenus should be elevated to the rank of ' Caesar,' should he adjudged the fillet and salutes and all other privileges which belong to this rank, and also that the largest town in Thessaly should be given to him. (In this town there is the magnificent church named after the great martyr Demetrius, where the myrrh which ever trickles from his venerable coffin works marvellous cures for those who approach it in faith.) The ambassadors were displeased with the terms but, since those they proposed were not accepted, and they observed also the rebel's great preparations against the city and the enormous army under him, and as they were pressed for time, they began to fear that if they captured the city, the Comneni would not grant even that which they now promised, so they asked that the conditions should be put in a Golden Bull and signed in red letters. To this Alexius the new emperor, consented and immediately summoned George Manganes, who served him as secretary, and ordered him to draw up this Golden Bull. But the latter deferred it for three days, always stringing together various excuses, saying once that after getting over-tired during the day he could not finish the whole letter at night, and at another time that a spark had fallen on what he had written at night and burnt it up. By making such and similar excuses and, true to his name, playing tricks, Manganes postponed writing by one means or the other. Pushing on further the Comneni quickly seized the place called Aretae. This is a district lying close to the city and overlooking the plain, and to persons standing below and looking up to it, it looks like a hill; on the one side it slopes down to the sea, on. the other, to Byzantium, but on the North and West sides it is exposed to all the winds; it has perennial supplies of clear, fresh water but is so utterly devoid of bushes and trees that you would have said the hill had been laid bare by woodcutters. Because of its pleasant situation and climate the Emperor Romanus Diogenes erected some fine houses suitable for kings for short periods of rest. When the Comneni were established there, they made attempts on the wall not by means of siege-engines or machines or stone-throwing instruments, since there was not time enough for those, but with light-armed troops, far-shooters, spearmen and fully-armed soldiers.

CHAPTER NINE

NOW WHEN BOTANIATES, saw the size of the army of the Comneni and its composition of men of all races, and that it was already approaching the gates of the city, and that Melissenus Nicephorus had reached Damalis with no less a force than theirs and was likewise a claimant for the throne, he knew not what to do, and was quite unfit to contend against two foes. For old age had chilled his spirit and made him over-fearful, though in youth he had been very brave, and now he only breathed freely as long as he was encircled by the walls, and he had already ideas of abdicating. Hence the citizens were naturally seized with alarm and unrest and thought the whole place could easily be captured from any side. The Comneni on their side thought the taking of the city would be difficult (for their forces were composed of various nationalities besides natives, and wherever there is a mixed crowd, their temper also is wont to be mixed), so Alexius, the newly-shod Emperor, seeing the city would be difficult to capture, and suspecting the unstable character of his soldiers, adopted a new plan which was by flattery and promises to suborn some of the guards of the walls, and by thus stealing, so to say, their goodwill, to capture the city. After thinking out these things all night he went into the Caesar's tent at early morning and told him his intention and asked him to accompany him on a tour round the walls in order to investigate the defences and their guards (who were chosen from different regiments), and to determine how it would be possible to take the city. The Caesar, however, was annoyed at this order, for he had only adopted the monastic habit very lately and naturally shrank from going near the walls for he felt he would be laughed at by the men on the walls and battlements. And so it fell out. For when he followed Alexius under compulsion, directly the men spied him from the walls they jeeringly called him "Father" and added some insulting remark. However he knitted his brows and though inwardly insulted, disregarded them but gave his full attention to the purpose in hand. For men of firm disposition can fix their mind on the matter before them and overlook external disturbances. He therefore found out which soldiers were on duty in the various towers. He learnt that in one place the "Immortals" were on guard (this is the most select regiment of the Roman army) and in another the Varangians from Thule[30] (by these I mean the axe-bearing barbarians) and in yet another the Nemitzi[31] (these too are a barbaric tribe who have been subjects of the Roman Empire from of old); and he thereupon advised Alexius not to make an offer to the Varangians or the Immortals. For the latter, being indigenous, naturally cherished a great affection for the Emperor and would sooner lose their lives than be persuaded to adopt any treachery against him. The Varangians, too, who carried their axes on their shoulders,

30 By some interpreted as the British Isles, by others as part of Scandinavia, particularly Thyland in Jutland.

31 Germans

regarded their loyalty to the Emperors and their protection of the imperial persons as a pledge and ancestral tradition, handed down from father to son, which they keep inviolate and will certainly not listen to even the slightest word about treachery. But if Alexius approached the Nemitzi he would perhaps not be far from the mark, but be lucky enough to gain entrance into the city through the tower where they kept watch.

Alexius listened to these words of the Caesar as if they came from an oracle and at once acted upon them. He sent one of his men to sound the leader of the Nemitzi carefully from the foot of the wall; the leader looked down from above and after a brisk interchange of questions and answers, he soon agreed to betray the city. So the soldier returned bringing the message and as soon as Alexius and his companions heard this unexpected news, they were delighted and very eagerly prepared to mount their horses.

CHAPTER TEN

AT THE SAME TIME the ambassadors from Melissenus were insistently demanding the Golden Bull which had been promised them, and Manganes was summoned to bring it. He said that he had indeed written the letter, but protested that the implements necessary for the royal signatures and sealing had been lost, pen and all! For he was a dissembler and clever at easily forecasting the future, at picking out what was advantageous from the past, and also accurately diagnosing the present and skilfully arranging matters to his own liking while he covered his doings as long as he wished. Thus Manganes postponed the writing of the Golden Bull in order to keep Melissenus in suspense, for he feared that if the Bull, which bestowed upon him the rank of Caesar, were dispatched more hastily than was wise, Melissenus would scorn that honour and cling at all costs to gaining the empire, as he had informed the Comneni, and venture on a very bold stroke. Such then was the art and wiliness of Manganes in postponing the writing of the Golden Bull for the Caesar. While these things were being arranged and time was pressing for entering into the city, the ambassadors became suspicious of some trick, and were still more insistent in their demands for the Golden Bull. But the Comneni said to them, "Since we practically have the city in our hands, we are going now to take possession of it with the help of God, so do you depart and take this news to your lord and master." And they added further, "If events do indeed turn out according to our hopes, he must come to us, and then all matters will easily be arranged in a manner agreeable both to ourselves and to him" - this was their answer to the ambassadors. Then they sent out George

Palaeologus to Gilpractus, the leader of the Nemitzi, to find out the latter's intentions, and if he discovered that he was ready to admit the Comneni, as he had promised, he was to give the pre-concerted signal, and directly they saw it they would hasten their entrance, while Gilpractus himself would quickly ascend the tower and open the gates to them. Palaeologus undertook this errand very willingly, for he was a man eager for military exploits and the sacking of cities, and the term "stormer of cities" which Homer applies to Ares, would fit him exactly. Next the Comneni got ready and drew up all their heavy-armed troops in a very clever way, and then, marching slowly, they approached the city in troops. But in the evening George Palaeologus approached the wall and receiving the signal from Gilpractus, he went up into the tower with his companions. Alexius meanwhile and his men were only a short distance from the walls and after throwing up a palisade, they encamped comfortably and remained at rest there for a brief period of the night. During the rest of the night, however, after posting the light-armed, they pushed on at a marching pace - the Comneni held the centre of the line with picked cavalry and the flower of the troops - and just at daybreak they stood outside the walls with the whole of their army. All the soldiers were fully armed as if for battle so that they might strike terror into the hearts of the citizens. But when Palaeologus gave them the signal from above and opened the gates, they rushed in pell-mell, no longer with military discipline, but just as each could, carrying their shields, bows and spears.

Now the day was Good Friday (the day on which we offer and feed upon our Mystical Passover) of the fourth "Indiction" in the month of April in the year 6589.[32] And as the whole army (which was composed of

32 i.e., of the Byzantine era – April 1, 1081 AD

foreign and native troops and had come together from home and neighbouring countries) knew that the city had for a long time been crammed with all kinds of riches which were continually imported from other lands and seas, they entered very quickly through the Charisian Gate and scattering in all directions along the main streets, the cross-roads and the by-lanes, they spared neither houses, churches nor even the innermost sanctuaries but amassed a large amount of booty and only desisted from killing, and in every way they acted throughout with the greatest recklessness and shamelessness. Indeed the worst feature was that not even the natives themselves abstained from these deeds but apparently forgot themselves, changed their manners for the worse and did themselves exactly the same things as the barbarians.

CHAPTER ELEVEN

ON BEING INFORMED OF these events, Nicephorus Botaniates realized that his own situation had become exceedingly difficult as the city was being besieged on the West, and Nicephorus Melissenus was encamped at the promontory of Damalis on the East; he did not know what to do but rather inclined to abdicate in favour of Melissenus. And when the city was already surrounded by the Comneni, he bade one of his most trusty attendants go and bring Melissenus through the fleet to the palace; and a certain very fierce guardsman was to accompany him. But before this project could be fulfilled, the city was taken. And Palaeologus, taking one of his servants with him, walked down to the sea, and finding a boat, got in at once and told the oarsman to row to the place where the fleet was usually anchored. When he was already drawing near to the other coast he saw the man sent by Botaniates to fetch Melissenus getting the fleet ready, and the guardsman was on one of the men-of-war. Recognizing the latter from afar as one of his former acquaintances, he sailed alongside the vessel, hailed him and asked the usual questions, "Whence he came and whither going" and then begged him to take him up into his ship. But the guardsman, seeing him with a shield and sword, was frightened and replied, "I would gladly have taken you, had I not noticed that you are fully armed." Hereupon Palaeologus at once consented to lay aside his helmet, shield and short sword, provided only the other would pick him up. Directly the guardsman saw him taking off his weapons, he allowed him to board his own ship, and took him in his arms and embraced him effusively. But Palaeologus, a man of energy, did not delay even for a moment before embarking on his task. Running up to the prow he began asking the rowers, "What are you doing? and where are you going, taking part in a business which will bring dire misfortune to yourselves? the city, as you see, has been taken. He who was once the ' Great Domestic' has been proclaimed Emperor; you see his soldiers and you can hear the shouts; and there will be no room in the palace for anybody else. Botaniates for his part is a fine man, but then the Comneni on theirs are far finer. Large too is the army of Botaniates, but our army is many times larger. You ought not therefore to betray yourselves, your wives and children, but rather take a good look at the city, notice that the whole army is already inside it and the standards fixed, listen to the loud shouts of acclamation, and while the late Domestic draws near to the palace as Emperor and is even now girding on the royal insignia, put your ship astern and go and join him, and thus assure him complete victory! “The crew were immediately convinced by his words and came over to his opinion, whereupon the guardsman grew angry and that warrior George Palaeologus threatened to put him into chains there and then on the deck or to throw him into the sea. Then Palaeologus at once started the cheering and the rowers joined in, but as the guardsman was angry and refused to do so, he had him bound to the deck and left him. After sailing a little further, he again took up his sword and shield, and then brought his ship to the place where the fleet lay, and soon he had all the sailors joining in cheers for the new Emperor. He happened, also, upon the man dispatched by Botaniates to take over the fleet and bring Melissenus through, so he straightway apprehended him and ordered the sailors to loose the cables. Next he sailed away from there with the fleet and reached the Acropolis where he led fresh shouts of acclamation. There he commanded the rowers to cease rowing and to stand by quietly and thus prevent the landing of any who were trying to cross from the East. Within a short time he saw a vessel putting in to the palace, and by bidding the rowers of his own boat row their hardest, he outstripped it. And when he saw his own father in it, he stood up and at once gave him the salutation due to parents. But his father did not look at him pleasantly, nor did he call him the "dear light of his eyes," as Odysseus of Ithaca once did on beholding Telemachus. On that occasion there was a banquet, suitors, a contest of strength, bows and arrows and the prudent Penelope set as prize for the victor, and Telemachus was not an enemy, but a son assisting his father; but on this there was fighting and war and the father and son were opposed in spirit. And each was well aware of the other's feelings, even though their opinions had not yet been manifested in action. So the father called his son a "fool" and asked him: "What have you come to do here?" and his son replied "As it is you who ask me, nothing!" To this the other answered, "Wait a little, and if the Emperor will follow my advice, I will let you know shortly." The aforesaid Nicephorus Palaeologus entered the palace where he found the soldiers dispersed in all directions intent on collecting booty, and judging that they could easily be overcome, he begged Botaniates to let him have the Varangians from the island of Thule, in order to drive the Comneni out of the city with their help. But Botaniates, having once for all despaired of his cause, pretended that he did not want civil war. "If perchance you will listen to me, Nicephorus, then I pray you go to the Comneni as soon as they are in the city and make overtures of peace to them." And so, though very unwillingly, he went.

CHAPTER TWELVE

THE COMNENI ON ENTERING the city had already gained confidence and halted near the square of the Great Martyr, George, called Syceotes, discussing whether they should first go and salute their mothers, according to custom, and then proceed to the palace; but the Caesar, being informed of this, sent one of his body-servants and upbraided them severely for their dilatoriness. So they hastened to the house of Iberitzes where Nicephorus Palaeologus overtook them and said, “The Emperor sends you this message: ‘ I am already an old man and a lonely one, and possess neither son nor brother nor any blood-relation, and if you are willing’ (here Nicephorus addressed his speech to the newly-made Emperor Alexius), ‘do you become my adopted son. And I will not prevent your giving whatsoever you have already promised to your fellow-soldiers, nor will I even share your royal power in any way; I merely ask to retain the name of Emperor, public acclamations and the red buskins, and further the permission to live quietly in the palace. The administration of the affairs of the Empire shall be handed over entirely to you.'" I response the Comneni said a few words, suggestive of agreement, which were repeated to the Caesar who thereupon made haste to get to them to urge them with threats to hurry to the palace. The Comneni. who were going out, met him who was on foot, entering the courtyard from the right and he censured them severely. As he was entering he also caught sight of Nicephorus Palaeologus who was approaching the house again from the left and said to him, "What have you to do here? and for what purpose have you come, kinsman? "to which the other replied, "My coming will accomplish nothing, meseems, but I come to bring the same message from the Emperor as this morning. For the Emperor is resolute to keep to the terms he has offered to treat Alexius as his son; he proposes to invest him with full imperial power so that he may administer the affairs of the Empire according to his pleasure, provided he himself may merely retain the name of Emperor and the red buskins and his purple clothing and the right of living quietly in the palace, as he is an old man now and needs repose.") Hereupon the Caesar with a fierce glance and heavy scowl said, "Get away and tell the Emperor that those offers would have been more useful before the city was captured; for the future ambassadorial messages are uttered out of place. Tell him too, 'As you are already an old man, get off the throne and take thought for your own safety.' "That was the Caesar's answer. Now when Borilus learnt of the entry of the Comneni and of the army's dispersal throughout the city, occupied with plundering and wholly intent on collecting booty, he determined to attack them, thinking they could easily be defeated owing to their scattered state (for the chiefs had been left alone with their kinsmen by blood or marriage and a few foreign soldiers). So he collected all the men who brandished their axes on their shoulders and those who hailed from Coma, and marching from the Forum of Constantine to the so-called Milestone, he drew them up there in ranks with utmost precision; so there they stood, in close order, ready for battle and keeping quiet for the time being.

The Patriarch at that time[33] was a truly holy man and poor, and had practised every species of asceticism such as the fathers of old who lived in the deserts and on the mountains used; he was also endowed

33 Cosmas

with the divine gift of prophecy and had at various times predicted various things in none of which he had been wrong; in a word, he was a model and type to posterity. This man was perfectly well aware of all that had befallen Botaniates, and now either by divine inspiration or at the suggestion of the Caesar (for this, too, was whispered, as the Caesar had long been his friend on account of his high standard of virtue) he counselled the Emperor to abdicate. "Do not begin a civil war," he said, "nor resist God's decree. Do not allow the city to be defiled with the blood of Christians, but yield to the will of God, and depart from our midst." The Emperor followed the Patriarch's advice, and fearing the army's insolence, he girt his clothes around him and went down to the great church of God, hanging his head; and in his very disturbed state of mind, he did not notice that he was still wearing the robes of an Emperor. But Borilus turned to him and catching hold of the mantle attached to his arm by a pearl clasp, pulled it off his dress remarking with a sneer and a grin, “Such a pretty thing truly suits me better now!” And the Emperor entered into the great church of Divine Wisdom[34], and stayed there for a time.[35]

34 Hagia Sophia

35 His abdication was on April 4, 1081

BOOK THREE

The Accession of Alexius and Interfamily Power Struggles

CHAPTER ONE

DIRECTLY THE COMNENI HAD taken possession of the palace they dispatched to the Emperor their niece's husband, Michael, who later became Logothete of the private treasure. With him went a certain Rhadinus who was then Prefect of the city, and by them the Emperor was conducted into a barque and taken a short distance to the famous Monastery of the Peribleptos where they both urged him to don the monastic habit. He, however, wished to defer this for a time, but they in their dread lest a rebellion should be manoeuvred by those two slaves and the soldiers from Coma during the prevailing disorder and confusion, urgently counselled him to be tonsured, and he yielded to their persuasions and forthwith assumed the "dress of angels." Such is Fortune's way! At one moment she exalts a man when she wishes to smile on him, and places a kingly diadem on his head, and purple shoes on his feet; at the next she frowns upon him, and in place of diadems and purple she clothes him in black rags. And this is what happened to the Emperor Botaniates. When asked once by an acquaintance if he easily bore the change, he replied, "Abstinence from meat is the only thing that bothers me, as for the rest I care very little."

In the meantime Queen Maria with her son, Constantine (whom she had by the ex-emperor Michael Ducas) still stayed on in the palace, for she was anxious about her fair-haired Menelaus, as the poet says; and her relationship gave her quite sufficient excuse for remaining, although there were some who, prompted by envy, suggested other reasons, and said she had anticipated matters by making one of the Comneni her son-in-law, and the other her adopted son. This consideration alone decided her to remain, and not a reason which is generally censured, nor the attractiveness and affability of the Comneni, on the contrary it was because she was in a foreign country, without kith or kin, or even a fellow countryman near her. She did not wish to quit the palace hurriedly for fear lest some evil should befall her son unless she first received a guarantee for his safety; for such accidents do occur during a change of dynasty. The child was very beautiful and quite young, being only in his seventh year and (I trust I may be allowed to praise my own relations when the nature of the circumstances demands it) in the opinion of those who saw him at that time he was unrivalled for his sweet disposition and his childish grace in all his movements and games, as those who were there with him afterwards said. He was fair-haired with a milk-white complexion, suffused in the right places with a delicate pink, like that of a rose just bursting its sheath ; his eyes were not light, but gleamed from under his eyebrows like those of a hawk's under a golden hood. As a result he affected all beholders pleasurably in one way or the other and seemed to be of celestial, rather than earthly, beauty - in short he exactly resembled a picture of Eros, as who beheld him might have remarked. This was the true reason of the Queen's remaining in the palace, Now I am by nature averse to fabricating tales and inventing slanders, though I know this is a common practice, especially if people are bitten by envy or malice, nor do I lend a ready ear to popular calumnies; moreover, in this matter I know from other sources the truth of the matter. For from childhood, from eight years upwards, I was brought up with the Queen, and as she conceived a warm affection for me she confided all her secrets to me. I have also heard many others discussing the course of events at this time, and they differed from each other, each one interpreting them according to his own state of mind or to the degree of good-will or hatred he bore the Queen, and thus I discovered that they were not all of the same opinion. Likewise I have heard her herself too narrating the occurrences, and the panic into which she fell about her son, when Nicephorus was deposed. Thus in my opinion and that of the real seekers after the truth, it was only anxiety for her son which detained the Queen in the palace for a short time then. I have said enough about Queen Maria. My father Alexius who had now grasped the sceptre came and dwelt in the palace, but left his wife, fifteen years' of age, with her sisters, mother and her imperial grandfather on her father's side in the ' Lower' palace as it was generally called from its site. And he himself with his brothers and mother and nearest male relations moved into the 'Upper' palace, which is also called 'Boucoleon' for the following reason. Not far from its walls a harbour had been constructed long ago of native stone and marbles, and there stood a sculptured lion seizing a bull-for he is clinging to the bull's horn, pulling his head back, and has fixed his teeth in the bull's throat. So from this statue the whole place, that is both the buildings there and the harbour itself, has been named Boucoleon.

CHAPTER TWO

AND NOW, as I said above, many people were suspicious of the Queen's staying in the palace, and began to whisper that the present holder of the sceptre would take her in marriage. The family of Ducas, however, did not imagine any such thing (for they were not biased by current opinion), but as they had long recognized the undisguised hatred the mother of the Comneni bore them, they lived in constant dread and suspicion of her, as I have repeatedly heard them tell, Therefore when George Palaeologus arrived with the fleet and started the acclamations, those in attendance on the Comneni bent down to them from the walls, and told them to be silent, fearing they might join the name of Irene to that of Alexius and acclaim them together. At this George waxed angry and shouted up to them, "It is not for you that I undertook this heavy conflict, but just for her you mention, Irene." And straightway he bade the sailors shout for Irene as well as Alexius. These doings cast dire terror into the souls of the Ducas family and furnished the malicious with material for ribald jokes against Queen Maria. Meanwhile the Emperor Alexius, who had never had any such idea (for why should he?), having taken over the Roman Empire, and being a man of unvarying energy, at once undertook the whole management of the affairs, and began directing everything from the centre, so to say. For he took possession of the palace at sunrise and before even shaking off the dust of combat or allowing his body any rest, he was wholly plunged in thought about military matters. His brother Isaac, whom he reverenced as a father, he made his confidant on all matters, as he did his mother, and they both assisted him in the administration of the common weal; not but what his great and active mind would have sufficed not only for the administration of one kingdom, but several. Alexius first directed his attention to the most urgent question and spent the rest of that day and the whole of the night in anxiety about the crowd of soldiers dispersed throughout Byzantium. For these were indulging their animal passions to the full, and he was devising a means of checking their undue licence without causing a revolt, and of ensuring peace for the citizens in the future. In any case he feared the recklessness of the soldiers all the more because the army was composed of many different elements, and he wondered whether they might not even be hatching some plot against himself. And the Caesar, John Ducas, was anxious to get rid of Queen Maria, and - drive her out of the palace as quickly as possible, and thus allay people's unjust suspicions, so first he tried in divers ways to win over the Patriarch Cosmas, imploring him to be on their side and to turn a deaf ear to the suggestions of the Comneni's mother, and secondly he very sensibly advised the Queen to ask the Emperor for a letter to assure her own and her son's safety and then to leave the palace, and in this instance he used what is called the "Patroclus" excuse.[36] For once before he had succeeded in providing for her, namely, after Michael Ducas' deposition, when he had advised the latter's successor, Nicephorus Botaniates, to take her in marriage, because she came from another country and had not a crowd of kinsfolk to give the Emperor trouble, and he had told Botaniates a great deal about her family and personal beauty, and often praised her to him. And certainly she was as slender of stature as a cypress, her skin was white as snow, and though

36 Cf. Iliad, 19: 302

her face was not a perfect round, yet her complexion was exactly like a spring flower or a rose. And what mortal could describe the radiance of her eyes? Her eyebrows were well-marked and red-gold, while her eyes were blue. Full many a painter's hand has successfully imitated the colours of the various flowers the seasons bring, but this queen's beauty, the radiance of her grace and the charm and sweetness of her manners surpassed all description and all art. Never did Apelles or Pheidias or any of the sculptors produce a statue so beautiful. The Gorgon's head was said to turn those who looked upon it into stone, but anyone who saw the Queen walking or met her unexpectedly, would have gaped and remained rooted to the spot, speechless, as if apparently robbed of his mind and wits. There was such harmony of limbs and features, such perfect relation of the whole to the parts and of the parts to the whole, as was never before seen in a mortal body, she was a living statue, a joy to all true lovers of the beautiful. In a word, she was an incarnation of Love come down to this terrestrial globe.

By use of the above-mentioned arguments the Caesar soothed and appeased the Emperor's mind, although many advised him to marry Eudocia. Of her it was whispered that in her desire to become "Empress" for the second time, she wooed Botaniates with letters at the time that he occupied Damalis and was hoping to be raised to imperial power. Others say that she did not do this for herself, but for her daughter Zoe Porphyrogenita; and perhaps she would have attained her desire, had not one of the servants, the eunuch, Leo Cydoniates, checked her by giving her much cogent advice. What this was it would not be right for me to detail as I am by nature averse to slander, so I will leave it to those who like to chronicle such things. However the Caesar John who had approached Botaniates on this subject with every kind of art, finally settled the matter by persuading him to marry the Princess Maria as I have already plainly stated and from henceforth John was allowed much freedom of speech in her presence. It took some days to arrange matters, and the Comneni did not want to drive her from the palace at once, seeing that they had received so many kindnesses at her hands during the time she was Empress, and also because of the intimacy between them which bad grown up owing to their mutual connection. Consequently many rumours indicative of varying dispositions were set afloat, some interpreting the facts in one way, others in another, according to the degree of good- or ill-will each individual bore her, for people are wont to judge according –their prejudices rather than according to the real facts. During this time Alexius was crowned without his Queen by the right hand of the Patriarch Cosmas. The latter, a reverend man full of holiness, had been elected to succeed the saintly Patriarch John Xiphilinus, who had died on the 2nd August of the thirteenth Indiction in the fourth year of the reign of Michael Ducas, the son of Constantine . The fact that the imperial diadem had not yet been conferred on the Queen, still further alarmed the family of Ducas, who now insisted on Queen Irene's being crowned too. Now there was a certain monk Eustratius, surnamed Garidas, who was building a house near the large church of God, and from this it seems, had gained a reputation for sanctity. He had already in former times been a frequent visitor to the mother of the Comneni and had predicted her son's rise to the throne. She was in any case fond of monks, and in this instance being soothed by flattering words, she daily showed him increasing confidence and had begun to plan his elevation to the patriarchal seat of the metropolis. Alleging as excuse the simple and unpractical mind of the reigning patriarch she persuaded some friends to suggest to him the idea of resigning in the form of advice which they pretended to offer as most conducive to his welfare. But the holy man was not blind to these machinations, and finally he swore by his own name and said, “By Cosmas, unless Irene receives the crown from my hands, I shall not resign from the patriarchate.” The men forthwith reported these words to the “Mistress,” for thus she was generally called now by the wish of the Emperor who was devoted to his mother. And so seven days after Alexius was publically proclaimed Empero, his wife Irene was also crowned by the Patriarch Cosmas.

CHAPTER THREE

NOW THE APPEARANCE OF this imperial couple, Alexius and Irene, was inconceivably beautiful and absolutely inimitable. No painter striving after the archetype of beauty, would have been been able to picture them nor would a sculptor be able so to compose the lifeless material. Even that well known canon of Polycleitus would have seemed to lack the first principles of art, if anyone looked first at these natural statues - I mean the newly-crowned couple - and then at Polycleitus' masterpieces. Alexius indeed was not especially tall but rather broad, and yet his breadth was well proportioned to his height. When standing he did not strike the onlookers with such admiration, but if when sitting on the imperial throne, he shot forth the fierce splendour of his eyes, he seemed to be a blaze of lightning, such irresistible radiance shone from his face, nay from his whole person. He had black arched eyebrows, from beneath which his eyes darted a glance at once terrible and tender, so that from the gleam of his eyes, the radiance of his face, the dignified curve of his cheeks and the ruddy colour that suffused them, both awe and confidence were awakened. His broad shoulders, muscular arms, mighty chest, in fact his generally heroic appearance, evoked in the multitude the greatest admiration and pleasure. From his whole person emanated beauty and grace and dignity, and an unapproachable majesty. And if he entered into conversation and let loose his tongue, you would have realized from his first words that fiery eloquence dwelt on his lips. For with a flood of argument he would carry the opinions of his hearers with him, for truly he could not be surpassed in discussion or action, being as ready with his tongue as with his hand, the one for hurling the spear, the other for casting fresh spells.

On the other hand, Irene, the Empress and my mother was only a girl at the time for she had not yet completed her fifteenth year. She was the little daughter of Andronicus, the eldest son of the Caesar, and of illustrious lineage, for she traced her descent from the famous houses of Andronicus and Constantine Ducas. She was just like some young, ever-blooming plant, all her limbs and features were perfectly symmetrical, each being broad or narrow in due proportion. She was so charming to look at as well as listen to that eyes and ears seemed unable to get their fill of seeing and hearing. Her face too shone with the soft glamour of the moon, it was not fashioned in a perfect circle like the faces of the Assyrian women, nor again was it very long like those of the Scythians, but it was just slightly modified from a perfect round. And the bloom of her cheeks was such that their rosy hue was visible even to those who stool afar off. Her eyes were blue, yet in spite of their gaiety, they were somewhat awe-inspiring, so that though by their gladness and beauty they attracted the eyes of all beholders, yet these felt constrained to close their eyes so that they knew neither how to resist looking at her nor how to look. Whether there ever existed such a person as the described by the poets and writers of old, I really cannot say, but the following tale I have often heard repeated, namely that, if in those olden days a man had said that this Empress was Athena in mortal guise or that she had glided down from heaven in heavenly brilliance and unapproachable splendour he would not have been far from the truth. The most surprising feature, seldom found in other women, was that she abashed the audacious, but by a single glance gave fresh courage to those abashed by fear. Her lips were generally closed, and thus silent she resembled a living statue of beauty, a breathing pillar of grace. She usually accompanied her words with appropriate gestures, displaying her forearm up to the elbow, and from the shape of her hands and fingers you would have thought they were wrought in ivory by some artificer. The pupils of her eyes resembled a calm sea shining with the intense blue of quiet deep water; the white surrounding the pupils was extraordinarily bright, thus giving the eyes an indescribable dazzling and exquisite beauty. This then was the appearance of Irene and Alexius. My Uncle Isaac, again, was like his brother in stature, and not very different from him in other respects, his complexion however was paler, and his beard less thick than his brother's especially round the jaws. Both the brothers often indulged in the chase if there was no great stress of business, but their chief pleasure they found in military, rather than in hunting, adventures. In an attack on an enemy, nobody ever outran Isaac, even when he was commanding a regiment, for no sooner did he see the enemy's lines than he forgot all else and hurled himself into their midst like a thunderbolt and quickly threw their men into disarray. For this reason he was captured more than once, when fighting against the Hagarenes in Asia. This characteristic of his, that in battle he would not be restrained, is the only one worthy of censure in my uncle.

CHAPTER FOUR

AS IT WAS NECESSARY in accordance with his promise to bestow upon Melissenus Nicephorus the dignity of 'Caesar,' and it was only right that his eldest brother Isaac should be honoured with some higher title and there was no second degree except that of ' Caesar,' the Emperor Alexius invented a new name by compounding the names of 'Sebastos'[37] and ‹Autocrator,' and bestowed upon his brother the title ‹Sebastocrator,' making him, as it were, a second Emperor, and exalting him a step above the ‹ Caesar ‹ who was now counted third in the acclamations, including the acclamation to

37 Greek for ‹Augustus"

the Emperor. Further he ordered that on the public festivals both the Sebastocrator and the Caesar should wear crowns which were, however, very inferior in grandeur to the diadem he wore himself. The imperial diadem, or tiara, was like a semi-spherical close-fitting cap, and profusely adorned with pearls and jewels, some inserted and some pendent ; on either side at the temples two lappets of pearls and jewels hung down on the cheeks. This diadem is the essentially distinctive feature of the Imperial dress. But the coronets of the Sebastocrators and Caesars are but sparingly decorated with pearls and jewels, and have no globe.

Simultaneously, Taronites who had married the Emperor's sister, was created 'Protosebastos' and 'Protovestiaire,' and soon afterwards he was gazetted 'Panhypersebastos,' and then sat with the Caesar. Besides these his brother Adrian was dignified with the title of most illustrious Protosebastos, and his youngest brother

Nicephorus, who had been promoted to be the 'great Drungaire' of the fleet, was now raised to the rank of the Sebasti. Now my father was the inventor of all these new honorary titles, some he made by compounding names, of which I gave an instance above, and the others by applying them to a new use. For names like 'Panhypersebastos ' and ' Sebastocrator ' and similar ones he compounded, but the dignity of ' Sebastos' he seems to me to have applied to a new use. For from olden times the epithet 'Sebastos'had been given only to the Emperors and the name 'Sebastos' was peculiar to them, and my father was the first to bestow it on several of lower rank. And if anyone were to reckon the art of ruling as a science and a kind of high philosophy, as if it were the art of all arts and the science of all sciences, then he would certainly admire my father as a skilful scientist and artist for having invented those new titles and functions in the Empire. Not but what the masters of the logical science have invented new names for the sake of clearness, but this man Alexius, the arch-scientist of Emperors, instituted them for the advantage of the Empire and often made innovations both in the apportioning of duties and in the bestowal of titles.

To return, however, to the revered Patriarch Cosmas, of whom we were speaking - a few days after he had solemnised the sacred rites in memory of the hierarch, John the Theologian, in the chapel in Hebdomon named after him, he resigned his high office, after gracing it for five years and nine months, and retired to the monastery of Callias. And after him the aforementioned eunuch, Eustratius Garidas, was put at the helm of the patriarchal government.

Now when his father Michael Ducas was ousted from the throne, Queen Maria's son, Constantine Porphyrogenitus, doffed the red buskins of his own accord and assumed ordinary black ones, but Nicephorus

Botaniates who succeeded his father as Emperor, bade him take off the black buskins and wear silk shoes of varied colours, as he felt some reverence for the young man, and liked him for his beauty and his high descent, for he grudged him indeed the splendour of entirely red buskins, but allowed him to have a few spots of red shewing in his woven shoes. Then after Alexius Comnenus had been proclaimed Emperor, the Queen Maria, Constantine's mother, in obedience to the Caesar's suggestion, demanded from the Emperor a written pledge, which would be inviolable by being written in red and sealed with a gold seal, to the effect that not only she and her son should suffer no harm, but further that her son should be the Emperor's partner, allowed to wear red buskins and a crown, and be acclaimed as Emperor together with Alexius himself. Nor did she fail in her request, for she received a Golden Bull granting all she asked. Next they took from Constantine the woven silk shoes he used to wear, and gave him red ones, and in the future he put his signature in red after that of Alexius to an deeds of gift and to Golden Bulls, and in processions he followed him, wearing the imperial diadem. Some persons assert that the Queen had made an agreement with the Comneni before their revolt that these privileges should be granted to her son. Matters being thus settled, she left the palace with a decent suite, to reside in the house built by the late Emperor Constantine Monomachus close to the monastery of the great martyr George (still popularly called 'Mangana'),and Isaac the Sebastocrator accompanied her.

CHAPTER FIVE

SUCH THEN WERE the arrangements made by the Comneni for the Queen Maria. The Emperor who from infancy had received a good education and always conformed to his mother's counsels, and was imbued with a deep-seated awe of God, was now tortured with remorse for the plundering of the city, which had taken place on his occupation of it, and brought suffering upon all the inhabitants. For indeed a smooth path occasionally drives a man to some act of madness if he has never in the smallest degree come into contact with rude shocks; but provided the man be one of the cautious and prudent-minded, when such a one has lapsed, his spirit is immediately smitten with fear of God, and overwhelmed and alarmed, and more especially so, if he has undertaken a great enterprise and risen to a proud station. For he is troubled by a dread that by acting ignorantly, audaciously and insolently he may call down the wrath of God upon himself, and be hurled from his throne and lose all he had hitherto possessed. For such was the stateof Saul long ago; when God, because of the King's presumptuousness, rent his kingdom in twain. Alexius was distraught with these reflections and vexed in soul, lest God should make him a scapegoat- for whatever crime had been committed anywhere in the city by any individual soldier- and the rabble which had surged through it at that time had been enormous-he counted as his own and reckoned that it was as if he himself had perpetrated the many deeds of shame. Thus he was wounded and sore stricken in mind; and his Empire and power, his purple robes and diadem encrusted with jewels, and his golden dress sewn with pearl she accounted, as was only right, as of no value compared with the indescribable calamity which had overtaken the Queen of Cities. For nobody, were he to attempt it, could adequately describe the evils which at that time had overwhelmed the city. Even the very churches and shrines and all property, both public and private, had been ruthlessly despoiled everywhere by everybody, one's ears were deafened by the cries and shouts raised on all sides-in fact, an onlooker would have said an earthquake was taking place. All these things Alexius revolved in his mind and was consequently vexed and harassed in spirit, and did not know how to stem the tide of his sorrow. For he was very quick in coming to the right appreciation of any evil deed. And although he knew that these occurrences under which the city had been so evilly entreated, were wrought by other men's hands and minds, yet he was also most keenly conscious that he himself had furnished the pretext for, and the beginning of, the calamity; although again the primary cause of Alexius' revolt had been the two slaves of whom I have spoken before. But even so he attributed the whole blame to himself, and was anxious and desirous to heal the wound. For he felt that only after the wound had been healed and the stain of guilt removed, could he set his hand to the affairs of state, and successfully direct and carry out his plans for the army and military operations. Accordingly he visited his mother, laid bare to her his creditable remorse and asked her how he could allay and gain relief from the anxieties which gnawed at his conscience. She embraced her son and listened to his words with gladness. And then with Alexius' consent she sent for Cosmas (who had not yet resigned his seat), and some of the leaders of the sacred synod and of the monastic body. Alexius placed himself before these men as a condemned criminal, as a humble suppliant, nay, more as a man arraigned before the magistrate and momentarily expecting the verdict which the judge will pronounce against him. He related everything, omitting no offence, or humiliation, or deed, or reason for his actions, but in fear and faithfulness he told everything and earnestly besought them to cure him of his sufferings and submitted himself to their punishments. Thereupon the priests subjected not only him but all his blood-relations, as well as the participators in the rebellion, to the same penances, prescribing fasting, sleeping on the ground, and the other accompanying rites for the propitiation of God. And they all accepted these penances and performed them zealously. Nor would their wives allow themselves to be exempted from these penances (for being very fond of their husbands why should they?) but of their own free will they put on the yoke of penitence. In those days you could have seen the palace full of weeping and mourning, mourning which was not reprehensible or indicative of weak minds, but commendable and a harbinger of that far greater joy which shall never cease. But the Emperor, such was his piety, went even further and wore sackcloth next to his skin underneath his imperial purple for forty days and nights. At night he lay on the ground with only his head raised on a stone and lamenting his faults as was right. After his penance was over, he resumed the management of state affairs with pure hands.

CHAPTER SIX

HE REALLY LONGED THAT his mother rather than himself should take the helm of the state, but so far he had concealed this design from her, fearing that if she became cognizant of it, she might actually leave the palace, as he knew she aimed at the higher life. Therefore in all daily business he did nothing, not even a trifling thing, without her advice, but made her the recipient and coadjutor of his plans, and gradually he stole a march upon her and made her a partner in the administration of affairs, sometimes too he would say openly that without her brain and judgment the Empire would go to pieces.

By these means he kept and bound his

mother more closely to himself, but hindered and thwarted her in her desires. She however looked towards her last abode and dreamt of a convent in which she might spend the remainder of her life in pious meditation. This was her intention, and she always prayed that her wish might be granted. Although she cherished this hope in her heart and steadfastly yearned towards a higher life, yet she was, an the other hand, perhaps more devoted to her son than most women. And so she wished to help her son to breast the stormy waters of government and to steer the ship as well as possible, whether she ran with a fair wind or were tossed hither and thither by the waves; and her desire to help was the stronger because her son had only just taken his seat in the stern and put his hand to the tiller, and had never before come in contact with a sea and waves and winds of such magnitude. By this metaphor I mean to indicate the very varied and disturbing troubles of Government. Thus her mother-love constrained her and she ruled conjointly with the Emperor, her son, and at times even took the reins alone and drove the chariot of Empire without harm or mishap. For besides being clever she had in very truth a kingly mind, capable of governing a kingdom. On the other hand, she was drawn in an opposite direction by her longing after God.

When in August of the same Indiction, Robert's crossing into Epirus forced Alexius to leave the capital he divulged his cherished plan, and gave effect to it, by entrusting his mother single-handed with the imperial government and by a Golden Bull he published his wishes to all the world. Since it is the duty of a historian not merely to catalogue roughly the deeds and decrees of good men, but wherever possible, to add details about the former and to expound the latter, I will adopt this course, and give the words of this Golden Bull, only omitting the scribe's embellishments. It ran thus: "Nothing is equivalent to a sympathetic and devoted mother nor is there any stronger bulwark, be it that danger is foreseen, or any other horror apprehended. For if she decides anything that decision will be a firm one; if she prays, her prayers will be a support and invincible guardians. Such a woman my saintly mother has proved herself actually to me, your sovereign, even from my immature years, and she has been mistress in everything to me, and nurse and upbringer. For though my mother herself was enrolled in the senate, yet her love for her son was her prime course and her confidence in that son was preserved intact. One soul in two bodies we were recognized to be, and by the grace of Christ that bond has been kept unbroken to this day. 'Mine' and 'thine,' those frigid words, were never spoken, and a matter of still greater import is that her prayers, of great frequency throughout her life, have reached & ears of the Lord and have raised me to my present position of sovereign. After I had taken the sceptre of empire, she could not bear to be dissociated from my work and from interesting herself in mine and the public weal, and now I, your sovereign, am preparing, with the help of God, for a sortie against the enemies of Rome, and with great care am collecting and organizing an army, yet I deem the administration of financial and political affairs the matter of supreme importance. And certainly I have found what is an unassailable bulwark for good government, that is, that the whole administration should be entrusted to my saintly and most deeply honoured mother. I, your sovereign, therefore decree explicitly by means of this same Golden Bull that, in virtue of her ripe experience of worldly matters (though she utterly despises them), whatever decrees she gives in writing whether the matter be referred to her by the president of the Civil Courts, or by the judges under him, or by any of all those others who prepare registers or demands or verdicts concerning public remissions of fines, these decrees shall have abiding validity just as if they had been dispensed by my own serene Majesty or ordered by my own word of mouth. And whatever solutions or whatever orders, written or unwritten, reasonable or unreasonable, she shall give, provided they bear her seal-the Transfiguration and the Assumption-these shall be accounted as coming from my sovereign hand. And in the mouth of him who, for the time being, presides over the financial department, as also with regard to promotions and successions to the judgeships of the higher and lower tribunals, and with regard to dignities, magistracies and gifts of immovable property, my holy mother shall have sovereign power to do whatsoever shall seem good to her. And further if any be promoted to judgeships or succeed to minor posts, if any receive the highest, lower, or lowest orders of merit, these they shall retain for ever unchangeably. And again with regard to increase of salaries, supplements to gifts, remission of taxes, and retrenchments and curtailments, these my mother shall settle absolutely. And to put it comprehensively, nothing shall be accounted invalid, that she shall order either by letter or by word of mouth. For her words and her commands shall be considered as given by me, your sovereign, and not one of them shall be annulled, but shall remain valid and in force for the coming years. And neither immediately nor in the future shall she ever be called to give an account or to undergo an examination by anyone whatsoever, either of her ministers or by the Chancellor for the time being, whether her decrees appear reasonable or unreasonable. In fine, whatsoever shall be done under confirmation of this same Golden Bull of that no account shall ever be demanded in the future."

CHAPTER SEVEN

SUCH WERE THE WORDS of the Golden Bull. Men may perhaps marvel that my father, the Emperor, should have shown so much honour to his mother in it, and handed over everything to her, whilst he himself, so to speak, took his hands off the reins of Government and whilst she metaphorically drove the chariot of state, he only ran alongside and merely shared with her the title of ruler. And this in spite of his having passed the years of boyhood and being of an age when characters like his are generally obsessed with the lust of power. He did certainly himself undertake the wars against the barbarians and all the labours and difficulties connected with those, but the whole administration of affairs, the choice of civil officers and the accounts of the income and expenditure of the Empire he entrusted to his mother. Very likely someone at this point would blame my father's management in transferring the administration of the Empire to the woman's apartments, but if he thoroughly understood this woman's high-mindedness and knew what virtue and intellect and remarkable energy she possessed, he would leave off blaming and turn his censure into wondering praise. For my grandmother was so clever in business and so skilful in guiding a State, and setting it in order, that she was capable of not only administering the Roman Empire, but any other of all the countries the sun shines upon. She was a woman of wide experience and knew the nature of many things, how each thing began and to what issue it would come, and which things were destructive of certain others, and which again would strengthen others; she was very keen in noting what should be done and clever in carrying it out to a sure end. And not only was she so remarkable intellectually, but her powers of speech too, corresponded to her intellect, for she was really a most convincing orator, not verbose or apt to drag out her speeches to a great length nor did the spirit of her subject quickly fail her, but she would start happily, and also end in the happiest way. For imperial authority had devolved upon her when she was of a ripe age, just when the powers of thought are at their height, and judgment has matured, and knowledge of affairs is correspondingly at its height, and from these management and administration gain their force. People of this age can naturally not only speak with more wisdom than the young, as the tragedian says, but they can also act more expediently. In earlier days too when she was still counted among the younger women, it was quite wonderful how she seemed to have "an old head on young shoulders." Anyone who had eyes to see could have gathered from her expression the fund of virtue and worth that lay in her. However, as I was saying, my father, when he had taken the sceptre, reserved for himself the contests and sweats of war at which his mother looked on, but her he established as mistress and like a slave he would do and say whatever she bade. The Emperor verily loved her exceedingly, and he hung on her counsels (so fond was he of his mother) and he made his right hand the servant of her wishes and his sense of hearing the listener to her words, and in every case the Emperor would agree or disagree according as she agreed or disagreed. To put it concisely, the situation was as follows, he indeed had the semblance of reigning but she really reigned-moreover she drew up laws, administered and directed everything ; all her orders, written or unwritten, he confirmed by his seal or by word-and thus it may be said, he was the instrument of Empire for her, but not the Emperor. He was satisfied with everything his mother arranged and decided and not only was he very obedient as a son to his mother, but he subjected his mind to her as to a master of the science of ruling. For he was convinced that she had reached perfection in all points and that in knowledge and comprehension of affairs she far surpassed all men of the time.

CHAPTER EIGHT

SUCH WAS THE BEGINNING of Alexius' reign, for to style him 'Emperor' at this time would be scarcely correct, as he had handed over the supervision of the Empire to his mother. Another person might yield here to the conventional manner of panegyric, and laud the birthplace of this wonderful mother, and trace her descent from the Dalassenian Hadrians and Charons, and then embark on the ocean of her ancestors' achievements-but as I am writing history, it is not correct to deduce her character from her descent and ancestors, but from her disposition and virtue, and from those incidents which rightly form the subject of history. To return once again to my grandmother, she was a very great honour, not only to women, but to men too, and was an ornament to the human race. The women's quarter of the palace had been thoroughly corrupt ever since Monomachus assumed the power of Emperor, and had been disgraced by licentious 'amours' right up to my father's accession. This my grandmother changed for the better, and restored a commendable state of morals. In her days you could have seen wonderful order reigning throughout the palace; for she had stated times for sacred hymns and fixed hours for breakfast and for attending to the election of magistrates, and she herself became a rule and measure for everybody else, and the palace had somewhat the appearance of a holy monastery. Such then was the character of this truly extraordinary and holy woman. In sobriety of conduct she as far outshone the celebrated women of old, as the sun outshines the stars. Again, what words could describe her compassion for the poor and her liberality to the needy? Her home was a refuge, open to any of her kinsfolk who were in want and equally open to strangers too. But above all she honoured priests and monks, and nobody ever saw her at table without some monks. Her character as outwardly manifested was such as to be revered by the angels, and dreaded by the very demons; even a single look from her was intolerable to incontinent men, mere wild pleasure-seekers, whereas to those of sober conduct she was both cheerful and gracious. For she understood the due measures of solemnity and severity, so that her solemnity did not in any way appear fierce and savage, nor on the other hand her tenderness slack and unchaste. This, methinks, is the due bound of orderliness, viz.: when kindliness has been mingled with elevation of soul. She was naturally inclined to meditation and was constantly evolving new plans in her mind, which were not subversive of the public weal, as some murmured grumblingly, but were its salvation and destined to restore the State which was now corrupt to its former soundness, and revive, as far as possible, the almost bankrupt finances. Moreover, although she was very busy with public business, she never neglected the rules of conduct of the monastic life, but spent the greater part of the night in singing hymns, and became worn out with continual prayer and want of sleep ; yet at dawn, and sometimes even at the second cock-crow, she would apply herself to State business, deciding about the election of magistrates and the requests of petitioners, with Gregory Genesius acting as her secretary. If an orator had wished to take this theme as the subject for a panegyric, who is there of those of old times of either sex distinguished for virtue whom he would not have cast into the shade ‘ lauding to the skies the subject of his panegyric (as is the way of panegyrists), for her actions, ideas, and conduct, as compared with others? But such licence is not granted to writers of history. Wherefore if in speaking of this queen we have treated great themes somewhat too slightly, let no one impute this to us for blame, especially those who know her virtue, her majestic dignity, her quick wit on all occasions and her mental superiority. But now let us return to the point from which we deflected somewhat to speak about the Queen.

Whilst she was directing the Empire, as we said, she did not devote the whole day to worldly cares but attended the prescribed services in the chapel of the martyr Thecla, which the Emperor Isaac Comnenus, her brother-in-law, had built for a reason I will now relate. At the time when the chieftains of the Dacians decided no longer to observe their treaty with the Romans arid broke it treacherously, then, directly they heard of this, the Sauromatoe (anciently called Mysians) also decided not to remain quiet in their own territory. Formerly they dwelt on the land separated from the Roman Empire by the Ister, but now they rose in a body and migrated into our territory. The reason for this migration was the irreconcilable hatred of the Dacians for their neighbours, whom they harassed with constant raids. So the Sauromatae seized the opportunity of the Ister being frozen over and by walking over it as if it were dry land, they migrated from their country to ours, and their whole tribe was dumped down within our borders and mercilessly plundered the neighbouring towns and districts. On hearing this, the Emperor Isaac decided to go to Triaditza and as he had formerly succeeded in checking the enterprises of the eastern barbarians, so he effected this stroke too with very little trouble. He collected the whole army and started on the road thither intending to expel them from Roman territory. And when he had set his infantry in battle-array, he led an attack against them, but directly they saw him, the enemy broke up into dissentient parties. Isaac, however, thinking it unwise to trust them overmuch, attacked the strongest and bravest part of their army with a strong phalanx, and on his approaching with his men, they became panic-stricken. For they did not venture so much as to look straight at him, as if he were the Wielder of the Thunder, and when they saw the phalanx' unbroken array of shields they turned faint with fear. So they retreated a short distance and offered to meet him in battle on the third day from then, but that very same day they deserted their camps and fled. Isaac marched to the spot of their encampment and after destroying the tents and removing the booty found there, he returned in triumph. When he had got to the foot of Mount Lobitzus, a violent and most unseasonable snow-storm overtook him, for it was the 24th September, a day sacred to the memory of the martyr Thecla. The rivers at once became swollen and overflowed their banks, so that the whole plain on which the royal tent and those of the soldiers stood, looked like the sea. In a short time all their baggage had disappeared, swept away by the raging torrents, and men and beasts were numbed by the cold. Thunder rumbled in the heavens, lightning was continuous with scarcely any interval between the flashes which threatened to set all the country around on fire. The Emperor in this dilemma knew not what to do; but during a short cessation in the storm, as he had already had a great many men carried off by the wildly rushing streams, he with a few picked men left his tent and went and stood with them under an oak tree. But because he heard a great noise and rumbling which seemed to proceed from the tree itself and the wind was rising quickly, he was afraid that the tree might be blown down by it, and therefore moved far enough away from the tree to ensure his not being struck by it if it fell, and there he stood dumbfounded. And immediately as if at a given signal, the tree was torn up by the roots and was seen lying along the ground; whereupon the Emperor stood amazed at God's solicitude for him. Tidings of a revolt in the East were now brought to him, so he returned to the palace. In gratitude for his escape he had a very beautiful chapel built in honour of the proto-martyr Thecla, at no little cost, richly furnished and decorated with various works of art ; there he offered sacrifices of a kind befitting Christians for his safe delivery, and for ' the rest of his life he attended divine service in it. That was the origin of the building of the chapel of the martyr Thecla, in which as I have said, the empress-mother of the Emperor Alexius regularly paid her devotions. I myself knew this woman for a short time and admired her, and all who are willing to speak the truth without prejudice, know and would testify that my words about her are not empty boasting. Had I preferred writing a laudatory article instead of a history, I could have greatly lengthened my story by different tales about her as I made plain before; now however I must bring my story back to its right subject.

CHAPTER NINE

ALEXIUS SAW THAT THE Empire was nearly at its last gasp, for in the East the Turks were grievously harassing the frontiers whilst in the West things were very bad, as Robert was letting out every reef in his endeavour to foist that Pseudo-Michael, who had appealed to him, upon the throne. This was in my opinion only a pretext and it was rather the lust for power which inflamed him and allowed him no rest; consequently he used Michael as a Patroclus excuse and fanned the smouldering ashes of his ambition into a mighty flame and began arming himself with all his might against the Roman Empire. He prepared' dromones"[38] and biremes and triremes and ‹ sermones ‹ and various kinds of freight-ships, fitting them out from the maritime districts and collecting as large forces as possible from the continent to further his purpose. Consequently the young and brave Emperor was desperate, and did not know which way to turn first, as each of his enemies seemed to be trying to begin war before the other, and thus he grew sorely vexed and disturbed. For the Roman Empire possessed only a very insufficient army (not more than the 300 soldiers from Coma cowardly and inexperienced in war, besides just a few a ary barbarian troops, accustomed to carry their swords (?) on their right shoulder).

38 ligh galleys

And further there was no large reserve of money in the imperial treasury with which to hire allied troops from foreign countries. For the preceding Emperors had been very inefficient in all military and warlike matters and had thus driven the State of Rome into very dire straits. I myself have heard soldiers and other older men say that never within the memory of man had any State been reduced to such depths of misery. The Emperor's position was, as you can judge, very difficult and he was distracted by manifold anxieties. However, he was brave and fearless and had acquired great experience of war, so he determined to bring the Empire out of this heavy swell back to anchor by quiet shores, and with the help of God to beat these enemies who had arisen against him into empty foam, as waves are beaten when they break on rocks. He decided that first of all it was necessary to summon quickly all the local governors in the East who were holding forts and cities, and making a valiant resistance against the Turks. So he immediately drafted letters to them all; to Dabatenus, temporary governor of Heraclea in Pontus and of Paphlagonia; to Burtzes, governor of Cappadocia and Coma, and to the other leaders. He first set forth the occurrences which by God's providence had raised him to the imperial throne, and saved him miraculously from imminent danger, and secondly he bade them make provision for their respective districts to ensure their safety and leave sufficient soldiers for this purpose, and with the rest to present themselves at Constantinople and also bring up as many newly-recruited men in the prime of life as possible. Next he saw that he must take whatever steps were possible to guard himself against Robert and to try and deter the chieftains and counts who were flocking to the latter's standard. About this time the messenger returned, whom

Alexius had dispatched before seizing the capital, to ask Monomachatus for help, and to beg him to forward some money. However the messenger only brought back letters detailing the reasons for which forsooth (this we have already related) Monomachatus could not help him as long as Botaniates still sat on the throne. After reading these letters Alexius was terrified lest on hearing of Botaniates' fall from the throne, Monomachatus should join Robert, and he became very despondent. He therefore sent for his brother-in-law, George Palaeologus, and dispatched him to Dyrrachium (a city in Illyria) praying him to use every possible device for driving Monomachatus out of the town without fighting, since his forces were too small to eject him against his will, and to lay what counter plots he could to Robert's plots. He also ordered him to have the bulwarks remade in a new way with most of the nails that held the beams together left out so that if the Latins scaled them with ladders, directly they set foot on the beams, the latter, together with the men on them, would give way and be dashed to the ground below. He also wrote to the chiefs of the maritime districts and even to the islanders urging them not to lose courage nor to be careless but to watch and be sober, take measures for their protection and be on the lookout for Robert. Otherwise he might by a sudden descent upon them, make himself master of all the maritime towns, and even of the islands, and after that cause embarrassment to the Roman Empire.

CHAPTER TEN

SUCH THEN WERE THE precautions taken by the Emperor for Illyria; and he seemed to have firmly secured the towns which at that moment lay directly in front, or at the feet, of Robert ; nor was he unmindful of the districts which lay in his rear. Therefore he first sent a letter to Hermanus, Duke of Lombardy, next to the Pope of Rome, followed by one to Erbius,[39] the Archbishop of Capua. Nay, he went even further and wrote to the princes, and to the various chiefs of the Frankish provinces, and by offering them moderate presents and by promising great gifts and dignities he tried to incite them to war against Robert. Some of these had already abandoned their alliance with Robert and others promised to do so, if they received further inducements! But as he knew that the King of Alamania[40] was the most powerful of them all and could do whatever he liked against Robert, he wrote to him more than once, and tried to win him over by honeyed words and promises of all sorts. And when he noticed that the King

39 Hervaeus

40 Germany

listened to persuasion and seemed likely to yield to his wishes, he sent Choerosphactes to him with yet another letter couched in the following words: - "Most noble and most truly Christian brother, it is the fervent prayer of our Majesty that your Excellency should prosper and advance to greater power. For will it not be fitting that he, a pious sovereign, should wish you all that is good and profitable now that he has learnt the piety that dwells in you? For your brotherly inclination and affection towards our Empire, and the labours you have promised to undertake against that evil-minded person, in order to make him, the guilty miscreant, the enemy of God and all Christians, pay due retribution for wicked plots, proves the true right-mindedness of your soul, and fully confirms the report of your piety. Our Majesty, prosperous in other respects, is exceedingly disturbed and agitated by the news about Robert. But if we are to place any trust in God and His righteous judgments, then the downfall of this most iniquitous man will be swift. For surely God will never allow the scourge of sinners to fall upon His own inheritance to such an extent. The gifts our Majesty agreed to send to your mighty Highness, to wit the 144,000 ‹nummi' and one hundred pieces of purple silk, are even now being sent under the care of Constantine, our Supreme Magistrate and Overseer of dignities, according to the arrangement made with your most faithful and high-bom Count Bulchardus. The sum of money agreed upon and now sent consists of coins stamped with the head of Romanus and of ancient quality. And when your Highness has accomplished the oath, the remaining 216,000 ‹nummi' as well as the stipend of the twenty dignities conferred, shall be sent to your Highness by your trusty servant Bagelardus, when you come down into Lombardy. In what manner it behoves the oath to be fulfilled has been explained to your Highness already; but Constantine, our Supreme Magistrate and Overseer, will expound still more fully, in accordance with our commands, each of the points we require and which must be confirmed by you on oath. For when the conference took place between our Majesty and the ambassadors of your Highness, the points of greatest importance were discussed but, as the envoys of your Highness said they had no mandate, for this reason our Majesty suspended the oath. Wherefore we pray that your Highness will fulfil the oath as your faithful friend Albert assured me solemnly you would do, and as our Majesty begs of you as a necessary corollary. The return of your most faithful and high-born Count Bulchardus was delayed because our Majesty wished him to see our beloved nephew, the son of the most fortunate Sebastocrator, our Majesty's much beloved brother, so that on his return he might report to you the precocious intelligence of the boy who is still of tender years ; for our Majesty considers external and bodily graces as of secondary account, although of these too he has his full share. Your envoy will tell you this for as he was residing in the metropolis, he saw the boy, and as was right had a conversation with him. And since God has not yet blessed our Majesty with a child, this dearly beloved nephew is to us as a son, and, God willing, there is nothing to prevent our being united by ties of blood, and being kindly disposed towards each other, as becomes Christians, or even becoming each other's intimates like relations, and then in the future through mutual assistance we shall become formidable to our enemies and, with the help of God, invincible. As a token of friendship we are sending your Highness together with the other presents a gold pectoral cross inset with pearls and a gold pyx which contains relics of several saints, each of which can be recognized by the card attached to it ; a chalice of sardonyx, a crystal goblet, a radiated crown of gold[41] and some ‹opobalsamum.'[42]. May God grant thee long life, enlarge the borders of thy power and make all those who rise against thee thy footstool. Peace be with thy Highness and may the sun of content shine upon all lands subject to thee, and may all thy enemies be brought to naught by the help of the Mighty Power above who will grant thee the victory over all, because thou dost worship His true name and art arming thy hand against His enemies."

CHAPTER ELEVEN

THESE WERE THE MEASURES he took for the Western part of the Empire and next he prepared himself against the immediate

41 lit. "a thunderbolt bound with gold. Finlay translates this as "a gold ornament containing a protective charm against thunder."

42 Balm of Mecca

danger that threatened; he continued to reside in the capital, busily devising by what possible means he might resist the enemy who were almost at the very gates of the Empire. My history has already told how at this time the godless Turks were living round the Propontis[43] and Solyman, the ruler of the whole of the East, was encamped around Nicaea (where he had his ‹sultanicium ‹ corresponding to our ‹ palace ‹) and incessantly sending out raiders to devastate all the country round Bithynia and Thynia, and they made incursions on horse and on foot even as far as the Bosporus (now called Damalis), and carried off much booty, and they all but attempted crossing the sea itself. The Byzantines saw them living fearlessly in all the little towns along the coasts and in the sacred precincts even, as nobody drove them out, for the inhabitants were absolutely panic-stricken and did not know

43 Sea of Marmora

what steps to take. When the Emperor saw this, he hesitated between different plans, and often changed his mind and finally chose the plan which he considered the best and executed it as far as was possible. He had recently recruited soldiers from among the Romans and from Coma, from these he chose ‹decurions' and put them in command of boats with some light-armed troops who only carried their bows and a shield, and with others who according to their custom were fully armed with helmets, shields and spears. He instructed them to row along the coasts of the Propontis secretly during the night and to jump out and make an attack upon the infidels at any point where they noticed that the latter did not much outnumber themselves and then to run back quickly to their respective boats. As he knew that his men were quite inexpert in war, he told the rowers to row without making any noise, and also warned them to be on their watch against the infidels who would be in ambush in the clefts of the cliffs. After they had executed this maneuver for several days, the barbarians did indeed gradually retire inland from the seaside districts. On being informed of this, the Emperor directed the soldiers to occupy the villages and buildings recently held by the Turks and to pass the night in them; and at break of day when for foraging or any other reason the enemy generally came out into the country, to make a sudden massed attack upon them, and be satisfied if they gained an advantage over them, however slight it might be, and not to risk restoring confidence to the enemy by seeking for further success, but to retire at once to the shelter of their forts. In consequence the barbarians after but a brief space of time again retreated to an even greater distance. Hereupon the Emperor gained courage, had the foot-soldiers put on horses and given spears to brandish, and made many cavalry raids upon the enemy, and no longer secretly during the night but in the daylight too. And those who had hitherto been decurions were now created captains over fifty and the men who had fought the enemy on foot at night with great fear now attacked them in early morning or at noon, and with confidence entered upon brilliantly successful engagements. Thus fortune now deserted the infidels and the power of the Roman Empire which had been temporarily obscured shone forth. For Conmenus not only drove them far back from the Bosporus and the whole seaboard, but also routed them out of the whole of Bithynia, Thynia and the province of Nicomedia and reduced the sultan to making urgent overtures for peace. As Alexius was hearing from many quarters of the tremendous onset Robert was preparing and of the immense number of troops he had collected, and that he was hastening on his march to the coast of Lombardy, he gladly received the proposal of peace. For, if even the hero Heracles could not fight two men at the same time, as the proverb suggests, much less could this young ruler, who possessed neither forces nor money and had only just taken over a statealready corrupt which had for a long time been gradually diminishing and had sunk practically to the lowest depths ; and all its money had been squandered without any useful result. This was the reason he felt himself compelled to agree to terms of peace after, by various methods, chasing the Turks away from Damalis and its coasts, and further buying them off with bribes. He fixed the river called Dracon as their boundary, and compelled them to promise never to cross it or make incursions into Bithynian territory.

CHAPTER TWELVE

IN THIS WAY THEN affairs in the East were lulled to rest. On reaching Dyrrachium

Palaeologus sent off a runner with the news about Monomachatus, which was that on hearing of Palaeologus' journey he had hurriedly betaken himself to Bodinus and Michaelas. For he was afraid because he had not obeyed Alexius' order but had sent back empty-handed the messenger whom the Emperor Alexius had sent with a letter asking for money before he commenced the rebellion he was meditating. In reality the Emperor did not intend to punish him further than by dismissing him from his position for the reason just given. When the Emperor learnt what Monomachatus had done, he sent him a Golden Bull granting him full immunity, and as soon as Monomachatus received it he returned to the palace.

Robert, meanwhile, had reached Hydruntum and after delegating the rule over that town and the whole of Lombardy to his son Roger, he sailed and occupied the port of Brindisi. When he heard of Palaeologus' arrival in Dyrrachium, he at once had turrets constructed on the larger vessels, built of wood and covered with hides. And he speedily had everything necessary for a siege packed on board the ships, and horses and fully-equipped cavalry he embarked on the cruisers, and with wonderful celerity he collected from an sides all the apparatus for war, for he was in a hurry to cross the sea. His plan was to surround Dyrrachium, when he reached it, with battering engines both on the land- and sea-side so as to strike dismay into the hearts of the inhabitants and also by thus hemming them in completely, to take the town by assault. Consequently when the Islanders and the dwellers along the coast by Dyrrachium heard of this plan, great confusion fell upon them. When Robert had everything completed to his liking, he loosed anchor; the freight-ships, the triremes and monoremes were drawn up in the battle array of nautical tradition, and thus in good order he started on his voyage. Meeting with a favourable wind he struck the opposite shore at Valona and coasting along it, came up to Buthrotum.[44] There he joined forces with Bohemund who had crossed earlier, and taken Valona by storm. He now divided the whole army into two parts, with the one he meant to sail to Dyrrachium, and commanded it himself, and Bohemund he put in command of the other half with which to march to Dyrrachium over land. After he had passed Corfu and was directing his course to Dyrrachium, he was suddenly caught in a most terrible storm off the promontory called Glossa. For a heavy fall of snow and the winds rushing down from the mountains churned up the sea violently. Then the waves rose and roared and the oars of the rowers were broken off as they dipped them; the winds tore the sails to shreds; the yard-arms were snapped off and fell on the deck, and the boats, crews and all, sank. And yet this was in summer

44 Butrinrto

when the sun had already crossed the tropic of Cancer and was hastening towards the Lion, just at the season which is called the Rising of the Dog Star. They were naturally all much disturbed and agitated and quite helpless to cope with such enemies. There was a frightful tumult, for men wailed and shrieked, called upon God to save them, and prayed to be allowed to see the dry land. The storm did not lessen meanwhile, it was as if God were pouring out his wrath upon Robert's insolent and overweening presumptuousness, and shewing him from the very start that the issue would not be successful. Some of the ships were lost, crews and all, others were dashed on the rocks and broken to pieces. The hides covering the turrets became stretched by the rain, so that the nails fell out of their holes and the weight of the hides soon dragged down the wooden turrets which in their fall swamped the ships. However, the boat which carried Robert was saved with difficulty, though sadly battered; and some of the freight-ships with all on board were also miraculously saved. The sea threw up many of the men and quite a number of pouches and other oddments which the sailors had taken with them and scattered them over the shore. The survivors buried the dead with due rites, and consequently they became infected with the horrible stench, as it was not easy for them to bury so many quickly. Now all the provisions had been lost and probably the survivors would have died of starvation, had there not been a luxuriance of crops and fruits in the fields and gardens.

Now the moral of all this was plain to all right-minded persons, but none of these occurrences daunted Robert, for he was quite fearless and only prayed, I believe, that his life might be spared long enough to allow of his fighting against his chosen enemies. Therefore nothing of what had happened deterred Robert from the object he had set himself; and so with the remaining troops (for some by God's almighty power had escaped from the peril) he reached Glabinitza on the seventh day. Here he stayed so that he and the other survivors from the storm at sea might recuperate, and that those he had left behind at Brindisi and others, whom he expected to come by sea from other places, might join him, as well as the troops who had started overland a short time before, the fury-equipped cavalry, infantry and the light-armed soldiers. When he had collected his whole army from land and sea, he occupied the plain of Illyria with an his troops. In his company there was a Latin, an envoy, as he said, from the Bishop of Bari to Robert, and he it was who gave me an account of all this, and assured me that he went through this whole campaign with Robert. And next, huts were put up inside the ruined walls of the city once called Epidamnus, and the soldiers lodged in them by battalions. In this city the Epirote King,

Pyrrhus, dwelt when he made an alliance with the Tarentines and began his fierce struggle with the Romans in Apulia. And at that time such a frightful slaughter took place that all to the last man fell a prey to the sword, and the city was left uninhabited. But in later years, as the Greeks say, and to this the inscriptions in the town bear testimony, the city was rebuilt by Amphion and Zethus in the style that it still retains, and its name was changed to 'Dyrrachium.' These few words about this city must suffice, and here I will conclude my third book and continue the tale of Robert's doings in the next.

BOOK FOUR

War with the Normans (1081-82)

CHAPTER ONE

THUS THE CONTINENT WAS now occupied by Robert, who pitched his camp in it on June 17th of the fourth Indiction with an exceedingly great number of horse- and foot-soldiers who formed a terrifying sight as well because of their equipment as from their strategic arrangement; for by this time the whole army had reassembled from all sides. And at sea rode his fleet composed of every kind of vessel with a different set of soldiers, highly experienced in naval warfare. The inhabitants of Dyrrachium were hemmed in on either side, that is by sea and by land, and as they could see Robert's innumerable troops, which exceeded all their expectations, they were overcome with fear. However, George Palaeologus, a brave man and expert in every sort of strategy, who had fought thousands of battles in the East and come out victor, was undismayed, and began fortifying the city. He built bulwarks according to the Emperor's suggestions, placed a number of stone-throwing engines on the walls, put fresh heart into the discouraged soldiers, set watchmen all along the wall, made the circuit of them himself every day and night, and exhorted the guard to keep unceasing watch. At the same time he sent the news by letter to the Emperor of Robert's incursion and his intention of besieging Dyrrachium. When the inhabitants of Dyrrachium saw the siege-engines outside and the enormous tower that had been constructed, overtopping even the walls of Dyrrachium-and encased in hides with catapults standing on the top of it-when they saw the whole circumference of the walls girt round by the army, and the allies flocking in from all directions to Robert, and the neighbouring towns being raided, and the tents increasing in number daily, then indeed dread fear fell upon them. For now they recognized Duke Robert's aim, and saw that he had occupied the plain of Illyria, not for the purpose of pillaging towns and country, collecting a large store of booty, and then returning to Apulia, as rumour had reported, but that he was really striving for the mastership of the Roman Empire, and was anxious to take

Dyrrachium by storm, to start with, so to say. So Palaeologus ordered the question to be asked from the walls: 'For what purpose had Robert entered their country?' He replied, "In order to restore Michael, my kinsman, who was expelled from the Empire, to his former high position, to wipe out the insults heaped upon him, and generally to avenge him." To this the besieged replied: "If when we see Michael we recognize him, we will immediately do obeisance to him and hand over the city." On hearing this Robert forthwith commanded Michael to be clad in magnificent robes and exhibited to the inhabitants of the city. So with a magnificent procession as escort and to the music of a band and cymbals he was shown to the townsfolk. But directly they saw him, they poured down a stream of insults upon him from the walls and swore that they certainly did not recognize him. Robert paid no heed, however, and went on with the work he had in hand. Whilst the men inside and outside the walls were thus bandying words with each other, a few made a sudden sortie from the city, engaged the Latins in combat, and after inflicting a slight loss upon them, reentered Dyrrachium.

There was a great diversity of opinion about the monk who was accompanying Robert. Some declared he was the cup-bearer of the Emperor Michael Ducas, others asseverated that he was indeed the Emperor Michael himself, the barbarian's kinsman by marriage for whose sake alone he had undertaken this great war; and yet another party contended that they knew positively that the whole thing was a fiction invented by Robert; nor, said they, had the monk come to him of his own accord. But Robert raised himself from extreme poverty and complete obscurity by physical energy and mental predominance and carved himself a kingdom by conquering all the towns and districts of Lombardy, and even of Apulia, as has been told in this history.

Very soon he coveted more, as is generally the rule with men of insatiable ambition, and decided he ought to make an attempt upon the cities scattered throughout Illyria, and then, if that venture was successful, to proceed still further. For covetousness, whenever it grasps at Empire. does not differ at all from gangrene, which can never be arrested once it has attacked a body, until it has passed right through and vitiated it entirely.

CHAPTER TWO

THE EMPEROR WAS KEPT informed of all these events by the letters of Palaeologus - namely, that Robert crossed the sea in June (as already told); that, in spite of being caught in a terrible storm and shipwrecked and subjected to God's wrath, he was nothing daunted, but took Valona at first assault with the forces he had brought with him; further, that innumerable troops from all quarters were rallying to his standard, as many as the flakes of a snowstorm in number; and that the lighter-headed were joining Robert because they believed that the impostor Michael was really the Emperor. Consequently Alexius was afraid and considering the magnitude of the task before him and realizing that the forces at his command were only equal to a small fraction of Robert's, he deemed it necessary to call upon the Turks in the East for help, and signified his desire to the Sultan. By promises and bribes he also solicited the aid of the Venetians (from them, it is said, the Romans had previously introduced the name "Venetian colour "in their horse races). Some things he promised, and others he offered to give at once, provided that they would equip their whole navy and with all speed sail to Dyrrachium with the object firstly, of protecting the city and secondly, of engaging in battle with Robert's fleet. And if they carried out his request, and by God's help gained the victory or (as may always happen) they were defeated, even then they should receive all he had promised, just the same as if they had conquered. And all their desires, provided only they were not injurious to the Roman Empire, should be fulfilled and confirmed by Golden Bulls. On hearing this the Venetians signified their desires through their ambassadors and received definite promises. Thereupon they got their navy ready with every kind of ship and started for Dyrrachium in good order. They passed safely over the high seas and reached the chapel built long ago to the Immaculate Virgin at a spot called Pallia, about eighteen stades distant from Robert's camp outside Dyrrachium. But when from the region of Dyrrachium they had viewed Robert's fleet fitted out with every species of military instruments they lost heart for the war. As soon as Robert knew of their arrival he sent his son Bohemund to them with the fleet to bid them 'hurrah' for the Emperor Michael and for Robert. However, they put off their hurrahing to the morrow. When night fell, as they were not able to approach the shore, and there was a calm, they tied the larger vessels together with ropes and constructed a so-called "sea-harbour," and built wooden towers at their mastheads and hauled up on to them by ropes the small boats which were usually towed together at their stems. In these they placed armed men and cut up heavy beams into pieces about a foot-and-a-half long and studded them with sharp iron nails and then awaited the approach of the Frankish fleet. At daybreak Bohemund came demanding their acclamations. But when the Venetians laughed at his beard, he could not stand their ridicule, and himself led the attack against the largest of their ships and soon the rest of the fleet joined in. A fierce battle commenced and as Bohemund was fighting very savagely against them, they threw down one of the bludgeons mentioned above, and knocked a hole into the ship on which Bohemund was. As the water was sucking down the vessel and they were in danger of sinking, some of the men actually jumped out into the water and were drowned whilst the rest still continued fighting with the Venetians, and were killed. And Bohemund being in imminent danger leapt on to one of his own boats and was saved. Then the Venetians took fresh courage and carried on the battle with greater energy until at last they routed the enemy and pursued them to Robert's camp. Directly they touched the land they jumped on to it and started another battle with Robert. When Palaeologus saw them he too rushed out from the citadel of Dyrrachium and fought on the side of the Venetians. After a fierce battle which surged right up to Robert's encampment, a large number of men were driven out from this and many too fell a prey to the sword. Afterwards the Venetians carried off much spoil, and returned to their ships and Palaeologus re-entered the citadel. And after taking a few days' rest the Venetians sent ambassadors to the Emperor to recount these happenings. He received them with great honour, as was natural, bestowed many benefactions upon them, and then dismissed them with a large gift of money for the Doge of Venice and his subordinate magistrates.

CHAPTER THREE

BUT ROBERT BEING OF a most warlike disposition, decided not to discontinue the war, but to fight on bravely. As it was winter he was unable to launch his ships, and moreover, the Roman and Venetian fleets kept a strict guard over the straits and prevented his reinforcements and commissariat from Lombardy reaching him. Now when spring had set in and the storms at sea had ceased, the Venetians were the first to slip their cables and take the water against Robert, and behind them sailed Maurix with the Roman fleet. A bitter combat ensued hereupon and Robert's men fled, which led to Robert's deciding to haul up his whole fleet. Then the islanders and the towns along the coast and whoever else had been paying tribute to Robert, took heart because of his misadventures, and after they heard of his defeat at sea did not readily pay the taxes he had imposed. So he resolved to carry on the war with greater diligence and fight again both on land and sea. But as he could not proceed to put his plans into action, for strong winds were blowing at the time and he feared shipwreck, he waited patiently for two months near the harbour of Hiericho and got ready everything that he needed for fighting again on land and sea. The Roman and Venetian fleets guarded the straits as far as possible and whenever the sea lent itself even slightly to the idea of sailing, they intercepted the ships which were trying to cross from Italy to Robert. Since it was not easily possible to collect the necessary provisions, not even from the mainland, for Robert's army which was encamped along the river Glycis, as the men from Dyrrachium caught those who came out from Robert's trenches for foraging or anything else, his men began to suffer from hunger, and besides this the inclement climate of the district did them great harm. So that in the course of three months a total of ten thousand men are said to have perished. The same disease also attacked Robert's cavalry-forces and destroyed many. In the cavalry nearly five hundred of the Counts and the most valiant picked men were carried off by illness and famine, whilst in the lower ranks countless horsemen perished. Now Robert's ships, as we have said, had been hauled up into the river Glycis, this was almost dried up by the drought, as a very hot summer had set in after the winter and the spring, and it had scarcely as much as water running down its bed as usual, and therefore he hardly knew how to drag them down to the sea again. But being of an inventive mind and a deep thinker, he had posts fixed along either side of the river, and connected with closely woven wattle-work, then behind these he had large trees cut down at the root, laid flat and sand strewn over them, so that the water was collected and flowed all together into one spot, that is the channel formed by the posts. Gradually the water formed pools and then filled the whole bed of the river and reached a fair depth, until finally it raised the ships which had hitherto been embedded in the soil so that they floated on the top. Then after this all was fair sailing and the ships were drawn down to the sea without any difficulty.

CHAPTER FOUR

WHEN THE EMPEROR HEARD what Robert had done, he wrote immediately to Pacurianus telling him of Robert's irresistible assault on, and capture of, Valona, and of his total disregard of the ills which had befallen him on land and sea, and even of that defeat which he had suffered at the first setoff. He therefore commanded Pacurianus not to delay but collect his forces more quickly and come and join him. That then was his message to Pacurianus. He himself at once set out from Constantinople in the month of August in the fourth Indiction, leaving Isaac in the capital to carry on the civil administration. If he heard any seditious talk among their enemies, as would be likely, Isaac was to scatter them,also to guard the palace and the city and try to dissipate the women's grief. As far as his mother was concerned, she did not require any consoling, I fancy, for she was very strong-minded, besides being so clever in business. Pacurianus, after reading the letter, appointed Nicholas Branas, a brave man with great military experience, as his lieutenant-general. He himself with his whole army and with the flower of the nobility of the Orestias, started quickly and hurried to join the Emperor. Immediately the latter arrived, he arranged the whole army in order of battle, appointed the bravest men leaders of the battalions, and told them to continue the journey in that same order wherever the nature of the ground permitted, so that by understanding the whole arrangement and each man knowing his exact place, they would not become confused in the heat of battle and would not easily or accidentally shift their place. Constantine Opus led the Guards, Antiochus the Macedonians,

Alexander Cabasilas the Thessalians, and Taticius, at that time 'Primicerius,'[45] the Turks of Achrida. He was extremely brave, and absolutely fearless in battle, although he was not descended from free-born stock; for his father, who was a Saracen, fell into the hands of John Comnenus, my paternal grandfather, on a foraging expedition. The leaders of the Manichaeans, who totalled two thousand eight hundred, were Xantas and Culeon, also of the same heresy. All these were very warlike and ever ready to spill their enemies' blood when opportunity offered, they were moreover audacious and insolent. Of the household troops (generally called "Vestiaritae ") and the Frankish regiments Panoucomites and Constantine Hubertopoulos, so called after his origin, were in command. Then after arranging his troops in this manner, he set out with all his forces against Robert. On his way

45 Chief of the household

he met a man coming from Dyrrachiurn and obtained from him a clearer account of the events there and learnt that Robert had moved up all the engines necessary for a siege and drawn them close up to the walls. George Palaeologus had led a counterattack by day and night, and then in despair had flung open the gates and commenced a fierce battle with the enemy. He had been severely wounded in various parts of the body, and most seriously by an arrow which had pierced his head near the temple. As he struggled in vain to pull it out he sent for an expert who cut off the end, I mean the tail end which is usually furnished with feathers, and the rest of it he left sticking in the wound. Then with his head bound up as well as possible under the circumstances, he rushed back into the midst of the foe, and continued fighting without flinching until the evening. When the Emperor heard this, he realized that Palaeologus was in need of immediate relief, and therefore marched on at greater speed. On reaching Thessalonica the news about Robert was fully confirmed in detail by several. He was told that Robert, ever alert, had not only set apart extra brave soldiers, but had also collected a heap of material from the plain of Dyrrachium and then pitched his camp within a dart's throw from the walls, while he had also disposed others of his troops all around on the mountains and valleys and slopes. At the same time many also spoke to him of Palaeologus' untiring industry. For Palaeologus had now planned to set fire to Robert's huge wooden tower, and had collected naphtha and pitch and faggots of dry wood and catapults on the walls, and was awaiting the enemy's attack. As he expected Robert the next day, he placed the wooden tower (which he had had made inside the town) in the direct route of the mighty one which would come from the outside; then the whole night through he made tests with the beam which was hung at the top of his tower and intended to be pushed against the door of the huge tower which would be brought up; for he wanted to see if it moved very easily and would really fall directly against the door and prevent this being readily opened. When he was satisfied that the beam moved easily and would accomplish its purpose, he confidently awaited the attack. On the following day Robert commanded all to take arms, and about five hundred foot and horse soldiers to place themselves in the tower, and when this had been pushed up to the walls, they at once tried to throw open the door at the top which they intended to use as a draw-bridge for crossing into the citadel. Then Palaeologus from the inside drove forward the enormous beam with the help of the large body of brave men and the machines he had got ready, and thus rendered Robert's tower useless, for the beam effectually prevented the door being opened. Next the Franks who were standing on the top of the tower were subjected to a continuous volley of darts which they could ill bear and therefore hid themselves. Hereupon he ordered the tower to be fired, and almost before he had spoken it went up in flames. The men on the top threw themselves down and those below opened the door at the foot and fled. When Palaeologus saw them fleeing he made a sortie through the postern gate with a troop of brave soldiers in full armour and of others who carried axes with which to cut down the tower. And herein too he was successful, for he burnt the upper part of it and the lower was entirely destroyed by a few blows of a stonecutter's tool.

CHAPTER FIVE

AND NOW, the informant continued, Robert was busily building a second mighty wooden tower, just the same as the other, and was getting ready battering-machines to use against Dyrrachium; from all this the Emperor recognized that the besieged in Dyrrachium were in need of speedy help, so set his troops in order and took the road to the town. When he arrived there and had settled his troops in an entrenched camp near the river Charzanes, he at once sent messengers to ask Robert for what purpose he was there, and what his object was. Then he moved on to the Chapel dedicated to the memory of Nicholas, greatest of all Bishops, four miles distant from Dyrrachium, and reviewed the nature of the land in order to pick out beforehand the most suitable spot for drawing up his phalanxes for battle. And that day was the fifteenth of October. There was a neck of land running out from Dalmatia to the sea and terminating in a promontory which was almost a peninsular, and on this stood the chapel I have mentioned. The side of this neck which looked towards Dyrrachium sloped very gradually down to the plain and had the sea on its left, and on its right a steep, overhanging mountain. To this spot he brought his whole army, and after having fixed his palisades, sent for George Palaeologus. However he had had long experience of such tricks and as he deemed it inexpedient he refused to come out and explained this to the Emperor. But on the Emperor's again summoning him more urgently, he replied, "I think it would be fatal for me to leave the city while it is being besieged, and I shall not come out unless I actually see the ring from Your Majesty's finger." The ring was sent and upon seeing it Palaeologus joined the Emperor with ships of war. Then the Emperor asked him all about Robert and after Palaeologus had given him a clear account, he asked whether it would be well for him to venture on a battle with Robert; but Palaeologus disagreed with this proposal. And others too who had gained military experience by long service opposed it strongly. They counselled endurance and embarrassing Robert by skirmishes and not allowing any of his men to come out from their quarters to forage; they suggested he should send orders to Bodinus and the Dalmatians and the other chiefs of the adjacent provinces to do the same, and assured him that in this way Robert could easily be, worsted. But the majority of the younger officers preferred a battle, and most vehement among them were Constantine Porphyrogenitus, Nicephorus Synadenus, Nabites, leader of the Varangians, and even the two sons of the late Emperor Romanus Diogenes, Leo and Nicephorus. At this moment the envoys sent to Robert returned and brought the latter's verbal message to the Emperor which ran, "It was certainly not against Your Majesty that I took the field, but simply in order to avenge the injustice done to my kinsman by marriage. But if you desire peace With me, I too shall gladly welcome it, though only on condition that you are ready to fulfil the conditions signified to you by my ambassadors." However his requests were absolutely impossible and injurious, moreover, to the Roman Empire, although he promised that if the Emperor granted him his requests, he would consider that he held Lombardy too from his hand, and that he would give military assistance, whenever required. But his real plan was clear from the fact that he made requests as if he himself desired peace, but by making impossible ones and not obtaining them he would have recourse to arms, and thus attribute the blame for the war to the Roman Emperor. Then after ineffectually making impossible demands, Robert convoked all the Counts and addressed them in these words, "You all know the injustice done to my kinsman by marriage by the Emperor Nicephorus Botaniates, and the dishonour put upon my daughter Helen by her being expelled from the Empire with him. As we could not put up with such things we marched out against Botaniates' country to avenge these wrongs. He however has been moved from the throne, and we now have to do with a young Emperor, who is a brave soldier and gifted with strategic knowledge far beyond his years, and with such a man we cannot go to war lightly. Now wherever there is division of command, confusion results from the diversity of opinions. Hence it is necessary that all the rest of us should obey one single commander who must consult us all and not act on his own judgment heedlessly and casually; the rest of us should openly express our views, but at the same time be ready to follow the advice of the elected commander. And here am I, one of you all, ready to obey whomsoever ye agree to elect." All approved of this proposition and declared that Robert had spoken wen, and then unanimously awarded him the first place. But he simulated indifference and for some time refused the honour, whereupon they insisted all the more. And finally he yielded, as if overcome by their persuasions, though in reality he had been aching for this all the time; but by piling one argument upon another and skilfully weaving a tissue of excuses, he made it appear to those who did not penetrate his intention, that he had been exalted against his will to the position which really he had coveted. Then he said to them "Listen to me, Counts and all the rest of you. We have left our own countries and are here in a foreign land, and we shall shortly have to fight against an Emperor who is very brave; although he has only recently assumed the reins of government, yet under the previous Emperors he came out conqueror in many wars and brought back to them the fiercest rebels as captives of his spear, therefore we must enter upon this war with our whole heart and soul. And if God should allot us the victory, we shall no longer be in need of money. Consequently we ought to set fire to all our baggage and equipment, scuttle our ships, and then enter into battle with him, as if we had been born in this place and intended to die here." To this all assented.

CHAPTER SIX

SUCH, YOU SEE, were Robert's plans and intentions. The Emperor's on the other hand were different, more subtle and more clever. Both the leaders, however, kept their troops in camp whilst meditating upon their strategy and tactics so that they might use their powers scientifically. And the Emperor was planning a sudden night-attack from both sides upon Robert's entrenchments. He commanded the whole native army to march by way of the salt-pits and attack from the rear, and he did not object to their undertaking this longer march as it would add to the unexpectedness of their attack. He himself intended to attack Robert from the front directly he ascertained that his other troops had arrived. Robert, however, left his tents standing empty, and crossing the bridge by night (on October 18th of the fifth Indiction) took possession with his whole army of the chapel built long ago to the Martyr Theodore. And there throughout the night they sought to propitiate the Deity, and also partook of the Immaculate Sacred Mysteries. In the morning he drew up his troops in order of battle and stationed himself in the centre of the line; the wing near the sea he entrusted to Amicetas (one of the illustrious Counts, brave in thought and deed), and the other to his son Bohemund, nicknamed Saniscus. When the Emperor learnt of this, as he was clever in hitting upon the best expedient in a serious crisis, he re-adapted his plans in accordance with these happenings, and drew up his lines on the slopes by the sea. After dividing his forces, he did not interfere with the barbarians who were starting to make their attack upon Robert's camp, but detained those of them who carried double-edged axes on their shoulders, and ordered them to discard their horses and with their leader, Nabites, to march in rows at a short distance in f ront of the regular army; this tribe all carried shields. The rest of the army he divided into phalanxes and himself took the centre of the line, on his right and left he placed respectively the Caesar Nicephorus Melissenus and Pacurianus, called the "Great Domestic." The space between himself and the barbarians who were walking he filled with a fairly large number of soldiers skilled in archery whom he planned to send on ahead against Robert, and so he told Nabites that when these archers wanted to ride out suddenly against the Franks and retreat again, he must immediately give them passage by withdrawing his men to either side, and then afterwards close up again and march on in close order. Having re-arranged the whole army in this manner, he himself started along the seacoast in order to attack the Frankish army from the front. The barbarians appointed for the rear attack, after passing through the salt-pits, made an assault upon the Frankish camp in conjunction with the garrison of Dyrrachium, who by the Emperor's command had opened their gates. As the two leaders were marching against each other, Robert ordered groups of cavalry to harass the Roman troops and thus perhaps draw away some of them. But even in this detail the Emperor did not fail, for he kept on sending large numbers of light-armed troops to oppose them. Then after a little preliminary skirmishing on either side, as Robert was leisurely following his men, and the distance between the armies was by now fairly short, some infantry and cavalry belonging to Amicetas' phalanx dashed out and attacked the extremities of Nabites' line. These however, resisted the attack very stoutly, so the others turned their backs (since they were not all picked men), threw themselves into the sea, and up to their necks in water, made their way to the Roman and Venetian ships and begged them for protection, which they did not receive. And now, as rumour relates, directly Gaïta, Robert's wife (who was riding at his side and was a second Pallas, if not an Athene) saw these soldiers running away, she looked after them fiercely and in a very powerful voice called out to them in her own language an equivalent to Homer's words, "How far will ye flee ? Stand, and quit you like men! "And when she saw they continued to run, she grasped a long spear and at full gallop rushed after the fugitives; and on seeing this they recovered themselves and returned to the fight. Meanwhile the axe-bearing barbarians and their leader Nabites had in their ignorance and in their ardour of battle advanced too quickly and were now a long way from the Roman lines, burning to engage battle with the equally brave Franks, for of a truth these barbarians are no less mad in battle than the Franks, and not a bit inferior to them. But they were already tired out and breathless, Robert noticed, and naturally so he thought, considering their rapid advance, their distance from their own lines and the weight of their weapons, and he ordered some of the foot to make a sudden attack on them. The barbarians having been previously wearied out, proved themselves inferior to the Franks, and thus the whole corps fell; a few escaped and took refuge in the chapel of Michael, the 'Captain of the Host,' as many as could crowded into the chapel itself, and the rest climbed on to the roof, being likely in this way, they imagined, to ensure their safety. But the Latins started a fire and burnt them down, chapel and all. Meanwhile the rest of the Roman army fought on bravely. But Robert like a winged horseman, dashed with his forces against the Roman phalanx, drove it back and split it up into several fragments. Consequently some of his opponents fell fighting in this battle, and others ensured their own safety by flight. But the Emperor Alexius stood fast like an impregnable tower, although he had lost many of his comrades, men pre-eminent for their birth or military skill. For instance, Constantius fell there, the son of the ex-Emperor, Constantine Ducas, not born while his father was still a private man, but born and reared in the purple and deemed worthy formerly by his father of the royal fillet. There fell too Nicephorus by name, but nicknamed Synadenus, a brave and very handsome man who strove to surpass all in fighting on that day. With him the aforementioned Constantius had often spoken about marrying his sister. Nay, Nicephorus the father of Palaeologus, and other well-known men fell too, and Zacharias received a blow in the chest which cost him his life. Aspietes and many other picked men also perished. The battle did not come to an end because the Emperor still maintained his resistance, therefore three of the Latins, one of whom was Amicetas already mentioned, the second Peter, son of Aliphas, as he himself asserted, and a third, not a whit inferior to these two, took long spears in their hands and at full gallop dashed at the Emperor. Amicetas missed the Emperor because his horse swerved a little; the second man's spear the Emperor thrust aside with his sword and then bracing his arm, struck him on the collarbone and severed his arm from his body. Then the third aimed straight at his face, but Alexius being of firm and steadfast mind was not wholly dismayed, but with his quick wit grasped in the flash of an instant the thing to do, and when he saw the blow coming, threw himself backwards on to his horse's tail. Thus the point of the spear only grazed the skin of his face a little and then, hitting against the rim of the helmet, tore the strap under the chin which held it on and knocked it to the ground. After this the Frank rode past the man he thought he had hurled from his horse, but the latter quickly pulled himself up again in his saddle and sat there calmly without having lost a single weapon. And he still clutched his naked sword in his right hand, his face was stained with his own blood, his head was bare, and his ruddy, gleaming hair was streaming over his eyes and worrying him, for his horse in its fright spurned the reins and by its jumping about tossed his curls in disorder over his face; however, he pulled himself together as much as possible and carried on his resistance to his foes. Soon however he saw the Turks fleeing and Bodinus, too, retreating without having fought at all. This ally had donned armour and arranged his army in battle-order and hovered about throughout the day as if to succour the Emperor, if need be, according to their mutual agreement; but evidently he was watching, purposing to help in the attack on the Franks if he saw victory incline to the Emperor; or, in the contrary case, to keep quite still and then beat a retreat. This being his intent, as events proved, directly he perceived that the Franks had gained a complete victory, he rode off home without having struck a single blow. The Emperor, seeing this and not finding any one to help him, turned his back upon the foe and fled. Thus did the Latins beat the Roman army.

CHAPTER SEVEN

ROBERT TOOK THE CHURCH of St. Nicolas where the Imperial tent and all the equipment of the Roman army were; and sent off all the strongest men he had to pursue the Emperor, whilst he stayed where he was, picturing to himself the capture of the Emperor-for such ideas inflamed his overweening pride. And the soldiers pursued the Emperor very smartly to a place called by the natives Kake Pleura, its situation is this - a river, named Charzanes, flows below and over one side impends a tall cliff. Between these the pursuers overtook him; some of them thrust him with their spears on the left side (they were nine altogether) and thus made him lean to the right. And he certainly would have fallen had he not managed to fix the sword, which he carried in his right hand, in the ground and support himself upon it. Moreover the rowel of the spur on his left foot caught in the edge of his saddle-cloth, (often called 'Hypostroma') and made it more difficult for the rider to move; with his left hand too he grasped the horse's mane and thus held on. And he was succoured by Divine interposition, which unexpectedly brought him aid from his enemies themselves. For Providence produced some more Franks on the right side who also raised their spears at him, and thus by thrusting the tips of their spears against his right side, they lifted the soldier and set him upright in their midst. And a strange sight it was to behold. For those on the left strove to overthrow him whilst those on the right fixed their spears against his right side as if opposing the others, and by spears set against spears, they kept the Emperor upright. When he had settled himself more firmly in the saddle and held his horse and also the saddle-cloth tightly between his thighs, the horse gave a signal proof of its mettle. (Alexius had once received this horse and a purple saddle-cloth as a gift from Bryennius, after he had taken him captive in battle at the time when Nicephorus Botaniates was still Emperor.) This horse, besides being very fiery and supple in the legs, was also remarkably strong and warlike, and now to put it briefly, inspired by Divine Providence, he suddenly leapt through the air and stood on the top of the cliff, springing up lightly like a bird, or, as the myth would say, with the wings of Pegasus.

Bryennius used to call this horse Sgouritzes[46]. Some of the barbarians' spears were hurled into the empty air as it were, and fell from their hands while others remained sticking in parts of the Emperor's clothes and, borne aloft, followed the horse. Alexius at once cut off the clinging spears. Not even now, when in such dire peril, was he disturbed in soul or confused in his calculations, but swiftly saw his best course and unexpectedly freed himself. The Franks on their side stood gaping, awestruck at what they had seen, and certainly it might well cause consternation; but when they saw Alexius riding off

46 a dark bay

down another road, they recommenced their pursuit. After showing his pursuers his back for some considerable time, he turned upon them and encountering one of them, ran his spear through his chest, and the man fell backwards to the ground. Then the Emperor turned his horse again and held on his former way. And so he met a number of the Franks who before had been chasing the Roman troops. When they saw him in the distance, they formed in close order and halted, partly to wind their horses, but also because they were anxious to take him alive and carry him off as booty to Robert. But when he saw that besides the men pursuing him there were now others in front as well, he had well-nigh despaired of safety; nevertheless he collected himself and noticing a man amongst the foe whom from his stature and gleaming weapons he judged to be Robert, he set his horse straight at him; and the other aimed his spear at him. So both joined combat, and launched themselves the one against the other in the intervening space. The Emperor first directing his hand aright, struck at his opponent with his spear, which passed right through his breast, and out at the back. Straightway the barbarian fell to the ground and gave up the ghost on the spot, for the wound was mortal. And next the Emperor dashed right through the middle of the company and rode away, for by slaying that one barbarian he had gained safety for himself. As soon as the Franks saw their hero wounded and hurled to the ground, they crowded round the fallen and busied themselves about him. And when those who had been pursuing the Emperor saw them, they, too, dismounted, and on recognizing the dead man, began beating their breasts and wailing. However, the man was not Robert, but one of the nobles, second only in rank to Robert. While they were thus occupied, the Emperor continued his flight.

Book Four

CHAPTER EIGHT

AND TRULY WHEN WRITING this, partly from the nature of history and partly because of the extravagance of the events, I forgot that it was my father's deeds that I was describing. In my desire to make my history free from suspicion, I often treat my father's doings in a cursory way, neither amplifying them nor investing them with sentiment. Would that I had been free and released from this love of my father, in order that I might have, as it were, laid hold upon the rich material and shown the licence of my tongue, how much at home it is in noble deeds. But now my zeal is hampered by my natural love, for I should not like to afford the public a suspicion that in my eagerness to speak about my relations I am serving them with fairy tales! Indeed very often I recall my father's successes, but I could have wept my life away in tears when recording and describing the many ills that befell him, and it is not without private lamentation and plaint that I quit the subject. But no elegant rhetoric must mar this part of my history, and therefore I pass lightly over my father's misadventures, as if I were an insensible piece of adamant or stone. I ought really to have used them as a form of oath, as the young man does in the Odyssey (for I am not inferior to him who says "No, by Zeus, Agelaus, and by my father's sufferings ") and then I should both really be, and be called, a lover of my father. However, let my father's woes be a subject of marvel and lamentation to me alone, and let us proceed with our history. Afterwards the Franks hurried back to Robert. When he saw them coming empty-handed and heard all that had befallen them, he blamed them all severely, and picked out one of them and threatened to scourge him, and cursed him for a coward and a fool at war. He asked why he had not also jumped up to the rock with his horse and either knocked down and killed the Emperor, or else caught him and brought him back alive, until the soldier thought the worst was in store for him. For that was Robert - on the one hand very courageous and adventurous, and on the other, full of bitterness ; wrath ever sat in his nostrils, and his heart was overflowing with anger and fury, and towards his enemies he always felt that he must either ran his foe through with his spear, or he exclaimed that he must get rid of himself in defiance of the thread of destiny, as they say. However, the soldier at whom Robert was hurling abuse, very clearly described the steepness and inaccessibility of the rock, and told him what a sheer ascent the rock made, and that the cliff was so steep and dangerous that no foot- or horse-man could possibly climb it without Divine intervention, let alone one engaged in battle and fighting, for even apart from fighting, it was impossible for anyone to attempt the ascent." If, "he continued, "you disbelieve me, go and try yourself, or send the most daring of your horsemen, and he will soon see the impossibility. But if anybody does really manage to climb that rock, be it with or without wings, then I am willing to submit to any terrible punishment and to be condemned for cowardice." Speaking like this amidst awe and astonishment, the barbarian appeased Robert's fury, made him forget his anger and moved him instead to wonder.

And the Emperor rode along the windings of the surrounding mountains and the almost impassable tracks, and after two days and nights made his way out of them and reached Achrida. On this journey be crossed the river Charzanes and rested a little in the secluded valley called Babagora, and his spirit was not broken by his defeat nor by the other accidents of the battle nor would he give way to the pain of the wound in his forehead ; and though inwardly he was consumed with sorrow for those who had fallen in the battle, especially for the, heroes who had fought so bravely, yet, above all, his mind was wholly occupied with the thought of Dyrrachium. For he reflected with pain that this town was left without a governor, as Palaeologus had been unable to re-enter it after the battle was lost. So he secured the safety of the inhabitants as far as possible by entrusting the custody of the Acropolis to the chiefs of the Venetian colonists there, and the care of the rest of the city to Comiscortes of Albanian origin to whom he transmitted orders by letter.

BOOK FIVE

War with the Normans (1082-83), Alexius' First Battle with Heretics, and John Italus

CHAPTER ONE

AND MEANWHILE ROBERT, entirely freed from anxiety, collected all the booty and the Imperial tent, and, with these trophies and with much exultation, settled down again in the plain which he had occupied before when besieging Dyrrachium. After a short rest he began to consider whether he ought to make another attempt on that city's walls, or postpone the siege to the following spring and for the present invest Glabinitza and Joanina, and winter there, while lodging all his troops in the sequestered vales that lie above the plain of Dyrrachium. But the inhabitants of Dyrrachium (the majority of whom were colonists from Amalfi and Venice, as already stated), on hearing of the Emperor's misfortune, and the terrible carnage, and the death of so many valiant men and the departure of the fleet and Robert's intention of renewing the siege in the coming spring-on hearing all this they began individually to deliberate what action they had better take to ensure their safety and not incur such risks again. Consequently they called an assembly where they openly stated their private opinions and after discussing the vital points they thought they had found the only path, as it were, out of a pathless wood, which was to decide to listen to Robert and surrender the city to him.

One of the colonists from Amalfi still further incited them to this course, so they allowed themselves to be persuaded by his arguments, and threw open the gates and gave Robert entrance. After taking possession, he sent for the troops and dividing them according to race, enquired of each soldier individually whether he had been seriously wounded or had perhaps received a slight scratch from a sword; at the same time he found out how many and what class of men had fallen in the preceding battles. And, during the winter which was then close at hand, he intended to collect a second army of mercenaries and recruit foreign troops, and at the coming of spring to march against the Emperor with his whole army. However, Robert was not alone in formulating such plans, although he congratulated himself on being the victor and winning the trophies, for the Emperor, worsted and badly wounded, was scared, so to say, and much depressed by this intolerable defeat and the loss of so many brave soldiers-but in spite of this as he never underestimated his own powers and had not slackened in his reasoning, his whole mind was intent on the problem of retrieving this defeat in the following spring. Both these men were clever at foreseeing everything, and in grasping the essentials' and there was no strategic trick unknown to them; they were conversant with every kind of siege, ambuscade and regular battles in the open field, swift and brave in actual fighting, and of all the leaders in the world they were the adversaries most alike in intellect and courage. The Emperor Alexius had, however, a slight advantage over Robert in that while younger he was no whit inferior to the other who was already in his prime, and used to boast that he could almost make the earth quake and throw a whole army into a panic by one single shout!

But these details can be left for a different kind of writing, and are sure to be mentioned by encomiasts. The Emperor Alexius allowed himself a short rest in Achrida, and after regaining his physical strength, went to Diabolis. Here he sought as far as possible to reinvigorate the survivors from their sufferings in the battle, and he sent for his remaining followers from all parts and told them to assemble at Thessalonica.

Now that he had made experience of Robert and the boldness of his large army, he condemned his own leaders for great negligence and cowardice (I will not add the soldiers for the majority of those who had been in the battle had had neither training nor military experience), and therefore he needed allies. But how was he to get them without money? For there was none in the Imperial Treasury which had been depleted so thoroughly and for no useful purpose by his predecessor, Nicephorus Botaniates, that the gates of the treasure-house were not even locked now, but carelessly left open for anyone who liked to walk through them; for all its contents had been squandered. Hence the present embarrassment of the Roman state, which was oppressed simultaneously by weakness and poverty.

At such a moment then what was the young ruler to do who had only lately put his hand to the helm? He must either in sheer desperation throw everything overboard and resign his command, so that, being blameless, he might not be blamed for being an inexperienced and unskilful general, or else in this extremity he must gain as many allies as possible and collect from some quarter or other sufficient money to pay them; he must also recall the scattered remnants of his army by offering bribes which would raise their hopes and cause those who were with him to stand firmly by him, and those away to become more eager to return, and then they would be able to put up a braver resistance to the Frankish hordes. As he did not wish to do anything unworthy of, or inconsistent with, his own military knowledge and bravery, he focussed his attention on these two points - the first was to collect allies from all sides, who would easily be allured by the promise of heavy largess, and the second, to request his mother and brother to procure money somehow from somewhere, and send it to him.

CHAPTER TWO

THESE TWO COULD NOT discover any other means of procuring money, so to begin with they collected whatever silver and gold articles they possessed and sent them to the imperial mint ; but first of all the Empress, my mother, deposited the sum that remained to her of her parents' patrimony, hoping thereby to instigate others to do the same ; for she was extremely anxious for the Emperor, seeing the straits into which his affairs had fallen. Secondly, they took from the persons who were well-affected towards the imperial family, and had voluntarily offered to advance money, as much gold and silver as each was ready to give, and sent it to be used partly for allies and partly for the Emperor himself. But these monies were far from sufficient even for the immediate need (for some of the soldiers asked for rewards on the plea that they had fought on the Emperor's side, and others who were mercenaries kept clamouring for higher pay); the Emperor urgently pressed for more, and thought that the goodwill of the Romans had vanished. His relatives were quite at a loss, and after discussing many schemes in public and in private, when they heard that Robert was again preparing for war, they turned in their despair to an examination of the ancient laws and canons dealing with the sale of Church property. And amongst them they found that it was lawful to sell the sacred properties of the churches for the ransoming of prisoners of war (for it was well known that the Christians who remained under the domination of the barbarians in Asia, and had escaped massacre, became defiled by their intercourse with the infidels). Therefore to furnish pay for the allies and the soldiers, they considered turning into coin a few church properties which served no purpose and were amongst those which had long been lying idle and neglected, and only afforded the populace an excuse for sacrilege and impiety. When they had come to this conclusion, the Sebastocrator Isaac went up to the great House of God where he had convoked an assembly of all the clergy. The members of the Holy Synod who were fellow-councillors with the Patriarch were astounded at seeing him and asked him what brought him there. He replied, "I have come to speak to you of a matter which will be of service in this terrible crisis, and will be the means of maintaining the army." Thereupon he began reciting the Canons about "superfluous Church vessels "and after saying a good deal about them, he concluded with the words, "I am compelled to compel those whom I do not wish to compel." And by putting forward various bold arguments he seemed likely to win over the majority. But Metaxas opposed him, advanced some very specious counter-arguments and even jeered at Isaac himself. But in spite of him, Isaac's proposal was carried. This decision became the subject of a very grave scandal to the Emperors (for I do not hesitate to call Isaac "emperor "even though he did not wear the purple), which lasted not only for the moment but for a considerable time. The head of the church of Chalcedon at this time was a certain Leo, not one of the especially wise or intellectual, but of very virtuous life, though his manners were rough and disagreeable. This man tore off the silver and gold ornaments on the doors of the church in Chalcoprateia, and rushed into the assembly and spoke his mind freely without so much as a reference to the financial condition or the extant laws regarding Church property. Moreover he behaved very insolently, and in a most disorderly manner, to the Regent, and each time he visited the capital he abused the latter's forbearance and kindness. And indeed when Alexius left the city the first time to march against Robert, and the Sebastocrator Isaac, his own true brother, was collecting money from every possible source, but always with the consent of the people and in accordance with the laws and justice, Leo aroused Isaac's wrath by his shameless behaviour. At last after many defeats and then after countless successful encounters with the Franks, the Emperor, by the sanction of Heaven, returned a crowned victor, and then he learnt that a fresh swarm of enemies, I mean the Scythians, were ready to descend upon him. Consequently the raising of funds was hurried on for similar reasons as before, even while the Emperor was residing in the capital, and at that time Bishop Leo attacked the Emperor most impudently. About this time a great controversy arose about the holy images, and Leo laid down the principle that we should adore the sacred images, and not only give them relative honour. On some points he argued reasonably and in a manner befitting his station, but on others he laid down the law wrongly, whether this was to be attributed to the heat of contest and his hatred of the Emperor, or to ignorance, I cannot say. He was incapable of making a precise statement with conviction as he was absolutely untrained in the science of reasoning. By the advice of malicious persons of whom there were a number in the Government then, he grew still bolder towards the Emperors and egged on by his friends he even resorted to insults and untimely blasphemies. The Emperor besought him to change his opinion about the images and also to desist from the enmity towards him, he also promised to restore even finer vessels to the churches and to do all that was necessary to repair the loss. The Emperor himself was already acquitted of blame by the more liberal-minded of the senate whom the partisans of the Chalcedonian called "flatterers." As a result of this behaviour, Leo was condemned to deposition from office.

As he did not knuckle under and did not keep quiet at all, but again disturbed the Church meeting, coming with a considerable crowd of followers, for he was absolutely irreconcilable and incorrigible, he was condemned by a unanimous vote after the lapse of some years and a sentenced exile was pronounced against him. The city of Sozopolis on the Black Sea received him and treated him with much care and consideration by order of the Emperor, none of which he accepted because of his grudge against the latter, I suppose.

This account of him must suffice.

CHAPTER THREE

WHEN IT BECAME KNOWN that the Emperor had escaped from the battle, recruits in large numbers flocked to him, and these he had carefully trained to ride very securely, to shoot very accurately, to fight in full armour and to lay ambuscades cleverly. He had also sent ambassadors again to the King of Alamania, of these Methymnes was the leader, and in his letter he urged him not to delay any longer, but to take the troops he had at hand, and occupy Lombardy with all haste, according to his promise. In this way Robert would be fully occupied and he himself would gain a respite during which he could reassemble his army and collect foreign troops and by their help drive Robert out of Illyria. He assured the King of Alamania that he would be deeply indebted to him if he would do this, and promised him that he would fulfil the marriage-contract which he had proposed through his ambassadors.

After arranging these matters he left Pacurianus, the Great Domestic in those parts, and himself returned to the capital, for the purpose of collecting foreign troops from all sides, and to arrange other matters connected with the times and the actual circumstances. Now the Manichaeans, Xantas and Culeon, with the men under them who totalled about two thousand five hundred, went off home unceremoniously, and when invited several times by the Emperor to return, they did indeed promise to come, but kept postponing their coming. But he persisted and made them written promises of gifts and honours, but even so they did not return. Whilst the Emperor was engaged in these preparations for an advance against Robert, a messenger came to tell Robert that the King of Alamania had all but arrived in Lombardy. Then Robert was in a dilemma and deliberated what would be the best thing to do. After much reflection, as he had left Roger to be ruler over his Kingdom when he crossed to Illyria, but had not yet assigned any territory to his younger son, Bohemund, he assembled all the Counts and picked men among the soldiers, and summoning also his son, Bohemund, nicknamed Saniscus, he made a public harangue and said, "You know, Counts, that when I settled to cross to Illyria I appointed my beloved first-begotten son Roger, ruler of my country. For I could not have started from there and undertaken a task of great magnitude if I had left my own country without a leader, a ready prize at the mercy of the first comer. But now that the King of Alamania has entered it with hostile intent, it is my duty to defend it as far as in me lies. For certainly the man who attacks the possessions of others, must not in any way be careless of his own. Consequently it is necessary for me to leave you, in order to look after my own country, and engage in battle with the King of Alamania. Therefore to Uds, my younger son, I hand over Dyrrachium, Valona and all the remaining towns and islands which I have won by my sword since my arrival. And I commend him to you and ask you to regard him as my substitute and to fight for him with all your heart and mind." Then addressing himself to Bohemund, he said, "And you, my very dear son, I enjoin you to treat the Counts with all honour and ask their advice on all occasions and not to 'play the master' by yourself, but to communicate everything to them. Above all, take care not to neglect the continuance of the war against the Roman Emperor, but see that you do not relax at all now that he has suffered a severe defeat and all but fallen a victim to the sword, and the greater part of his army has been wiped out in the battle. (And truth to tell," he continued, "he came near being captured alive and only escaped from our hands after being terribly wounded). Therefore take care lest by gaining a respite he should recover and resist you more bravely than before. For he is not one of the common herd, but has been nurtured from childhood on wars and battles, he has travelled over the whole of the East and the West, and how many rebels he hunted down and brought back captive to the preceding emperors, you can learn yourself from many informants. Therefore if you lose heart at all and do not march against him with firm resolve you will lose all that I personally have won by great effort, and you yourself will undoubtedly reap the fruits of your own laziness. And now I am leaving immediately to drive the King of Alamania out of our country and thus firmly establish my son Roger in the dominion I gave him." After thus bidding his son farewell, Robert embarked on board a monoreme and reached the opposite coast of Lombardy, and from there hurried on to Salernum, which had formerly been appointed the residence for those who attained ducal rank. He stayed there until he had collected a large force and as many mercenary troops from surrounding countries as possible. Meanwhile the King of Alamania in accordance with his promise to the Emperor, was already hastening to take possession of Lombardy. Robert on hearing this news hurried to Rome to join his army with the Pope's and to deter the King of Alamania from carrying out his intention. As the Pope was not at all unwilling, they both set out against the King. He for his part was on his way to invest Lombardy when he heard the whole story about the Emperor-namely, that he had suffered a heavy defeat, that part of his army had been butchered and the rest scattered abroad, that the Emperor himself after surviving many dangers had been seriously wounded in several parts of his body whilst fighting magnificently, but had made a marvellous escape owing to his boldness and courage. On receipt of these tidings the King turned his horse and rode back to his native land, considering this a victory in that he had not exposed himself to danger uselessly. So this man took the homeward road; and Robert, when he had reached the King's encampment, did not trouble to pursue him himself but separated a large detachment from his troops and sent it in pursuit of the King of Alamania. He himself gathered up all the booty and made his way to Rome with the Pope. After establishing the latter firmly on his throne and in return being nominated King by him, he returned to Salernum there to repose himself from the many fatigues of war.

CHAPTER FOUR

SHORTLY AFTERWARDS BOHEMUND came to him, bearing witness on his face of the defeat he bad sustained. We will now relate how fate had dealt him this blow. The young man, mindful of his father's counsels and being moreover naturally fond of war and of confronting dangers, steadily pursued the war with the Emperor. Taking his own soldiers with him and accompanied by all the picked men of the Romans and by the chiefs of the districts and towns which had been subdued by Robert (for these threw themselves heart and soul into Bohemund's cause once they had given up the Emperor's case as hopeless), he marched through Bagenetia to Joanina. Here he first drew trenches in the vineyards outside the town and disposed all his troops in convenient positions, and then set up his own tent inside the town. He made a survey of the walls and recognising that the citadel was in a dangerous condition, he not only hastened to restore it as far as was possible, but he even built a second very strong one in another part of the walls where he thought it would be of more use; he also sent out raiding parties to plunder the surrounding country and towns. Thereupon the Emperor without the slightest delay, collected all his troops, and hurriedly left Constantinople in the month of May. When he arrived at Joanina, it was the right season for fighting. As he recognized that his own armies were but a fraction of Bohemund's forces and knew besides from his previous battles with Robert that the first onset of the Frankish cavalry upon their opponents was quite irresistible, he judged it would be best to have an attack by missiles made first upon the enemy by a small picked body of peltasts. By this means he would gain some idea of how much military experience Bohemund possessed, and by several partial attacks he would be able to form some opinion of the general state of affairs, and then, with the knowledge he had gained, engage in battle against the Franks with greater confidence. The two armies were burning with impatience to attack each other. But the Emperor dreading the irresistible first shock of the Latin cavalry hit upon a new device. He had wagons built, smaller and lighter than the ordinary ones, and four poles fixed to each, in these he placed heavy infantry so that when the Latins came dashing down at full gallop upon the Roman phalanx, the heavy-armed infantry should push the wagons forward and thus break the Latins' line.

When the hour of battle approached and the sun had already risen in its brilliance above the horizon, the Emperor drew up his regiments in order of battle and himself took the command of the centre. As soon as the engagement began, Bohemund shewed that he was not unprepared for the Emperor's scheme, but, as if he had foreknowledge of it, he adapted himself to this happening, for he divided his own troops into two divisions, avoided the waggons and attacked the Roman ranks on either flank. Then lines were confounded with lines and men fought men, face to face. After many had fallen on either side in the fierce fight, Bohemund certainly carried off the victory. The Emperor for his part stood like an unshaken tower with darts thrown at him from before and behind, for at one minute he would ride against the advancing Franks, engage in close fights with a few, giving and receiving blows and killing, and at another minute he would be shouting to, and rallying, the fugitives. Finally, however, when he saw his ranks split up into numerous portions, he deemed it wise to seek safety for himself too, not, as some might say, to save himself, nor was he shaken by cowardice, but in order that he might make a second, braver resistance to the valiant Franks, if only he could escape the immediate danger and rally his powers. As he was fleeing from the enemy with a few companions, he fell in with some Franks and again shewed himself the imperturbable general. For after exhorting his companions, he rode down upon the enemy impetuously as if determined either to die that day, or carry off the victory by force; with his own hand he struck and killed one of the Franks, and the followers of Ares with him wounded many and routed the rest. In this way he escaped from immeasurably great dangers, and once again reached safety by passing through the Swamps to Achrida. There he stayed and after recalling a fair number of the fugitives to his standard, he left them all in those parts with the Great Domestic and himself went to the Bardares. But not for the sake of rest, for unlike other royalties he did not allow himself imperial ease and repose. There he assembled his regiments and mercenaries again and started on his march against Bohemund, with a new device in his head for overcoming the Franks. For he prepared iron caltrops, and on the eve of the day on which he expected a battle, he had them spread over the intermediate part of the plain, where he guessed the

Frankish cavalry would make their fiercest onslaught, thus aiming to break the first irresistible attack of the Latins by piercing the feet of their horses. And he ordered the Roman spearsmen who held the front line, to ride forward at a measured pace in order not to be lamed by the caltrops, and to part to either side and then turn ; the light-armed troops were to send a heavy shower of darts on the Franks from a distance, and the left and right wings were to fall upon them in a vehement charge. These indeed were my father's plans but they did not escape Bohemund. For this is what happened: whatever plans my father made against him in the evening, the Frank knew by the morning. So he skilfully modified his plans in accordance with what he had been told, and engaged in battle but did not, as was his custom, begin with a frontal attack, but forestalling the Emperor's intention, he raised the din of battle on either flank, bidding the front ranks keep still for a time.

Then the battle became a hand-to-hand fight, the soldiers of the Roman army turned their backs to the Latins and had not even the courage to look them in the face again, as they had been thoroughly frightened beforehand by their previous defeat. Thus the Roman lines were thrown into utter confusion, even though the Emperor remained undaunted in hand and heart and offered brave resistance, wounding many and sometimes too being wounded himself. But when he saw that his whole army had disappeared and he was left with just a few, he decided not to incur danger by carrying on a hopeless fight. For when anyone after heavy travail has no longer the strength to make a stand against his enemies, he would be a fool if he thrust himself into certain danger. Now after the left and right wings of the Roman phalanx had turned to flight, the Emperor was still maintaining the combat against Bohemund's army, bearing the whole brunt of the battle himself. But on comprehending his unquestionable danger, he deemed it his duty to save himself, so as to be able to fight once again against his conqueror, and prove himself a very formidable opponent who would not allow Bohemund to reap a complete victory. For such was his character, whether conquered or conquering, fleeing or pursuing, he never was cowed, nor caught in the snares of despair. Moreover, he had very great faith in God and ever had His name on his lips, though always refraining from oaths. Now being tired out as just said, he too turned his back and was pursued by Bohemund and a few Counts. In so doing he asked Goules (he was my father's servant) and the others with him, "How far shall we flee? "With these words he turned his horse, drew his sword and hit the foremost of his pursuers in the face. When the Franks saw this and recognized that he was quite reckless of his own safety, and as they knew from experience that men reduced to such a state of mind are invincible, they were stricken with fear and ceased their pursuit. And so freed from his pursuers he escaped danger. Even in flight he did not entirely lose heart but managed to reassemble some of the fugitives and others he jeered at, though the majority naturally affected not to notice it. Having in this wise escaped from peril he re-entered the capital for the purpose of mustering new armies and again taking the field against Bohemund.

CHAPTER FIVE

AFTER ROBERT'S DEPARTURE FOR Lombardy Bohemund, obedient to his father's behests, carried on the war against the Emperor, and continually rekindled battles and engagements. Further, he sent Peter, the son of Aliphas, with the Count of Pontoise to besiege various towns, with the result that Peter at once took the two Polobi, and the aforementioned Count of Pontoise took Scopia, and on being invited by the Achridians, he quickly reached Achrida. But after staying there some time and accomplishing nothing, for Ariebes was guarding the citadel, he went away to Ostrobus ; from that town too he was sent away empty-handed so passed through Soscus and Serbia and came to Beroea. And after attacking several places repeatedly without success, he reached Moglena via Bodina and there rebuilt a small fort which had long lain in ruins. There he left a Count, nicknamed "the Saracen," with an ample garrison and betook himself to a spot on the river Bardares called the Asprae Ecclesiae. And whilst he was spending three months there, three of the foremost Counts, namely the Count of Pontoise, Reboldus and a certain Gulielmus were detected in a plot for deserting to the Emperor. The Count of Pontoise indeed, became aware of this and escaped and reached the Emperor, but the other two were captured and by the Frankish law condemned to ordeal by battle. Gulielmus was defeated and unhorsed and Bohemund imprisoned and blinded him; the other, Reboldus, he sent to Lombardy to his father, Robert, by whom he too was deprived of his sight. Then Bohemund left Asprae Ecclesiae for Castoria. The Great Domestic on hearing this, occupied Moglena, seized and immediately put to death the 'Saracen' and reduced the fort to complete ruin. Bohemund, meanwhile, left Castoria and came to Larissa where he hoped to winter. When the Emperor reached the capital, as already mentioned, he at once set to work-being, as he was, a strenuous worker and never allotting himself any rest-and asked the sultan for troops as well as for some generals with long experience. The latter consequently sent him 7,000 men with highly experienced leaders, among whom was Camyres who surpassed all in long experience. While the Emperor was arranging and preparing these matters, Bohemund selected a certain portion of his own army, all Franks in full armour, sent them out and they took Pelagonia, Tricala and Castoria off-hand. Then Bohemund himself with his whole army entered Tricala and dispatching a detachment of brave men took Tzibiscus at first assault. After this he approached Larissa on the festival of St. George the Martyr with all his troops, encircled the walls and proceeded to besiege it. Now the defender of this city was the son of the Emperor's hereditary servant, Leo Cephalas, and he put up a stout resistance to Bohemund's engines for six whole months. He at once informed the Emperor by letter of the barbarian's attack. But the Emperor did not immediately start on his march against Bohemund, though burning with impatience, but had to postpone his departure because he was recruiting mercenaries from all quarters. At length after equipping them all fully, he set out from Constantinople. When he was close to the territories of Larissa and had passed over the hill of the Cells, he left the public highroad and the hill, Cissabus, so-called locally, on the right and marched down to Ezeba ; this is a Vlach village situated close to Androneia. From this he marched on to a large village, generally called Plabitza, situated somewhere near a river called ... here he pitched his camp, entrenching it just sufficiently. Then on again through the gardens of Delphinas, and beyond them to Tricala. And here a messenger bearing a letter from Leo Cephalas (of whom I have already spoken), found him. He wrote very freely as follows: "Know, O Emperor, that up to the present by evincing extreme zeal I have kept this fortress from being taken. Now we are deprived of all foods allowed to Christians and have begun those which are not fitted for us, but even those are now giving out. Therefore please make haste if you wish to help us and if you could possibly drive away our assailants, then thanks be to God. But, if not, I, at least, have done my duty; and shortly (for how is it possible to struggle against nature and its imperious demands?) we must bow our heads to necessity and we intend to surrender the fort to the enemy who are pressing us hard and literally throttling us. But if this calamity should eventually come to pass, then may I be accursed! But I now take the liberty of speaking openly to your Majesty. If you do not hasten with all speed to extricate us from this danger, as we are unable to support the overwhelming burden of warfare, as well as famine, any longer; if you, our Sovereign, do not hasten to bring help when you have the power to do so, then, I say, you will certainly not escape the imputation of betrayal." From this the Emperor realized that in one way or another he must overcome the foe; and he was oppressed by anxieties and speculations. And for a whole day during which he invoked the aid of God, he worked hard at the problem of how best to set ambuscades. He also sent for an old man, a native of Larissa, and sought information from him about the lie of the land. With intent eyes and pointing with his finger too, he questioned him carefully about the places where ravines broke through the plain, and whether any thick coppices grew beside them. He asked these questions of the Larissaean because he wished to lay an ambush and defeat the Latins by craft ; for he shirked an open battle in the field as in several engagements he had been worsted and had gained experience of the Frankish method of attack. At sunset, the Emperor, who had toiled all day long, betook himself to sleep and a vision appeared to him. He seemed to be standing in the church of the Protomartyr Demetrius and heard a voice say "Do not grieve nor groan, tomorrow you shall conquer." He thought the voice fell upon his ears from an icon suspended in the temple on which the martyr Demetrius was painted. He awoke full of joy because of the voice of his vision, made his prayers to the martyr and promised besides that, if victory should be granted him, he would travel to Thessalonica and at several stades' distance from the town he would dismount and proceed on foot at a smart pace and do obeisance to him in his church. Then he summoned the generals, captains and his relatives and commenced the discussion by asking their individual opinion, and next explained the plan he had formed. And this was to entrust all the divisions to his relatives; as chief commanders he appointed Melissenus Nicephorus and Curticius Basileios, also called 'Little John'; this man was an outstanding figure renowned for his bravery and military skill, a native of Adrianople. But not only the divisions did he entrust to them but also all the royal standards. Moreover he enjoined them to draw up the army on the same plan as he had drawn it up in the foregoing battles, and advised them first to try the vanguard of the Latin army by a skirmishing attack, then to raise their battle-cry and make a general attack. But directly the troops were fully engaged they were to turn their backs to the Latins and flee precipitately as if making for Lycostomium. Whilst the Emperor was giving these orders, suddenly all the horses in the army were heard to neigh. Astonishment seized them all; however, the Emperor and the more intelligent of his audience at once interpreted it as a good omen.

After he had given them these injunctions he left them to the right of Larissa, and after waiting for the sunset, he ordered some picked men to follow him, and went through the narrow pass of Libotanium, skirted Rebenicus and through the so-called "Allage "he reached the left side of Larissa; there he explored the nature of the ground and finding a slight depression, he crouched down with his companions. At the same time when the

Emperor, as just related, was on the point of entering the defiles of Libotanium in his haste to place an ambush, the leaders of the Roman divisions selected and sent forward a detachment of the Roman troops against the Franks to draw the latter's attention to themselves and not allow them leisure to spy out whither the Emperor was going. So the Romans descended to the plain, attacked the Franks, and after a short battle, stopped, as night completely prevented further fighting. On reaching the desired spot the Emperor bade all dismount and kneel down and hold their reins in their hands; and he himself accidentally alighted on a bed of germander and bending down likewise lay the rest of the night on his face.

CHAPTER SIX

AT SUNRISE BOHEMUND SAW the Roman troops drawn up in array, and the royal standards and the silver-studded spears and the horses with their royal red saddle-cloths, drew up his own army against them as well as he could, dividing his forces into two, and leading one half himself and over the other he put Bryennius[47] as commander, who was one of the most illustrious Latins and called ‹Constable' by them. After thus disposing his own forces, he again followed his usual mode of procedure and thinking the Emperor was where he saw the imperial ensigns in the middle of the line, he dashed down upon this deception like a whirlwind. After a short resistance his opponents turned their backs and he rushed after them in mad pursuit as in our previous descriptions. Meanwhile the Emperor saw his own troops fleeing far, and Bohemund in mad pursuit of them, and when he judged that Bohemund was at a safe distance from the Roman camp, he jumped on his

47 Count of Brienne, Constable of Apulia

horse, bade his followers do the same, and fell upon Bohemund's encampment. Once inside it he slew a number of the Latins he found there and carried off all the booty; then he took another glance at the pursuers and pursued. And observing that his own men were really pretending flight and Bohemund chasing after them and behind him Bryennius, he called George Pyrrhus, a famous archer, and having detached other brave men, and a goodly number of peltasts he ordered them to ride quickly after Bryennius, and when they overtook him, not to start a close fight, but rather aim at the horses from a little distance and direct showers of arrows upon them. They did thus overtake the Franks and showered arrows upon the horses so that the horsemen were reduced to great difficulties. For every Frank is invincible both in attack and appearance when he is on horseback, but when he comes off his horse, partly due to the size of his shield, and partly to the long curved peaks of his shoes and a consequent difficulty in walking, then he becomes very easy to deal with and a different man altogether, for all his mental energy evaporates, as it were. This, I fancy, the Emperor knew, and therefore ordered them not to trouble about the riders, but to disable the horses. As the Franks' horses fell, the men with Bryennius were thrown into frightful confusion, and from this large whirling mass a tall, thick cloud of dust rose almost to the sky, so that its density could almost be likened to the darkness ‹that could be felt ‹ which befell Egypt long ago. For their eyes were blinded by the thick dust which also prevented their seeing whence and by whom the arrows were shot. So sent three Latins to report the matter to Bohemund. These found him standing on a little island in the river called Salabrias, eating grapes and also making a boastful pun which is still popularly quoted. For he kept repeating with his barbaric pronunciation of "Lycostomium "that they had driven Alexius "into the wolf's mouth." Thus does arrogance mislead many even with regard to things directly before their eyes, and before their feet. But when he heard the news sent by Bryennius and realized the craftiness and the victory won by guile he was naturally, indeed, furious with the Emperor, but in no wise cast down, so brave was he. A few selected Franks in full armour who were with him, then mounted a small hill opposite Larissa. Directly our heavy troops caught sight of them they demanded very eagerly to be allowed to attack them, but Alexius restrained them from this enterprise. Nevertheless quite a number from the different divisions and of various types did join together and mounted the hill and attacked the Franks, who immediately rushed at them and killed about five hundred. Then the Emperor guessing at the spot where Bohemund was likely to pass, dispatched brave soldiers with the

Turks and Migidenus as chief commander, but as they drew near, Bohemund set upon them and beat them and pursued them to the river.

CHAPTER SEVEN

AS DAWN BROKE ON the following day Bohemund crossed the river we have mentioned with his attendant Counts, Bryennius himself among them, and when he found a swampy place in the neighbourhood of Larissa and a tree-covered plain between two hills which ran out into a very narrow pass (this is called a "cleisura "), the plain was named "the palace of Domenicus," he entered by the pass and fixed his palisades there. The next day at dawn the leader of the phalanx, Michael Ducas, my maternal uncle, caught him there with all the army. This man was celebrated for his prudence, and in beauty and stature surpassed not only all his contemporaries, but all who have ever been born! (for all who saw him were amazed); he was, too, very quick and almost unrivalled in his conjectures of the future, his investigations of the actual and in taking action accordingly. The Emperor gave strict injunctions to this man not to let all the troops enter the mouth of the "cleisura"; but to leave the mass of them outside in squadrons, and to pick out a few of the Turks and Sauromatians who were skilled archers and allow these to enter, and to command them to use no weapon but their arrows. These entered and made cavalry attacks on the Latins, and the men outside, burning for a fight, vied with each other as to who should enter the mouth. Bohemund, who was an expert in strategic science, commanded his men to form in close order and to stand quietly and protect themselves with their shields. When the Protostrator saw the men under him gradually melting away and entering the mouth of the pass he went in himself. And Bohemund seeing them come rejoiced as 'a lion who has met with mighty prey,' to use a Homeric expression, even so he, when he saw the men and the Protostrator Michael with his own eyes, dashed at them with all his forces in an irresistible rush, whereupon they immediately turned and fled. Uzas (who was thus named after his race), a man famous for his bravery and skilled, as Homer says, 'in wielding, now right now left, the tough bull's hide that formed his target,' bent to the right as he was coming out of the entrance and, turning sharply, hit the Latin following him, who straightway fell headlong to the ground. But Bohemund pursued the fugitives as far as the river Salabrias. During the flight this same Uzas pierced Bohemund's standard-bearer with his spear and plucking the standard from his hands waved it aloft a minute, and then lowered it to the ground. When the Latins saw their standard lowered, they were confounded and fled along another path by which they reached Tricala which had already been seized by some of Bohemund's men who were fleeing to Lycostomium. And there they entered the town and stayed awhile and afterwards seized Castoria. But the Emperor soon left Larissa and entered Thessalonica and with his usual sagacity very soon began sending offers of rich rewards to the Counts in Bohemund's train on condition that they would ask Bohemund for the pay he had promised them, and that if he could not pay them, they should persuade him to journey down to the sea and ask his father Robert for it, or better still, cross the sea himself to fetch it. If they accomplished this, they should all enjoy his respect and numberless benefits. And if any of them were willing to serve under him as mercenaries, he would enrol them in his army and give them the pay they required, and to those who preferred to return to their own homes, he would give a safe passage through Hungary. In response to the Emperor's suggestion, the Counts unfeelingly demanded their pay for the last four years, but as Bohemund had not got it, he temporized awhile. However on their insisting in their reasonable demands, he did not know what to do, so appointed Bryennius Governor of Castoria, as well as Peter, son of Aliphas, who was guarding Polobi; and himself journeyed down to Valona. On receipt of this news, the Emperor packed up and entered the Queen of Cities in triumph.

CHAPTER EIGHT

WHEN HE ARRIVED HE found the church in a very perturbed condition, and did not even have a short period of relaxation. But as he was a true apostle of the church, and now found it vexed by the teachings of Italus, although he was anxious to march against Bryennius (the Frank who had taken Castoria, as we have said) yet even under these circumstances he did not neglect his faith. For at this time the doctrines of Italus had obtained a great vogue and were upsetting the church. Now this Italus (for it is necessary to give his history from the beginning) was a native of Italy and had spent a considerable time in Sicily; this is an island situated near Italy. For the Sicilians had rebelled against the Roman rule and were preparing for war against them and invited the Italians to join them; amongst those who came was the father of Italus who brought his son with him, although he was not of military age, and the boy accompanied and tripped along with him and received a military education, as is the custom of the Italians. That is how Italus spent the early years of his life, and that was the first foundation of his education. When the famous George

Maniaces during the reign of Monomachus mastered and subdued Sicily, the father of Italus with his child only escaped with difficulty and betook themselves in their flight to Lombardy which was still under the Romans. From there (I do not know how) this Italus came to Constantinople, which was not ill supplied with teachers of every subject and of the art of language. For from the time of Basil Porphyrogenitus down to the Emperor Monomachus, the study of letters, although neglected by the many, had nevertheless not entirely died out; it blazed up again and revived and was seriously pursued by the lovers of letters in the reign of the Emperor Alexius. Before that time men for the most part lived luxuriously and amused themselves, and due to their effeminacy they busied themselves with quail-hunting and other more disgraceful pastimes, and treated letters, and in fact any training in arts, as a secondary consideration. Therefore when

Italus found the majority of this character he consorted with the scholars, gloomy men of uncouth habits (for such were to be found in the capital even then) and after he had gained an education in letters from them he later associated with the renowned Michael Psellus. This man had not studied very much under learned professors, but through his natural cleverness and quick intelligence and further by the help of God (which he had obtained by his mother's ardent supplications, for she often spent whole nights in the church of God weeping and making invocations to the holy picture of the Virgin on her son's behalf) he had reached the summit of all knowledge, was thoroughly acquainted with Greek and Chaldoean literature and grew famous in those days for his wisdom. Italus, then, became this man's disciple, but he was never able to plumb the depths of philosophy for he was of such a boorish and barbarous disposition that he could not endure teachers even when learning from them. He was full of daring and barbarous rebelliousness and even before learning a thing, imagined he surpassed everybody else and from the very start he entered the lists against Psellus himself. Being well versed in dialectics he caused daily commotions in public meeting places by stringing together sophistical quibbles, putting forward something of the kind and then maintaining an argument to match it. The reigning Emperor, Michael Ducas, and his brothers, made a friend of him; they certainly placed him after Psellus in their estimation, yet they were fond of him, and used him in literary contests; for the Ducases, the Emperor's brothers, and even the Emperor Michael himself, were very literary. Italus would always cast heated, furious glances at Psellus when the latter, like an eagle, soared above his quibbles.

What happened next? The war of the Latins and Italians with the Romans broke out, and the occupation of Lombardy, nay even of the whole of Italy, was under consideration. The Emperor of that time sent Italus to Epidamnus on the supposition that he was his friend and an honest man, and understood Italian affairs. Then to cut my story short, he was detected in treachery to us and an official was sent to expel him, and Italus getting wind of this, escaped to Rome. Later, as was his nature, he repented and sent imploring letters to the Emperor who ordered him back to Constantinople and gave him as dwelling-place the monastery called Pege, and the church of the Forty Saints. Later when Psellus left Byzantium after taking the tonsure, Italus became the foremost teacher of all philosophy and was styled the highest, 'Hypatus,' of philosophers and he gave lectures explaining the books of Aristotle and Plato. He was generally supposed to be very learned. and he undoubtedly was far cleverer than all others in expounding that most wonderful philosophic system, the Peripatetic, and especially the dialectics of it. But for other branches of literature he had not a very good head, for he stumbled over grammar and had never tasted the nectar of rhetoric. Consequently his language was not adaptable nor at all polished. For the same reason, too, his character was austere and entirely unadorned with grace. His studies too had contracted his brows and he literally exhaled harshness. His writings were crammed full of dialectic exordiums and his language in disputations redounded with 'attempted proofs,' more so in his discourses than in his written works. He was so strong in his arguments and so difficult to beat that his opponent would automatically be reduced to silence and to despair. For he would dig a pit either side of his question and hurl his interlocutor into a well of difficulties. Such skill the man had in dialectics, and by a rapid succession of questions he would overwhelm his opponents by confusing and daunting their minds. And it was impossible for anyone, who had once argued with him, to free himself from these labyrinths. In other ways he was most unrefined, and subject to violent temper; and this fierce temper annulled and obliterated the credit he gained from his learning. For in arguments this man used fists as well as words and he did not allow his interlocutor simply to lose himself in embarrassment nor was he satisfied with sewing up his opponent's mouth and condemning him to silence, but forthwith his hand flew out to tear his beard and hair, and insult quickly followed insult, in fact the man could not be restrained in the use of his hands and tongue. The only unphilosophic trait he had was that after the blow his anger left him, tears and evident remorse followed. If it would interest anyone to know his appearance, his head was large, his brow very prominent, his face open, his nostrils wide and of free exhalation, his beard rounded, his chest broad and his limbs well-knit together, in stature shorter than the very tall. His pronunciation was such as you would expect of a Latin who had come to our country as a young man and learnt Greek thoroughly but was not quite clear in his articulation, for he mutilated his syllables here and there. This want of clearness in his utterance and his dropping the last letters did not escape even ordinary people and made rhetoricians call him 'rustic' in his speech. As a result, although his writings were crammed with dialectical commonplaces, drawn from all sources, they were decidedly not free from faults of composition and solecisms scattered broadcast.

CHAPTER NINE

THIS MAN THEN WAS the acknowledged master of all philosophy and the youth flocked to him. (For he expounded to them the doctrines of Plato and Proclus, and of the two philosophers, Porphyry and Iamblichus, but especially the rules of Aristotle; and he gave instruction in the system to those who wished, as affording a serviceable tool and it was on this that he rather prided himself and to this he devoted his attention.) Yet he was unequal to exerting a very good influence on his pupils as his violent temper and his general instability of character stood in the way. And look, I pray, at his pupils-there were Solomon John, and an Iasitas and Serblias and others devoted to learning maybe; most of them I saw myself later, as they often came to the palace. They knew no literary subject accurately, but would pose as dialecticians, making ungainly movements and mad contortions of their limbs, they understood nothing sound but put forth ideas, even those about metempsychosis, in a shadowy way and other similar equally monstrous notions. Is there any learned man who on visiting the court has not seen that holy couple, utterly absorbed in their study of the interpretation of the Divine writings both at day- and nighttime? I mean my royal parents. And here I will tell a little tale, for the laws of oratory allow that. I remember the Empress, my mother, when breakfast was already on the table, carrying a book in her hands and poring over the writings of the didactic Fathers, especially those of the philosopher and martyr Maximus. For she was not so much interested in the physical disputations as in those about the dogmas, because she wished to gain true wisdom. And I was often seized with wonder at her and one day in my wonder I said to her, "How can you spontaneously rise to such sublime heights? for I tremble and dare not listen to such things even with the tips of my ears? For the purely abstract and intellectual character of the man makes one's head swim, as the saying goes."She smiled and said "I know that kind of quite laudable dread; and I myself do not touch these books without a tremor and yet I cannot tear myself away from them. But you wait a little and after you have dipped into other books, you will taste the sweetness of these." The remembrance of these words pricks my heart and I have plunged into an ocean, so to speak, of other tales. But the rules of history forbid them, therefore let us run back to the tale of Italus - when he was at the height of his popularity with the students, some of whom I have named, he treated them all with contempt and turned many of the feebler-minded to rebellion and made not a few of his own pupils tyrants. And I could mention several of them, had not time obliterated their names from my memory. All this took place before my father was elevated to the throne. On his accession he found all education here in a very poor way and the regular study of letters apparently banished afar, he lost no time in raking the ashes together to see whether some live sparks might perchance be bidden under them. Those who were inclined to learning (and they were but few and had not passed beyond the vestibule of Aristotelian philosophy) he did not cease from encouraging but bade them prefer the study of the sacred writings to Greek literature. He found Italus throwing everything into confusion and leading many astray, so he deputed the Sebastocrator Isaac to examine him, as he was very literary and accustomed to undertaking important duties. When Isaac found that Italus was as report said, he openly censured him in a public meeting and then passed him on to the ecclesiastical tribunal by order of the Emperor, his brother. But Italus was unable to hide his own ignorance, and there he vomited forth doctrines quite foreign to the church's, and in the midst of the ecclesiastical dignitaries he did not cease from acting like a buffoon, and doing other things of a boorish and uncultured nature; the president of the church then was Eustratius Garidas who condemned him to detention within the precincts of the great church in the hopes of bringing him to a better state of mind. But, report says that Garidas would more quickly have shared the other's evil doctrines than brought him back to the right path, and Italus won him over entirely to his side. What was the consequence? The whole population of Constantinople surged into the church, shouting for Italus. Probably he would have been thrown down from the top into the middle of the church, had he not escaped to the roof of the sacred edifice and hidden himself in some hole he found. But as the wrong doctrines he had promulgated were much discussed by some of the courtiers, and not a few nobles had been corrupted by those pernicious dogmas, the Emperor's soul was vexed; and the heretical doctrines taught by Italus were summarized in eleven chapters and dispatched to the Emperor. Then the Emperor made Italus recite these chapters from the pulpit in the great church with his head uncovered, and pronounce a curse upon them, while all the congregation listened and repeated the curse. When this had been done, Italus still remained uncontrollable, and again taught these same doctrines to many quite openly, and on being reprimanded by the Emperor, he turned away abruptly and rudely, then he himself was excommunicated. Later on, when he professed penitence, his sentence of excommunication was lightened somewhat. And although his doctrines are still recited and cursed, his name is only mentioned indirectly, as it were, and secretly, and the anathema pronounced on him by the church is not pronounced in a voice audible to the congregation. For in his later years he changed his opinions and repented of the error into which he had been led. Furthermore, he denied a belief in metempsychosis and retracted his insulting words about the holy icons of the saints; he also remodelled his teaching about “ideas “so as to make it conform to orthodoxy, and it was quite evident that he condemned himself for having formerly strayed from the straight path.

BOOK SIX

Norman West, Death of Robert Guiscard, and The Turks

CHAPTER ONE

NOW BRYENNIUS WAS HOLDING Castoria, as told above, so the Emperor who was eager to drive him out and regain possession of the town, called up his whole army again and after fully equipping them with weapons necessary for a siege and also those for engagements in the open he took the road leading to the fort. The situation of the town was as follows: there is a lake called Castoria, into which a promontory runs, which widens out towards the end and terminates in rocky hills. On this neck of land towers and connecting walls were built in the shape of a camp, hence the town's name of Castoria. On arrival the Emperor thought it would be wisest in the first place to made an assault upon the towers and walls with his battering-machines. But as it was impossible to get the soldiers near the walls except from a definite base, he first made a palisaded camp, next built wooden towers and bound them together with iron bands and then from these, as if from a fort, he commenced the battles against the Franks. The siege-engines and catapults he drew up outside the town and then by day and night he fought and broke down part of the walls. However, the besieged resisted most determinedly (they did not surrender even when a breach had been made in the wall) so the Emperor, seeing that he could not achieve his object in that way, conceived a plan which was both daring and clever. It was to put some stout-hearted men into boats and make war from both sides simultaneously, that is, from the land and from the lake. As there were no boats he had some light skiffs loaded on wagons and introduced to the lake by means of the narrow causeway. He had noticed that the Latins who mounted the hills at one side, ascended quickly, whereas those who descended at another point spent a longer time over the descent ; so he put George Palaeologus in the boat with some plucky soldiers and told him to row to the foot of the hills and when he saw the predetermined signals then to mount to the ridge at the back of the enemy and enter the town by the uninhabited and easier road.

Afterwards directly he saw that the Emperor had commenced battle with the Latins on the land-side, he himself was to come as quickly as possible, for the Latins would not be able to carry on the fight equally well on two sides, and as soon as it slackened a bit on one side, they would then more easily be defeated on that same side. George Palmologus therefore anchored off the shores below the hill we have mentioned and stood there ready armed ; he posted a look-out above to watch for the signal to be given by the Emperor and told him directly he saw it, to pass on the same to him. As early as daybreak the Emperor's soldiers raised their war cry and hastened to engage the Latins in battle on the land-side. The lookout seeing the prearranged signal, signified it to Palaeologus by another signal, whereupon he and his men immediately rushed up the ridge and joined in the fight. When Bryennius saw the besiegers outside and Palaeologus raging against them inside he did not surrender even then, but called upon the Counts to be bolder in their resistance. But they behaved very shamelessly to him and said, "You see how calamity is piled upon calamity I Each one of us for the future must secure his own safety, some of us by joining the Emperor and others by returning to their own country." Straightway they translated their words into action; they petitioned the Emperor to have one standard posted near the shrine of Saint George (for a church dedicated to this martyr had been built there) and a second by the road to Valona. "Thus," said they, "those of us who wish to serve your Majesty, can gather at the turn of the road leading to the church of the martyr, whilst those who desire to return to their own country can assemble near the other on the road to Valona." And with these words they immediately deserted to the Emperor. But Bryennius, being a brave man, absolutely refused to go over to the

Emperor, but took an oath never to take up arms against him again, on condition that the Emperor gave him safe conduct to the frontiers of the Roman Empire and there set him free to go to his country. The Emperor at once granted him his request and himself took the road for Byzantium crowned with victory.

CHAPTER TWO

HERE I MUST INTERRUPT the thread of the story a while to relate how the Emperor suppressed the Paulicians. He could not bear the thought of entering the capital without having first subdued these rebels, but as though presiding over a second victory after a first, he caused the mass of the Manichaeans to complete the cycle of his achievements. For it was not even right to allow those descendants of the

Paulicians to be a blemish, as it were, on the brilliant trophy of his western victories. He did not wish to effect this by warfare, as in the clash of battle many lives on either side would be sacrificed, further he knew from of old that these men were very spirited and breathed defiance against their enemies. For this reason he was eager only to punish the ringleaders, and to incorporate the rest in the body of his army. Hence he proceeded against them adroitly. He knew those men's love of danger and irrepressible courage in battle and therefore feared that, if they became desperate, they would commit some terrible outrage; and for the moment they were living quietly in their own country and so far had abstained from raids and other forms of devastation; therefore on his way back to Byzantium he asked them by letter to come and meet him and made them many promises. But the Manichaeans had heard of his victory over the Franks and naturally suspected that those letters were misleading them by fair promises; nevertheless, though reluctant, they set out to meet him. Alexius halted close to Mosynopolis, pretending that he was waiting for other reasons, but in reality he was only awaiting their arrival. When they came he pretended that he wished to review them and write down each individual's name. So he presided with a grim face and commanded the chiefs of the Manichaeans not to ride past promiscuously but in parties of ten, promising a general review shortly, and then when their names had been inscribed, to enter the gates in that order. The men whose duty it was to take them captive were all ready and after taking away their horses and weapons, locked up the chiefs in the prisons assigned them. Those who came after were in complete ignorance of these doings and therefore entered the town little knowing the fate awaiting them. In this manner then he captured them, and their property he confiscated and distributed among the brave soldiers who had shared in the battles and dangers that had befallen him. The official who undertook this distribution went to Philippopolis and drove even the women from their homes and incarcerated them in the citadel. Within a short time the Emperor took pity on the imprisoned Manichaeans, and those who desired Christian baptism were not refused even this boon. So having overreached them by every kind of device he discovered the authors of this terrible madness, and these he banished and imprisoned in islands. The rest he released and gave them permission to go whithersoever they wished. And they, preferring their mother country to any other, hastened back to it to put their affairs into what order they could.

CHAPTER THREE

ALEXIUS THEN RETURNED TO the Queen of Cities. The mutterings against him in the highways and byways (about his appropriation of Church-treasures) did not escape his notice, and the hearing of them wounded his soul because the number of backbiters railing against him had increased greatly although he had not committed any serious offence. For in a time of dire need and world-upheaval and because of the emptiness of the royal treasury he had recourse to that measure and regarded it as a loan, and most assuredly not as robbery, nor was it the plot of a tyrannical master as his slanderers asserted. Further, he intended after the successful termination of the wars he had on hand, to restore to the churches the ornaments he had taken. So on his return to the Queen-City he could not endure being made the subject of discussion by those who wished to disparage his methods. On this account he summoned the church to a very large conference in the palace of Blachernae before which he would first present himself as defendant, and as such make his defence. The whole senate was present with the military and all the clergy wondering what this immense gathering was for. The fact was that it was nothing but an enquiry into the rumours which were being bruited about against the Emperor. The priors of the monasteries were present and before them were set up their books (these are generally called 'brevia') in which lists were written of the treasures in each church. In appearance the Emperor, seated on his royal throne, was the judge, but in reality he was about to be examined. First the gifts bequeathed to the holy houses in former times by various donors were read out and then the things that had been taken away later or even by the reigning Emperor. And when it appeared that nothing else had been taken away except the gold and silver ornaments which lay on the tomb of the Queen Zo6 and a few other vessels of no great use for the sacred services, the Emperor openly proclaimed himself as the culprit, and as judge anybody who liked. And after a little while changing the tone of his speech, he continued, "I found the Empire surrounded on all sides by barbarians and absolutely deficient in resources for opposing these enemies who were pressing hard upon her; you know in how many dangers I was involved and only narrowly escaped being slain by a barbarian's sword. And verily the foes who attacked us from either side were many times more numerous than we. You axe not ignorant of the incursions of the Persians nor of the raids of the Scythians, and you have not forgotten the spears from

Lombardy that were whetted against us. But the money had disappeared together with the arms, and the circle of our rule had been contracted to an indivisible centre. How the whole army has grown, been thoroughly trained, collected from all parts and welded into one, you know; and that all these things require much money, you all know, and also that what I took was spent usefully after the example of the famous Pericles and for the preservation of our honour. But, if to the censorious among you we appear to have offended against the canons, that is not surprising. For we read that the prophet among kings, David, when reduced to the same need, ate the holy bread with his soldiers, and this, though it was not lawful for a layman to touch the food reserved for the priests. And besides this we learn from the sacred canons that on several occasions holy things were allowed to be sold for the ransom of prisoners of war. If then, when our country was enslaved, when the cities, and even Constantinople itself, were in danger of being captured-if then under this frightful compulsion I laid hands on just a few things which did not at all partake of the dignity of sacred things and used them for our liberation, then, I aver, I have given my detractors no just cause of accusation." With these words he changed his manner of speech, proclaimed himself guilty and himself condemned himself. Then he ordered the guardians of the 'brevia' to unroll them again with the object of making a clear statement of what had been taken. And he immediately awarded a fairly large sum of gold to the Chapter of the Church of the Antiphonetes to be paid yearly by the trustees of the public fund; and this payment has remained unchanged to this day; for the tomb of the Empress aforementioned was there. And to the church in Chalcoprateia, he allotted an annual sum of gold from the royal treasury sufficient to pay the regular choristers of that church dedicated to the Virgin.

CHAPTER FOUR

AT THE SAME TIME a plot against the Emperor was discovered, organized by the leaders of the senate and the chief officers in the army, and it was divulged to the Emperor. The accusers were confronted with the instigators of the plot and denounced them. Thus their conspiracy was revealed and the legal penalty awaiting them for this offence was heavy, but the Emperor did not wish to impose this punishment upon them, but decreed confiscation of their goods and exile against the ringleaders and to this extent only did he take vengeance for this plot. Now I must return to the point in my history where I broke off.

When Alexius was raised to the rank of

Domestic by Nicephorus, Botaniates, he took a certain Travlos, a Manichaean into his staff of intimate servants and after he had honoured him with Christian baptism, he married him to one of the Empress' maidservants. Now this man had four sisters and when he heard of their being driven from their homes with all the other women and imprisoned, and deprived of all their belongings, he was indignant and could not bear it, but began to consider how he could free himself from the Emperor's power. His wife got to know this and seeing her husband ready to run away she revealed the matter to the man entrusted with the supervision of the Manichaeans. This fact did not escape Travlos and so one evening he sent for all those whom he had made participators of his secret to come to him. All his kinsmen rallied round him and they took possession of Beliatoba ; this is a little town situated on the top of the hill which overlooks the valley below Beliatoba. Finding this deserted, they looked upon it as their own property and fixed their dwellings there, then they made daily sallies from it, sometimes even as far as their own town, Philippopolis, and returned laden with much booty. But Travlos, not satisfied with this, made a treaty with the Scythians who dwelt by the Danube, and won over the chieftains round Glabinitza and Dristra and the neighbouring districts, and at the same time betrothed himself to the daughter of one of the leading Scythians ; this he did because he desired with all his might to vex the Emperor by an inroad of the Scythians. The Emperor received daily news of his doings and with an eye to the future, he did his best to reconcile him by letters and promises as he suspected the evil that would be wrought by him Nay, he even issued and sent him a Golden Bull guaranteeing him security and perfect freedom. However, 'a crab never learns to run straight' ; so Travlos remained the same man as before, continuing to seek the friendship of the Scythians, to send for more from their own countries, and to lay waste all the surrounding regions.

CHAPTER FIVE

WHEN THE EMPEROR HAD settled this matter of the Manichaeans as a secondary business, he secured their allegiance by a treaty

Bohemund, meanwhile (for we must return to him now), was still lingering in Valona; when he received the news concerning Bryermius and the other Counts, and heard that some had preferred to serve the Emperor, and the others had dispersed in different directions, he sought his mother country, crossed to Lombardy and found his father at Salernum, as already said, and by inveighing bitterly against the Emperor, aroused his father's ire against him. When

Robert saw him with disastrous tidings plainly written on his face, and realized that the great hopes be had placed in him had fallen ‘ wrong side up like a shell,’ he stood dazed for some time, as if struck by lightning. After enquiring about everything and finding that all had happened contrary to his expectations, he was overcome by dejection. Yet even at this crisis he did not meditate anything ignoble or unworthy of his personal bravery and daring; but was rather stirred up all the more to fight, and anxieties and cares, heavier than the former ones, oppressed him. For the man was a firm upholder of his own designs and conceptions and would never willingly give up anything he had once planned-in a word ‘ he was undaunted and thought he ought to be able to accomplish everything at the first attempt. So he soon composed himself and on recovering from his deep despondency he sent messengers in every direction to announce that he was crossing again to Illyria to fight against the Emperor, and summoned all his friends. In a short time a multitude of soldiers assembled from all parts, both horse- and foot-, all splendidly equipped and eager for action. Homer would have described this multitude 'as being like tribes of swarming bees.' And they flocked together from distant towns just as much as from nearer ones. Thus Robert made great preparations in order to avenge his son's defeat, and finally sent for his other sons, Roger and another called Gidus[48]. (The Emperor Alexius wanted to make this son secede from his father, and had sent to him secretly with an offer of marriage and promises of high preferment and an extravagant sum of money; Gidus had lent a willing ear, but so far had kept the matter to himself.) To these two sons Robert entrusted all the cavalry and dispatched them with orders to take Valona

48 Guido

speedily; they crossed and did this at once. Then they left a small number of soldiers as garrison in Valona, marched on with the rest, reached Buthrotum and took this too at the first assault. Robert on his side took his entire fleet, and sailed along the coast opposite Buthrotum, and reached Brindisi with the intention of crossing to Illyria. But when he found out that the strait was narrower at Hydrunturn he crossed from that port to Valona. Then with his whole fleet he coasted along from Valona to Buthrotum and was reunited with his sons. As Corfu, which he had conquered before, had revolted again, he left his sons in Buthrotum and sailed for Corfu himself with his whole fleet. So much for Robert - the Emperor when he received the tidings, did not lose heart at all but began preparations for renewing the war against Robert and urged the Venetians by letter to furnish a large fleet, promising them they should have their expenses paid many times over.

He himself equipped biremes and triremes and all manner of piratical vessels and sent them out against Robert with hoplites on board skilled in naval warfare. When Robert heard of the arrival of the fleets he, as was his nature, wanted to force on an engagement, so loosed cable and entered the port of Cassope with his whole fleet. The Venetians had anchored in the harbour of Pasaxi and stayed there a little and on hearing of Robert's arrival, they too quickly made for the port of Cassope. A fierce engagement ensued and a fight at close quarters in which Robert was defeated. But fond of war as he was, and ever lusting for a fight, he would not give in after defeat, but got ready for a second battle and that a more serious one. This the admirals of both the fleets learnt and, emboldened by their recent success, attacked him again on the third day and gained a brilliant victory over him, and after it sailed back to the harbour of Pasari. Then, as so often happens in such cases, they were either overelated by their previously gained victories or they thought they had driven the vanquished to despair, and consequently relaxed as if they had completed their task, and held Robert in contempt. For they detached all the quick-sailing ships and sent them to Venice to carry the news of Robert's complete defeat. Whenen Robert heard of this from a certain Venetian, Peter Contarinus by name, who had lately deserted to him, he fell into deep despondency and found life scarcely tolerable. He soon, however, thought better of it and recovering his spirits again attacked the Venetians. These were panic-stricken by his unexpected arrival; they at once bound together their larger vessels with ropes in the neighbourhood of the harbour of Corfu, and having thus constructed what is called an 'open sea harbour ' they drove the smaller vessels into it; then armed and awaited his coming. When he came, the battlc began, and it was a terrible one and fiercer than the two former for the men fought more madly than before. So the battle waxed fiery; and neither side would yield, but on the contrary fought face to face. The Venetians had previously consumed all their provisions and consequently the boats were empty but for the soldiers; so the boats, owing to their lightness, floated about as if upheld by the surface of the water, which did not come up even to the second stripe; the soldiers rushed in a mass to the side of the ships facing the foe, and so were drowned; they numbered about thirteen thousand. The other ships were taken, crews and all. After this signal victory Robert in a fit of harshness treated many of the prisoners most cruelly, for he had the eyes of some gouged out, the noses of others cut off, and some he deprived of their hands and feet, or both. About the rest he sent word to their fellow-countrymen that whoever wanted to ransom a friend for a price might come without fear.

At the same time he asked whether they wished for peace; and this is the answer they sent: “Know, Duke Robert, that even if we were to see our women and children slaughtered by you, we should not renounce our allegiance to the Emperor Alexius, and certainly we shall never cease succouring him and fighting bravely for him.” After a short lapse of time the Venetians equipped some ‘dromones’ and triremes and various other small, quick-sailing craft and advanced against Robert with a stronger force. And when they found him stationed at Buthrotum they joined battle with him and gained a great victory over him, killing many and drowning more; and they very nearly captured his legitimate son, Gidus, and his wife. Then they sent word to the Emperor of the brilliant victory they had gained over Robert. He paid their services by liberal gifts and preferments, and honoured the Doge of Venice with the title of ‘Protosebastos ’ with the salary attached, and on the

Patriarch he bestowed the title 'Hypertimius ' with its corresponding salary. Moreover he decreed that a large sum of gold should be apportioned yearly to all the churches in Venice from the royal treasury, and to the church named after the evangelist and apostle Mark he made all the shopkeepers in Constantinople, who were natives of Amalfi, pay tribute. He also gave the Venetians all the wharfs running from the old Hebraic anchorage to that called Bigla and all the anchorages between these two, as well as much real property, not only in the capital and in the town of Dyrrachium, but wherever they asked for it. But greatest gift of all, he ordered that their merchandise should not be taxed in any of the countries under Roman sway, so that they could trade freely where they liked, and not pay even an obol, neither for customs nor for any other tax required by the Treasury, but should be exempt from all Roman authority.

CHAPTER SIX

AS FOR ROBERT (for my tale must return to the point where it digressed and be kept within the bounds of historical narration) he did not rest even after this defeat. But as he had already sent one ship with his son to Cephalenia as he wished to take possession of the town on it, he brought his remaining ships, with the whole army, to anchor near Boditza and himself sailed for Cephalenia in a galley with one bank of oars. And before he could join his son and the rest of his forces, whilst he was lingering near Ather (which is a promontory of Cephalenia) he was seized with a violent fever. As he could not bear the burning of the fever, he asked for cold water. His men dispersed in various directions to seek water when a native said to them, "You see the island there, Ithaca. On that a large town was built long ago called Jerusalem, and now it has fallen into ruins from age; in that town there was a spring whose water was always fit for drinking and very cold." Robert was overcome with fear on hearing this for by connecting Ather and the town of Jerusalem he understood that his death was imminent. For many years before some soothsayers had prophesied to him the kind of thing flatterers are wont to tell princes, As far as Ather you shall bring all countries under your sway, but from there you shall depart for Jerusalem and pay your debt to nature." Whether the fever killed him or whether he died of pleurisy, I have no means of saying for certain. At all events he died in six days. His wife Gaïta reached him just in time to see him die and his son weeping over him. News of this calamity was, then sent to the son whom Robert in his lifetime had already designated heir to his dukedom. On hearing the sad tidings he was overcome at first by uncontrollable grief, but soon summoning reason to his aid and collecting himself, he sent for all his followers and, whilst weeping inconsolably for his father, he told them what had happened, and then made them take the oath of allegiance to himself. Next he crossed with them all to Apulia. During the crossing he was caught in such a severe storm, although it was summer, that some of the ships were wrecked, and others dashed on the shore and beaten to pieces. The ship carrying the corpse was also half wrecked and the crew only just managed to save the coffin, and convey it safely to Venusia. Robert was buried in the old monastery dedicated to the Holy Trinity, where his brothers had been buried before him. Robert died in the twenty-fifth year of his reign as duke and at the age of seventy. The Emperor, on hearing of Robert's sudden death, was greatly relieved by having such a burden lifted from his shoulders; and very quickly turned his attention to the Normans who were still in possession of Dyrrachium.

He aimed at sowing dissension amongst them by letters and other devices, as he thought that would be the easiest means of regaining the city. He also persuaded the Venetians who happened to be in the capital to advise the Venetians, Amalfians and other foreigners who were in Epidamnus to submit to his will and surrender Dyrrachium to him. And he himself did not cease making promises and offering bribes with a view to their surrendering Dyrrachium. to him. The Latins allowed themselves to be persuaded (for their whole race is very fond of money and quite accustomed to selling even their dearest possessions for an obol) and with high hopes in their hearts they formed a conspiracy and first of all slew the man who had originally suggested betraying the fort to Robert, and next his fellow-conspirators; and then they went to the Emperor, and handed over the fort to him and in return received immunity of every kind from him.

CHAPTER SEVEN

A CERTAIN MATHEMATICIAN NAMED Seth who boasted much of his knowledge of astrology had forecast Robert's fate by an oracle, after his crossing to Illyria, written this forecast on a paper, sealed it and entrusted it to some of the Duke's intimates, bidding them keep it till a certain time. After Robert's death they opened it by the astrologer's order and the prophecy was as follows: "A great enemy from the west shall fall suddenly after having stirred up great confusion."This caused everybody to marvel at the man's knowledge; and in truth he had delved very deeply into this branch of science, and if I may be allowed to make a short break in the course of my history, the following are the facts about astrological prophecies. The discovery is fairly recent, and the science of it was not known to the ancients. For this method of divination did not exist in the time of Eudoxus, the greatest of all astronomers, neither did Plato have any knowledge of it, and even the astrologer, Manetho, had not brought it to perfection. Now these (astrologers) observe the hour of the birth of the persons about whom they intend to prophesy, and fix the cardinal points and carefully note the disposition of all the stars, in short they do everything that the inventor of this science bequeathed to posterity and which those who trouble about such trifles understand. We, also, at one time dabbled a little in this science, not in order to cast horoscopes (God forbid!), but by gaining a more accurate idea of this vain study to be able to pass judgment upon its devotees. I do not mention this for the sake of boasting, but to prove that during my father's reign many of the sciences made great progress, as he honoured both philosophers and philosophy itself, but towards this teaching of astrology he showed some hostility, I believe because it tended to make people of a guileless nature reject their faith in God and gape at the stars. This was the cause of the Emperor's waging war against the teaching of astrology. Yet in spite of this there was no dearth of astrologers at that time, for the Seth I have mentioned flourished then, and there was also a famous Egyptian, Alexandreus, who was a strong exponent of the mysteries of astrology. He was consulted by many and used to give most accurate forecasts in many cases, not even using the astrolabe, but made his prophecies by a certain casting of dice. There was nothing magical about that either, it was an art practised by the Alexandrians (or by Alexandreus). When the Emperor saw how the young people flocked to him and regarded the man as a species of prophet, he himself consulted him twice and each time Alexandreus gave very correct answers. But the Emperor was afraid that harm might come to many from it and that all would be led away to the vain pursuit of astrology, so he banished him from the capital, assigned Raedestus as his dwelling-place and showed great consideration for him, and his means of living were amply supplied from the imperial treasury. Nay more, the great dialectician, Eleutherius, also an Egyptian by birth, cultivated this art too and carried it to such perfection that he yielded the palm to no one. Later again, a man called Catanances from Athens came to the capital, anxious to carry off the first prize among astrologers and when questioned by some about the date of the Emperor's death, he foretold it as he thought, but was proved wrong in his prognostication. It happened, however, that the lion which was kept in the palace died that day, after four days' fever, so the vulgar considered that the prophecy of Catanances had been accomplished. After some considerable time he again foretold the date of the Emperor's death and was mistaken;

yet the Emperor's mother, the Empress Anna, died on the very day Catanances had foretold. Because Catanances had made repeated mistakes in his predictions about him, the Emperor did not like to banish him as he was self-convicted, and also it might seem that he banished him in anger. But now let us return to the point in our history where we abandoned it, otherwise we shall be thought to be stargazers, obscuring the main theme of our history with the names of astrologers.

Now Robert, as rumour insisted and many said, was a most exceptional leader, quick-witted, good-looking, courteous in conversation, ready too in repartee, loud-voiced, easily accessible, very tall in stature, his hair always close-cut, long bearded, always anxious to maintain the ancient customs of his race. He preserved his perfect comeliness of countenance and figure until the end, and of these he was very proud as his appearance was considered worthy of kingship, he showed respect to all his subordinates, more especially to those who were well-disposed towards him. On the other hand he was very thrifty and fond of money, very business-like and greedy of gain, and, in addition to all this, most ambitious; and since he was a slave to these desires, he has incurred the serious censure of mankind. Some people slander the Emperor and say he was faint-hearted and began the war with Robert too soon. For if, as they allege, he had not attacked Robert before the right time, he could have defeated him easily, as Robert was being worried on all sides by the so-called Albanians and by the natives of Dalmatia sent by Bodinus. These remarks came from the backbiters who stood out of shot and hurled envenomed darts from their lips against the fighters. For all acknowledge Robert's bravery, remarkable skill in warfare and steadfast spirit; and he was a man who could not be conquered easily but only with extreme difficulty, and after a defeat he seemed to rise again with renewed vigour.

CHAPTER EIGHT

THE EMPEROR, as related above, returned to the capital in triumph with the Latins from Count Bryennius' army who had deserted to him on the first of December in the seventh Indiction. He found his wife in the pangs of childbirth in the room which had of old been set apart for the Empresses' confinements, our forefathers called it the'purple' room, and from it the name 'Porphyrogeniti'[49] has become current in the world. And at dawn on a Saturday a female child was born to them who was exactly like her father, they said; that child was I. And once upon

49 born in the purple

a time, I heard the Empress, my mother, relate that three days before the Emperor's entry into the palace (for he was returning then from the war with Robert and his other numerous battles and labours) she began to feel pains, so she made the sign of the cross on her womb and said, "Wait a little, child, for your father's coming! "When she said that, the ‹Protovestiaire,' her mother, scolded her severely and said angrily, "How do you know whether he will come within a month? and how will you be able to bear the pains so long ? "Thus spake her mother, but the Empress' command took effect, which signified that even in the womb I felt that affection for my parents which was manifested so conspicuously in the future. For afterwards as I grew up and reached years of discretion I became sincerely devoted to my mother and also equally to my father. And many can bear witness to this fact, above all those who know my history. And further testimony to it are the many struggles, anxieties and even dangers which I suffered because of my deep love for them, as I spared neither my honour, money, nor even my life; for devotion to them so fired me that I even risked my life for them several times. But no more of this. Let me return to the events which took place after my birth. All the ceremonies usual at the birth of an Emperor's child were performed most lavishly, that is to say, acclamations and presents and honours given at such a time to the heads of the Senate and the army, so that all were more joyful and exultant than ever before and loud in their praises, especially the Empress' relations who could not contain themselves for joy. And when a certain number of days had passed, my parents honoured me with a crown and royal diadem. Now Constantine, the son of the ex-Emperor, Michael Ducas, of whom I have often spoken, was regent together with the Emperor, my father, and with him signed all deeds of gifts in red ink; and wearing a tiara, accompanied him in all processions, and was acclaimed second in all acclamations; as I too was now to be acclaimed, the leaders of the acclamations shouted out “Constantine and Anna “together at the time for acclamations. And this continued for a good long time, as I have often heard my relations and parents subsequently say. This was perhaps symbolic of what should befall me later, whether it can be called good, or on the contrary, ill fortune. When a second daughter was born to their majesties, bearing a likeness to her parents, and also showing signs of the virtue and wisdom which were to distinguish her later, they much desired to have a son as well, and their prayer was granted. For during the eleventh Indiction a son was born to them. Thereupon my parents were indeed overjoyed and no trace of sadness remained, as their desire had been fulfilled. The whole populace too rejoiced, seeing their masters so happy, and congratulated each other and were delighted. Then you would have seen the palace full of rejoicing and no shadow of sorrow or even care, for all the well-disposed rejoiced from the bottom of their heart, whilst the others feigned delight. A people, as a rule, is ill-affected to its rulers, but by much pretence and flattery win the favour of their superiors. However on this one occasion universal joy could be witnessed, as one and all were really pleased. The child had a swarthy complexion, broad forehead, lean cheeks, a nose neither snub nor aquiline but something between the two, very black eyes which betokened, as far as one can judge from an infant's face, a quick intelligence. As my parents naturally wished to raise this child to the rank of Emperor and leave him the empire of the Romans as his inheritance, they deemed him worthy of being baptised and crowned in the great church of God. This is what happened to us children, ‹born in the purple’ from the very starting-point of our birth. What befell us later, shall be narrated in due order.

CHAPTER NINE

THE EMPEROR ALEXIUS HAD driven away the Turks from the shores of Bithynia and the Bosporus and the Northern provinces and made a truce with Soliman, as I have recounted earlier; then he rode off to Illyria where after many hardships he utterly defeated Robert and his son, Bohemund, and thus delivered the West from an overwhelming catastrophe. On his return from those parts he found that the Turks under Apelchasem[50] were not only overrunning the East, but had penetrated as

50 Abul-kassim

far as the Propontis and the maritime towns there. And this is the right point at which to tell how the Ameer Soliman on leaving Nicaea had left this Apelchasem behind as governor ; how Puzanus was sent into Asia by the sultan of Persia, and defeated and killed by Tutuses[51], the brother of the sultan; and how Tutuses himself after the defeat of Puzanus, was strangled by his second cousins. A certain Armenian, Philaretus by name, conspicuous for bravery and sagacity, had been raised to the rank of Domestic by the former Emperor, Romanus Diogenes, and when he saw the latter's downfall and heard further that he had been deprived of his sight, it was more than he could bear, for he loved him with an exceeding love, so plotted rebellion and made himself master of the province of Antioch. But as the Turks daily laid waste the surrounding country so that he had no peace, he meditated desertion

51 or Tutush or Toutoush

to the Turks and circumcision, which they practise. But his son vehemently opposed him and tried to divert him from this mad enterprise, but his better counsels were not accepted. In his grief at his father's refusal he travelled for eight days to reach Nicaea, and there gained access to the Ameer Soliman (who had just attained the rank of Sultan) and roused him to undertake the siege of Antioch and incited him to war against his father. Soliman lent him a ready ear, and when starting for Antioch he left Apelchasem as Governor of Nicaea and also appointed him General-in-Chief over all the other Generals. Then with Philaretus' son in his train he rode for twelve nights (for he reposed in the day) and by the unexpectedness of his arrival took Antioch at first assault. At the same time Charatices secretly pillaged Sinope as he had found out that a large sum of gold and money belonging to the imperial treasury had been stored there. The Grand

Sultan[52] had a brother, Tutuses, who ruled over Jerusalem, the whole of Mesopotamia, and Aleppo and as far as Baghdad, and was hoping to secure Antioch; when he noticed that the Ameer Soliman was on the point of rebelling, and had already won the province of Antioch for himself, he encamped with his whole army midway between Aleppo and Antioch. On the Ameer Soliman's coming out to meet him, a tremendous battle broke out at once, and when it came to hand to hand fighting, Soliman's troops turned their backs and fled in disorder. In spite of all his protestations Soliman could not restrain them from flight, so seeing his imminent danger he turned aside from the battle and when he thought he had reached a safe spot, he placed his shield on the ground, and throwing himself to the ground, sat down on it. However he had not escaped the notice of his fellow tribesmen; and some of

52 i.e. Malek Shah

the satraps followed him and said his uncle Tutuses had sent for him. He refused to go as he scented danger. But the satraps insisted and being unable to restrain them by force, as he was alone, he drew his sword from its sheath and plunged it deep into his bowels; and thus the wretched man died wretchedly. And the survivors of Ameer Soliman's forces at once joined Tutuses. On hearing of these doings the Sultan feared that Tutuses was growing too powerful, so he sent a Chiauss to the Emperor to ask a Roman princess in marriage for himself and promising, if this were granted, to fetch away the Turks from the maritime towns, to restore him his forts, and to help him wholeheartedly. The Emperor received him, read the Sultan's letter but eluded the question of marriage; and seeing that the Chiauss was a man of understanding he asked him of his origin and parentage. On the latter replying that his mother was an Iberian but his father a Turk, the Emperor took a great deal of pains to persuade him to accept Christian baptism. The Chiauss consented to this and pledged himself to the Emperor not to return home, after he had received holy baptism. Since he had received instructions from the Sultan by letter that, if the Emperor were willing to arrange a marriage for him, he should drive out all the satraps who held the maritime towns by shewing them the Sultan's letter treating of this question, the Emperor suggested to the Chiauss to make use of this letter and after he had expelled them all by shewing them the Sultan's writing, to return to the capital again. The Chiauss with great alacrity went first to Sinope and by shewing Charatices the Sultan's epistle he drove him out of the town without an obol of the Emperor's money in his pocket. This is what happened. As Charatices was going out of Sinope, he desecrated the church dedicated to our Immaculate Lady, the Mother of God, and forthwith he was delivered by the hand of God, as it seemed, to an avenging demon, and fell to the ground foaming at the mouth, and so he went out of the town mad 1 The jurisdiction over Sinope the Chiauss handed to Constantine Dalassenus whom the Emperor had sent down there for that purpose, then he successively visited the other towns, shewed the satraps the Sultan's letter, and thus drove them all out and handed the town over to the Emperor's satraps. This business finished, the Chiauss returned to the Emperor, and after receiving holy baptism and revelling in rich presents he was appointed Duke of Anchialus.

CHAPTER TEN

WHEN THE SUICIDE OF Ameer Soliman became known throughout the whole of Asia, each satrap who was governor over a town or fortress, took that respective place and made it his own. For at the same time that the Ameer Soliman entrusted the Government of Nicaea to Apelchasem on his departure for Antioch, he also apportioned the seacoast, and Cappadocia, in fact the whole of Asia, to various satraps, for each man to guard his own portion until such time as he, Soliman, should return. Now Apelchasem who was then archsatrap in Nicaea, where the Sultan's palace was, took possession of the town and transferred Cappadocia to his brother, Pulchases, and then lived a carefree life, expecting soon to assume the dignity of 'Sultan,' in fact looked upon it as a certainty. The man was capable and intrepid, and would not be satisfied with what he had, so sent forth foraging parties to lay waste the whole of Bithynia as far as the Propontis. The Emperor then tried his former plan, that is, he dissipated the foragers and forced Apelchasem to sue for terms of peace. But as he found that the latter continued making secret designs against him and postponing the truce, he decided it was necessary to put a strong army in the field against him. So the Emperor sent Taticius (whom I have frequently mentioned) with a respectable force to Niceaa, warning him to use discretion in attacking the enemy if by chance he fell in with any outside the town. Taticius went off and marshalled his army in line of battle close to the walls as no Turks were to be seen then, but they suddenly threw open the gates and a body of about two hundred of them rode down upon him. When the Franks (of whom there were a goodly number) saw them, they dashed straight at them in a tremendous onrush with their long spears in their hands, and after wounding a large number, drove the rest back to the fort. The next day Taticius stood there with his army in the same formation until sunset, and since no Turk shewed himself outside the gates, he marched back to Basileia and pitched his camp at a distance of twelve stades from Nicaea. During the night a countryman came to him and assured him that Prosuch was approaching with fifty thousand men, and had been sent by the newly elected Sultan, Pargiaruch. As others confirmed this report, Taticius, seeing that his forces were insufficient against large numbers, cancelled his former plans and thought it better to preserve his whole army safe and sound rather than lose it altogether by fighting against forces infinitely more numerous and far stronger than his own. Consequently his thoughts turned to the capital, and he settled to return to it via Nicomedia. Now Apelchasem from his watchtower saw him turn off to Constantinople and already on the march, so came out and followed him, intending to attack him if he espied him encamping in some suitable spot. And he overtook him at Prenetus, surprised him and started a violent fight. Taticius quickly drew up his men and allowed the Franks to begin the battle and make the first charge against the enemy. And they, long spears in hand, rode at full gallop and hurled themselves like fire upon the barbarians, cut the phalanxes to pieces and routed them completely. Afterwards Taticius regained the capital by way of Bithynia. Apelchasem, however, could not keep quiet, for he was obsessed with the desire of annexing the Roman Empire, or, if this was impossible, of extending his rule over all the coast-lands and islands as well. In pursuit, then, of these plans he determined first to build some buccaneering vessels, as he had taken Cius (a town on the coast of Bithynia) and when the ships were nearing completion, he thought his plans were maturing well. But he was not unobserved by the Emperor, who quickly fitted out whatever biremes, triremes and other vessels he had at hand, set Manuel Buturnites in command and sent him with injunctions to make haste and burn Apelchasem's half-built ships, no matter in what condition he found them. Moreover, he sent Taticius with a considerable army against him by land. These two left the City, and Apelchasem soon saw Butumites approaching by sea at great speed, and heard that others were bearing down upon him by land; he judged the ground, where he happened to be, unsuitable, as it was rough and narrow, and altogether ill-adapted for his archers, as it would not allow them to act against the Roman cavalry; so he moved his camp in order to place his troops on suitable ground. This place he found, and by some it is called Halycae and by others Cyparission. Butumites, meanwhile, arrived by sea and set fire to Apelchasem's ships more quickly than can be told. On the following day Taticius too came by land and drawing up his troops in a convenient position, did not cease from mom till eve for fifteen whole days, either skirmishing or engaging the troops of Apelchasern in close combat. But as Apelchasem would not yield but maintained a determined resistance, the Latins grew weary and, although the ground was not to their advantage, yet they worried Taticius to allow them, even unaided, to undertake a pitched battle with the Turks. Finally, although against his own judgment, yet as he saw daily reinforcements coming to Apelchasem, he gave way to the Latins. And about sunrise he set his forces in array and joined battle with Apelchasem. In it many of the Turks were killed, but most were taken prisoners, and still more fled without giving a thought to their personal baggage. And Apelchasem himself rode straight to Nicaea and only just escaped. Taticius' soldiers collected a large amount of booty and returned to their own camp. On receiving this news, the Emperor, clever as he was in winning the souls of men and in softening a heart of stone, at once dictated a letter to Apelchasem advising him to abstain from such vain enterprises and not to beat the air but to come over to him and thus exchange a life of labour for the enjoyment of bounteous gifts and honour. Therefore Apelchasem, when he further heard that Prosuch was besieging towns held by various satraps and would soon be at Nicaea with the object of besieging it, made a virtue of necessity, as the saying is, and boldly accepted the Emperor's offer of peace, although he guessed the latter's purpose. When the truce between them had been concluded, the Emperor who was already scheming to obtain another advantage, and could see no other way of gaining his end, invited Apelchasem to the capital to receive gifts of money, enjoy a life of luxury to the full and then return home. Apelchasern accepted and on his arrival in the capital was treated with much kindness. The Turkish rulers of Nicaca still held Nicomedia (which is the metropolis of Bithynia) and as the Emperor wished to expel them from that town, he thought it well to build a second small citadel near the sea, while the terms of peace were being arranged. Consequently he had all the materials necessary for the construction of the fort, as well as the builders, loaded on transports and dispatched them under Eustathius, the 'Drungaire' of the fleet, to whom he had revealed his secret and entrusted the building. He conjured him to treat any Turks who might pass, very kindly, and give them their fill of needful things, at the same time signifying to them that Apelchasem knew of the building of the forts, but he was to ward off all vessels from the shores of Bithynia to prevent Apelchasem's hearing anything. To Apelchasem. the Emperor gave money every day and was profuse in his invitations to him to come to the baths, or horse-races or the chase, and further to view the monuments set up along the highroads. Moreover he gave orders to the charioteers to prepare an equestrian display in his honour in the theatre which Constantine the Great built long ago: and he urged him to go every day and watch the horses being tested, all this was to get time for his builders while Apelchasem wasted his days in the capital. But when the fort was finished and his purpose accomplished, he loaded him with further gifts, honoured him with the rank of "Sebastos" and after again confirming the treaty, sent him home in great state by sea. When the building of the fort was revealed to Apelchasem, although he was wounded deeply by the raising of it, yet he pretended to know nothing and said not a word about it. A similar tale is told of Alcibiades-for he in a similar manner had outwitted the Lacedoemonians when they refused to allow Athens to be rebuilt after it had been destroyed by the Persians. For he told the Athenians to rebuild their city while he went on an embassy to Sparta. There the embassy wasted its time, thus giving the builders an opportunity and after the trick had been successful, the Lacedaemonians learnt of the complete rebuilding of Athens. And the Paeanian[53] somewhere in his writings also mentions this clever deception. So my father's plan was similar, though more sagacious than that of Alcibiades. Forhefawned upon this barbarian with horse-races and other delights and by delaying him from day to day he managed to complete the fort and when the work was quite finished he dismissed him from the capital.

CHAPTER ELEVEN

MEANWHILE PROSUCH HAD come up with an enormous army, as was expected, and was besieging Nicaea, as the countryman who came by night to Taticius said, and for three months he persevered in the siege. Then when the townsmen and

53 Demosthenes

even Apelchasem himself saw that things had come to a distressful pass, and that they would be unable to hold out much longer, they sent a message to the Emperor begging him to come to their aid and saying that they preferred to be called his servants than to yield to Prosuch. He immediately picked out the best of the troops that happened to be on the spot, gave them standards and silver-studded sceptres and sent them away to carry succour. Now he did not send this army to help Apelchasem exactly, but in his own heart he hoped that his help might afterwards turn out to be the ruin of Apelchasem. As two enemies of the Roman power were fighting against each other, it was necessary to help the weaker, not in order that he might grow more powerful, but that he might beat off the other, and then he, the Emperor, would take away the town from the former and make it his own, which at present was outside the orbit of Empire; after that he would gradually take another and yet another and thus enlarge the boundaries of the Roman Empire which had become very restricted; more especially since the sword of the Turks had grown so powerful. For there was a time when the limits of the Roman rule were the two pillars which bound east and west respectively, those on the west being called the ' pillars of Heracles,'those on the east the 'pillars of Dionysus' somewhere near the frontier of India. It is hardly possible to define the Empire's former width. Egypt, Meroë, all the Troglodyte country, and the region adjacent to the torrid zone; and in the other direction far-famed Thule, and the races who dwell in the northern lands and over whose heads the North Pole stands. But in these later times the boundary of the Roman rule was the neighbouring Bosporus on the east and the city of Adrianople on the west. Now, however, the Emperor Alexius by striking with both hands, as it were, at the barbarians who beset him on either side and starting from Byzantium as his centre, enlarged the circle of his rule, for on the west he made the Adriatic sea his frontier, and on the east the Euphrates and Tigris. And he would have restored the Empire to its former prosperity, had not the successive wars and the recurrent dangers and difficulties hindered him in his purpose (for he was involved in great, as well as frequent, dangers). His idea then, as I said at the beginning, in sending an army to Apelchasem, the tyrant of Nicaea, was not to rescue him from danger, but to gain a victory for himself; fortune, however, did not favour him. For the matter fell out thus. The troops that were sent reached a small town called after the lord George ; and the Turks immediately opened their gates to them. Then the soldiers went up to the battlements of the wall above the East gate, piled up the standards and sceptres, shouting at the same time and then continuously chanted their war cries.

This noise absolutely terrified the besiegers outside who crept away during the night, thinking that the Emperor himself had come and thereupon the Roman forces returned straightaway to the capital. For they were not a strong enough force to withstand an assault by the Persians who were expected to come up shortly from the depths of the Turkish Empire.

CHAPTER TWELVE

THE SULTAN ON HIS side was awaiting the return of his Chiauss; when he noticed that he delayed his return, and then heard all he had done, how he had expelled Charatices by stratagem from Sinope, had accepted Christian baptism and been sent to the west by the Emperor with the title of Duke of Anchialus, he was vexed and distressed. So he resolved to send Puzanus for a second time with troops against Apelchasem, and also to give him a letter for the Emperor treating of the question of alliance by marriage. The tenor of the letter was as follows: "O Emperor, I have heard of thy doings. I know that no sooner hadst thou taken up the reins of government, than thou wast involved in many wars, and that now when thou hast just quelled the turbulent Latins, the Scythians are preparing war against thee, and that Ameer Apelchasem has broken the treaty, made by thee with Soliman, and is ravaging Asia right up to Damalis. If therefore thou art anxious for Apelchasem to be driven out of those countries and to have Asia and even Antioch itself under thy rule, then send me thy daughter as bride for my eldest son. If thou dost this, there will be no more stumbling-blocks in thy path, but thou wilt easily accomplish everything with me as thy coadjutor, not only in the East, but even in Illyria and all the West by means of the forces I shall send thee, and nobody will be able henceforth to stand before thee." This was the tenor of the Persian Sultan's letter. After Puzanus reached Nicaea and made not only one, but several attempts to take it, which were foiled by Apelchasem's valiant resistance, as he had obtained the help he had begged from the Emperor, he turned his attention to the capture of other towns and forts, so left Nicxa and pitched his tents near the Lampe (which is a river near Lopadium). After his departure Apelchasem loaded as much gold as they could carry on fifteen mules and set off to the Sultan of Persia, taking this gift with him in order not to be dismissed from his governorship. He came upon the Sultan encamped near Spacha, and as the latter did not deign even to see him, he employed mediators. And as these worried the Sultan, he said "As I have once for all bestowed the province on the Ameer Puzanus I have no intention of taking it away from him again. Let the man go and carry his money to Puzanus and say what he likes to him, and whatever Puzanus settles, will satisfy me." Thus after remaining a considerable time there and taking a great deal of trouble all to no purpose, he started, presumably to go to Puzanus and met the two hundred satraps whom the latter had sent after him, for his exit from Nicaea had not passed unnoticed. These took him prisoner, threw a noose woven of bowstrings round his neck and strangled him. Now in my opinion this deed was not due to Puzanus, but to that Sultan who had ordered his men to dispose of Apelchasem by some such means. That is the story of Apelchasem. The Emperor read the Sultan's letter but did not think the offer contained therein worthy of consideration at all. And how could he have done so ? For if the Emperor's little daughter, as the letter demanded, had been betrothed to the barbarian's eldest son, she would assuredly have been unhappy. if she had gone to Persia and become mistress of a kingdom which would have brought her greater wretchedness than the worst poverty. But God forbade it nor did the Emperor ever intend that such a thing should happen, not even if his fortunes had sunk to the lowest ebb. Directly after he first heard the letter he burst into laughter at the barbarian's presumption with the remark that "Some demon put this into his mind." This is what the Emperor thought of the marriage. But as he considered it expedient to keep the Sultan's mind in suspense by feeding him on vain hopes, he sent Curticius and three others as ambassadors to him with letters, in which he pretended to entertain the idea of peace and to agree to his requests, whilst, on his side, he made other demands which would occasion further lapse of time. But before the ambassadors sent from Byzantium had reached Chorosan they heard of the Sultan's murder, and so returned. For Tutuses, the Sultan's brother, had killed the Ameer Soliman and also his own brother-in-law, who had marched against him from Arabia with an army, and as a result became puff ed up with conceit ; consequently when he learnt that the Sultan had already begun negotiations for peace with the Emperor, he contemplated murdering his brother.

So he sent for twelve Chasii, as they are called in Persian, who breathe murder, and sent them off quickly in the guise of ambassadors to the Sultan, having first suggested to them a way of killing his brother. "Go," he said, "and first have it proclaimed that you have certain secrets to reveal to the Sultan, and, when you have been granted an audience, go up close to him as if you wanted to whisper in his ear, and then slay him quickly." Then these ambassadors, or rather assassins, went off in very high spirits to kill the Sultan, just as if they had been invited to a dinner or a festivity. On arrival they found him drunk, and everything was made easy for them, because the guards entrusted with the watch over the Sultan were standing at some distance, so they approached him, and drawing their swords from under their arm, promptly dispatched the wretched man. For the characteristic of these Chasii is to rejoice in bloodshed, and to consider it a treat to be allowed to thrust their swords through a man's entrails. And if, perchance, others were to attack them at that very minute, and mince them up like sausage-meat, they reckon that kind of death an honour, for they inherit and hand on to their children this trade of assassination, as a species of ancestral heritage. Not one of those fellows returned to Tutuses as they would have lost their own lives in expiation for this crime. Puzanus however, on hearing of it, returned to Chorosan with all his forces; and as he was nearing it, Tutuses, the brother of the murdered Sultan, encountered him. At once a close conflict began, as both armies fought bravely and neither would yield the victory to the other, and then Puzanus fell, mortally wounded, after fighting bravely, and causing consternation to his foes; and his men scattered in flight in different directions, each one thinking only of his own safety. Tutuses entered Chorosan as victor and felt as if he had already risen to the rank of 'Sultan,'and yet danger menaced him. For Pargiaruch, the son of the murdered Sultan, Tapares, met him in battle and rejoicing, as the poet says, 'like a lion who has fallen in with mighty prey,' he attacked him with all his might and main, cut up the whole of Tutuses' forces and vigorously pursued the fugitives. And Tutuses himself, who was puffed up with pride like Novatus[54], perished too. When Apelchasem had gone to Chorosan with his money to see the Sultan, as was related earlier, his brother Pulchases surprised Nicaea and held it. On receipt of this news the Emperor made him offers of extravagant rewards, provided only he would quit the city and hand it over to him. Pulchases indeed was willing, but hesitated, as he had his eye

54 a heretic whose pride had been proverbial

upon Apelchasem; he sent message upon message to the Emperor, keeping him in suspense, but really waiting for his brother's return. In the interval something like this happened. Before his murder by the Chasii he Sultan of Chorosan had managed to secure the great Soliman's two sons, and after his death they ran away from Chorosan and quickly found their way to Nicaca, where the inhabitants gave them an ovation and received them with the greatest joy. And Pulchases willingly handed over Nicaea to them as being their rightful inheritance, and the elder of the two, Clitziasthlan[55] by name, was elected Sultan. He sent for the wives and children of the men then staying in Nicaeea, and bade them live there, and made this city the dwelling-place, as one might say, of the Sultans. After making this arrangement in Nicaca, he deposed Pulchases from his post, appointed the arch-satrap, Mahomet,

55 Kilidje Arslan

chief over the satraps in Nicaea, and leaving him in charge set out for Melitene.

CHAPTER THIRTEEN

SO MUCH ABOUT THE Sultans. Elchanes, the archsatrap, with the troops under him, seized Apollonias and Cyzicus (both these are on the coast) and then laid waste all the country along the sea. On being informed of this the Emperor assembled a number of the boats he had (for the fleet was not ready yet), put siege-engines in them and brave soldiers, appointed Euphorbenus Alexander, one of the most illustrious for lineage and famous for valour, over the expedition and sent him against Elchanes. On reaching Apollonias he at once besieged it, and after six days and nights, for he did not at all stop the work at night, he made himself master of the outer circuit of the fort, which is now usually called the 'exopolos.' But Elchanes held on stoutly to the citadel as he expected relieving forces. And indeed Alexander found out that a large barbarian army was advancing to the assistance of Elchanes, and seeing that his own men were but a small fraction of this new army, he decided that, as he could not conquer, it would be wiser at least to keep his men unharmed. Since his affairs were in a precarious state and no road of safety remained, he led his men off towards the sea. They embarked in their boats, and intended to sail down the river to the sea. But Elchanes guessing Alexander's intention took possession beforehand of the exit from the lake and the bridge over the river, on which a shrine to the memory of Constantine the Great was built of old by St. Helena, and from this the bridge took, and still takes, its name. At the exit from the lake then and on this bridge he posted some of his bravest men on either side with orders to watch for the passing of the fleet. Thus all our men who were on board these small vessels fell straight into Elchanes' ambush as they passed through the mouth of the lake, and losing their heads at sight of the sudden danger they drove the ships to land and jumped ashore. The Turks overtook them and a serious battle commenced. Many of the leaders were captured and many too fell into the river and were swept away in its eddies. The Emperor could not brook this defeat, so sent out a considerable army under Opus to march overland against them. Opus reached Cyzicus and took that without trouble; then he picked out three hundred adventurous men used to storming cities and dispatched them to Poemanenum. This city, too, they took at first onset and killed some of the inhabitants on the spot and sent the rest as prisoners to Opus, and he, as promptly, sent them to the Emperor. He then left Cyzicus and went on to Apollonias which he beset closely. As Elchanes had no longer adequate forces to contend against him, he surrendered the city of his own free will, and he and all his blood-relations deserted to the Emperor, hence he enjoyed countless privileges, and obtained the greatest of all, namely, holy baptism. Some refused to join Opus, for instance, Scaliarius and he who later was created 'Hyperperilampros' ... (for these belonged to the number of illustrious satraps), but when he heard of the Emperor's benevolence and liberal gifts to Elchanes, they came over to him too, and obtained their heart's desire. For the Emperor was essentially a most religious man, and in his life and speech the high priest of all piety. He was very fond, too, of teaching our doctrines and was a real missionary by choice and in his manner of speech; he wanted to bring into the fold of our church not only the Scythian nomads, but also the whole of Persia, as well as the barbarians who inhabit Libya and Egypt and follow the rites of Mohamed.

CHAPTER FOURTEEN

ENOUGH HAS BEEN SAID about the Turks. I now intend to relate a second attack on the Roman Empire, more terrible and greater than the first, and I again resume the story at the beginning, for one subject has come up after another as wave follows wave.

A certain Scythian tribe, who were daily harried by the Sauromatx, left their homes and travelled down to the Danube. It was, of course, necessary for them to make terms with the dwellers on the shores of the Danube, so by common consent the chieftains met for a conference ; there were Tatus and Chales and Sesthlabus and Satzas (for I must give the names of the highest born of these, although the elegant appearance of my history is spoiled by them), the last named was chief over Dristra, the others over Bitzina and neighbouring towns. After having made a truce with the chiefs the Scythians proceeded fearlessly to cross the Danube, and to ravage the surrounding country and also took a few small towns. And in between when they rested a little, they commenced to plough and sowed millet and wheat. But that fellow, Travlos, the Manichaean, with his followers, and his co-religionists who dwelt in the town on the ridge of Beliotaba, with whom this history has dealt at some length already, heard of these Scythians and so brought to birth the plan they had been hatching so long, for they seized the rough roads and passes, sent for the Scythians to help them and then started to devastate the Roman territory. For these Manichaeans are by nature 'ever greedy of war' and, like dogs, ' ever thirsty of human blood.'

On hearing of this, Alexius sent orders to Pacurianus, the Domestic of the West, to take an army and march against them; for he knew he was the ablest man for training and organizing and marshalling it; with him was to go Branas, another very gallant commander. Pacurianus found that the Scythians had scaled the mountain-pass and planted their palisades this side of Beliotaba, and when he saw their countless host he at once shrank from battle with them, thinking it better to keep his own troops quiet for the present rather than to risk a battle with the Scythians and be defeated and lose many. However, Branas, who was of a very adventurous and daring nature, did not approve of this plan. So the Domestic to avoid the imputation of cowardice for postponing the battle, yielded to Branas' impetuosity, bade his men arm, and after drawing them up in line of battle marched against the Scythians, himself holding the centre of the line. But ' since the Roman army was not equivalent even to a small fraction of the opposing host, they were all panic-stricken at first sight. However they did attack the Scythians, and many were killed in the fight and Branas himself fell, mortally wounded. The Domestic fought desperately and made fierce onsets on the foe, but was dashed against an oak and killed on the spot. And the rest of the army scattered in all directions. On receiving these tidings the Emperor mourned for all the fallen, both individually and collectively. But he was most grieved at the Domestic's death and shed floods of tears, for he loved him exceedingly even before his elevation to the throne. Yet in spite of it all he did not lose heart, but called Taticius and sent him with sufficient money to Adrianople to give the soldiers their pay for the year and to collect troops from all quarters so that he might raise a fresh army large enough for the war. He ordered Hubertopoulos to leave an adequate garrison in Cyzicus and taking the Franks only with him to lose no time in joining Taticius. When Taticius saw the Latins and Hubertopoulos, he took courage and as he had already collected a sufficiently large army, he immediately marched straight against the Scythians. When near Philippopolis he pitched his camp on the edge of the river which flows by Blisnus. But when he beheld the Scythians returning from a raid and bringing back much booty and captives, although the baggage had scarcely been brought into the camp, he selected a division of his army and sent it to attack them, then he armed himself, bade all do the same, drew up his lines and then followed the soldiers he had sent ahead. As he observed that the Scythians with their spoils and captives were rejoining the main Scythian body on the bank of the Eurus (?), he divided his army in two and bidding both divisions raise the war-cry he attacked the barbarians amidst loud shouts and clamour. As the conflict grew fierce, the majority of the Scythians were slain but many saved their lives by running away.

Then Taticius gathered up all the booty and returned victorious to Philippopolis. There he quartered his whole army and then meditated from what direction and in what manner he could best attack the barbarians again. As he knew that their forces were innumerable he sent out spies in all directions, so that through them he might be kept informed of the Scythians' movements. The spies returned and reported that a great multitude of the barbarians was near Beliotaba and ravaging the country. Taticius who expected the Scythians to come, and had not sufficient forces to pit against such numbers, was at a loss what to do and in great perplexity. Nevertheless he whetted his sword and put courage into the army for a battle. Soon a spy ran in, announcing the approach of the barbarians and adding that they were already close at hand. Taticius quickly snatched up his arms and getting the whole army ready, crossed the Eurus immediately and disposed his regiments in battalions and having formed his plan of battle waited, his own station being the centre of the line. The barbarians who drew themselves up in the Scythian fashion and arrayed themselves for battle, seemed to be eager for a fight and to wish to provoke their opponents to a battle. But really, both the armies were afraid and tried to avoid an engagement ; the Roman army quaked before the overwhelming numbers of the Scythians, while these for their part were alarmed at the sight of all our men in full armour, and the standards, and splendid clothing and the glitter shining over all and gleaming like starlight. Alone amongst them all the adventuresome Latins, so daring in battle, wished to be the first to attack, and they whetted their teeth and their swords at the same time. But Taticius restrained them ; for he was very levelheaded and very clever in forecasting the trend of events. So both the armies stood, each waiting for the other to make a movement, and not a single soldier from either army daring to ride out into the intervening space; when the sun began to set, each of the generals returned to his own encampment. This was done for two days, the generals got ready for battle and drew up their men in battle formation, and, as neither hazarded battle against the other, at dawn of the third day the Scythians retreated. Directly Taticius learnt this he hurried after them; but 'on foot after a Lydian chariot', as they say. For the Scythians passed through Sidera (that is the name of a valley) before him, and as he did not overtake them there, he led back all his forces to Adrianople. There he left the Franks and dismissing the soldiers to their homes, he himself returned to the capital with a portion of the army.

BOOK SEVEN

War with the Scyths (1087-90)

CHAPTER ONE

AT THE APPROACH OF spring Tzelgu (the supreme commander of the Scythian army) crossed the passes above the Danube with a mixed army of about eighty thousand, composed of Sauromatians, Scythians, and a number from the Dacian army (over whom the man called Solomon was leader), and plundered the towns round about Chariopolis. And after entering Chariopolis itself and carrying off much booty, he settled down in a place called Scotinum. On receipt of this news Nicolas Mavrocatacalon and Bebetziotes (who got this name from his country) occupied Pamphylum. with the forces under their command. When they saw the villagers from the districts around hurrying in to the towns and fortresses in their extreme fear, they moved from the place called Pamphylurn and occupied the small town of Cule with their whole army. Behind them came the Scythians and directly they discovered the track of the Roman army (this is the word used by soldiers) they followed almost in their footsteps one might say. At dawn of day Tzelgu drew up his own forces and contemplated battle with Mavrocatacalon. But the latter climbed up with a few chosen comrades to the pass overlooking the plain to spy out the barbarian forces; and seeing the multitude of the Scythians, he deferred the battle, although madly impatient for it, as he realized that the Roman army was numerically far inferior to the Scythian horde. He returned to the camp and discussed with all the officers of the army and with Joharmaces himself the advisability of attacking the Scythians. As they all urged him to do so and his own inclination lay in that direction, he divided the troops into three portions, bade them sound the attack and engaged the barbarians. In the combat many Scythians fell wounded, and no fewer were killed; and Tzelgu himself who had fought valiantly and thrown the ranks into confusion, received a mortal wound and gave up the ghost. Still more fell as they fled into the stream running between Scotinum and Cule and were trampled under foot by each other and drowned. Having gained this brilliant victory over the Scythians, the Emperor's officers returned to the capital. Here the Emperor bestowed on them appropriate gifts and honours and afterwards they left with the newly appointed Domestic of the West, Adrian Comnenus, own brother to the Emperor

CHAPTER TWO

IN THIS MANNER, then, the Scythians were driven out from the districts round Macedonia and Philippopolis, but they returned and encamped beside the Ister and settled along its banks and plundered our territory as freely as if it were their own. When the Emperor heard this, he could not endure the idea of their settling within the Roman frontiers, and at the same time he was afraid of their crossing the passes again and perpetrating worse mischief than before. Consequently he made his preparations, fitted out the army well and marched to Adrianople and thence to Lardea, which lies in the plain between Diabolis and Goloë. Here he appointed George Euphorbenus general and dispatched him by sea to Dristra. Then the Emperor stayed in those parts for forty days and summoned troops from all sides. When he had collected a large army, he deliberated whether he should traverse the defiles and commence warfare with the Scythians, "for," said he, "we ought not to allow them immunity at all," and there was justice in this remark in the case of these barbarians. For the incursions of the Scythians did not begin in one of the four seasons and cease in the following, for instance, starting in summer and finishing in autumn, or even in winter (or late autumn); nor was this evil limited to the cycle of one year, but for several years past they had been troubling the Empire, although in the plethora of subjects I have only mentioned them occasionally. Neither could they be split up by double-dealing, although the Emperor had often tried to seduce them in various ways; but not one deserted to him even in secret, so unswerving was their loyalty up to that time. Now Nicephorus Bryennius and Gregorius Mavrocatacalon whom the Emperor had ransomed for forty thousand pieces of money when taken by the Scythians, did not at all approve of waging war along the Ister with the Scythians; but George Palaeologus and Nicolas Mavrocatacalon and all the young, vigorous men pressed the Emperor hard and urged him to cross the passes of the Hoemus and start war with the Scythians on the Danube. Of this same opinion were also Nicephorus and Leo, the two sons of the Emperor Diogenes, who were born to him in the purple room after his elevation to the throne and were consequently styled "Porphyrogeniti." This purple room was a certain building in the palace shaped as a complete square from its base to the spring of the roof, which ended in a pyramid; it looked out upon the sea and the harbour where the stone oxen and lions stand. The floor of this room was paved with marbles and the walls were panelled with it but not with ordinary sorts nor even with the more expensive sorts which are fairly easy to procure, but with the marble which the earlier Emperors had carried away from Rome. And this marble is, roughly speaking, purple all over except for spots like white sand sprinkled over it. It is from this marble, I imagine, that our ancestors called the room "purple."

Now, as I was saying, when the trumpet with its loud summons directed all to the road of the Haemus Mountains, as if to march against the Scythians, Bryennius, who had tried his utmost to dissuade the Emperor from this attempt and had not succeeded, remarked sententiously, "If you cross the Haemus, Emperor, you will certainly find out whose horses are the swiftest." When somebody asked what he meant by those words, he replied, "When you all flee." For although this man had had his eyes dug out for rebellion, yet he was recognized as by far the cleverest strategist, and most skillful and ingenious in the arrangement of troops. How this Bryennius was deprived of his sight for desertion, or rather rebellion, against the Emperor Botaniates, and how, when captured by Alexius Comnenus, at that time the great Domestic of the Eastern and Western armies, he was handed over to Borilus with his eyes uninjured - I must refer those who wish to know further details to the history of the great Caesar. For this Caesar became the son-in-law of Alexius when the latter was already Emperor, and he was the descendant of that Bryennius. But at this point my soul is convulsed and filled with sorrow, for he was wise in counsel and a very distinguished orator. For everything, strength, swiftness, physical beauty, in fact all good qualities of mind and body combined to adorn this man. For in him nature begot and God fashioned a man most eminent in all ways, and just such a hero as Homer depicted Achilles among the Achaeans, one could say my Caesar was shining forth amongst all those beneath the sun. And this Caesar, who was an expert in military matters, had not neglected letters, but had read every book and applied himself to every branch of learning, and drawn therefrom all the wisdom of our own and of other times. And later he devoted himself to history, and at the suggestion of my mistress mother, I mean the Empress Irene, he composed a work well worthy of attention and worth reading, for he arranged a narrative of my father's deeds before he took up the reins of government. In this history he gives an accurate account of the facts concerning Bryennius; and there too he narrates his grandfather's many vicissitudes, and his father-in-law's brilliant exploits, and assuredly he never falsified anything for he was related to them both, to the latter by marriage and to the former by blood. I have already mentioned his book in the earlier chapters of this history.

Now the Scythians saw that George Euphorbenus was on his way against them coming up the Ister with a large army and a fleet. This river flows down from the western mountains, and after a series of cataracts empties itself into the Pontus Euxinus[56] through five mouths; broad and with a strong current it flows through a vast plain, and is navigable for even the largest and most heavily laden vessels can be carried on its waters. It has not only one name, for in its upper reaches and near its source it is called the ‹Danube,' whilst in the lower and at its mouths, the ‹Ister.'

To resume, when a portion of the Scythians saw George Euphorbenus coming up this river, and were told that the Emperor too was already marching towards them overland, with a very considerable army, they recognized that it would be impossible

56 Black Sea

for them to fight against both and so looked about for a way of escape from this imminent danger. Accordingly they sent a hundred-and-fifty Scythians as ambassadors to discuss terms of peace, and also to insinuate a few threats and perhaps to promise that if the Emperor acceded to their requests, they would furnish him with thirty thousand horsemen, whenever he required them. But the Emperor, awake to the Scythians' treachery, knew that this embassy was merely to circumvent the immediate danger, and that, at the next opportunity, they would kindle the latent sparks of their malice into a mighty conflagration; therefore, he refused to receive the ambassadors. In the course of the discussion a certain Nicolas, one of the Emperor's secretaries, came up to him and whispered in his ear, "You may expect an eclipse of the sun to take place today," and on the Emperor expressing a doubt, he swore with an oath that he was not lying. Then the Emperor, with his habitual quick-wittedness, turned to the Scythians and said, "I appoint God as judge; and if a sign appears in the heavens this day, you will know for a surety that I have good reason for suspecting, and therefore not receiving, your embassy because your leaders are not sincere in their overtures for peace. If, however, no sign appears, I shall stand convicted of having been wrong in my surmise." Before two hours had passed, the light of the sun failed, and the whole of its disc was darkened by the moon's passing over it. At that sight the Scythians were terrified, and the Emperor handed them over to Leo Nicerites (he was a eunuch, brought up among the soldiers from babyhood, and much respected) and ordered him to take a sufficient guard and conduct them to the Queen of Cities. And Leo started very willingly on the road to Constantinople. But the barbarians who were throughout intent on regaining their liberty, slew the guards who were keeping a very careless watch over them when they reached little Nicaea, and returned by devious paths to those who had sent them. Nicerites with three others escaped with difficulty and rejoined the Emperor at Goloë.

CHAPTER THREE

AFTER HEARING LEO'S TALE, the Emperor was afraid that the ambassadors would stir up the whole Scythian army and attack him suddenly; but he did not require a dream to urge him to battle, as Atreus' son, Agamemnon, did, for he was seething with lust of combat, so he led his legions through the vale of Sidera, and encamped near the Bitzina, a river running down from the adjacent mountains. Here a good many of his soldiers were killed, for in foraging they had strayed too far from the camp and many were captured besides. At dawn the Emperor quickly made for Pliscoba and from there he ascended a mountain peak called Simeon, and also locally 'the Scythians Parliament House.' Here a similar accident occurred to soldiers who, whilst foraging, were at a distance from their camp. On the following day he marched along a river flowing at about a distance of twenty-four stades from Dristra and there he piled the baggage and erected his palisades. Here the Scythians made a massed attack upon the Imperial tent and killed not only a number of the light-armed troops but also captured some of the Manichaeans who had fought most courageously. Hence a great din and confusion arose in the army and even the imperial tent was overturned by some horse-soldiers careering about wildly, and this fact was looked upon as a bad omen by the Emperor's ill-wishers.

However, the Emperor drove off the barbarians with a detachment of the army to some distance from his tent, so that they should not cause confusion again, then he mounted his horse and quelled the tumult, immediately broke up the camp and marched with all his troops in good order to Distra (this is the best-known of the towns near the Danube) in order to besiege it with engines. Accordingly he set to work, invested the town on all sides, and after breaking down one side of the walls, he entered with his entire army. But the two citadels of this town were still held by the kinsmen of a man called Tatus who had left the town shortly before to try and win over the Comans to come to the help of the Scythians. On the point of leaving and when bidding farewell to his friends this Tatus said, “I know for certain that the Emperor will come and besiege this town. Therefore directly you see him advancing into this plain, make haste to be the first to seize the hill which overlooks it, for it is the most advantageous position, and erect your palisades there, so that the Emperor may not be able to carry on the siege at his leisure, but be obliged to turn his attention to what is happening in his rear through fear of the injury you may do. And throughout the day and night keep on sending relays of troops against him." But the Emperor, hitting upon the right plan, abandoned the siege of the citadels (for it was an arduous and lengthy task), left the town and entrenched himself near a stream, not far from the Ister, and deliberated whether it would be wise to attack the Scythians. Paheologus and Gregorius Mavrocatacalon were for deferring war with the Patzinaks and advised taking an army and capturing the large town Pristhlava. "For," said they, "if the Scythians see us marching in good order fully accoutred, they will certainly not dare to attack us. And should perchance a few horsemen without chariots risk an engagement, you may be sure they will be worsted, and then in future we shall have the large town of Pristhlava as our well-fortified stronghold." This important town, which is situated on the Ister, did not always bear this barbaric name, but a Greek one, for it both was, and was called, a great city, namely, Megalopolis. But from the time that Mocrus, King of the Bulgarians, and his descendants, and finally Samuel, the last of the Bulgarian dynasty (as Zedekiah of the Jewish) overran the West, the town acquired a double name, retaining 'great' from the Greek language and adding a Slavic word, and was universally spoken of as 'Great Pristhlava.' "If we have this town as a place of refuge," said Mavrocatacalon's adherents, "and harass the Scythians by daily skirmishes, we shall be punishing them the whole time and not allowing them to come out of their own camp at all either to forage or to fetch any other necessaries." During the bandying of arguments the two young sons of Diogenes, Nicephorus and Leo, who were inexperienced in the difficulties of warfare, slipped off their horses and took off their bridles, gave them a slap and drove them into a field of millet with the remark, "Do not be afraid, Emperor, we will cut them to pieces with our swords." The Emperor who was very adventurous and liked to be the first to start a battle, did not take into consideration the arguments of those who protested against fighting, but put George Cutzomites in charge of the Imperial tent and all the baggage and dispatched him to Betrinum; then he enjoined the army not to light a lamp or fire that evening, but to keep the horses ready and watch till sunrise. He himself left his tent at daybreak, divided his forces and set them in order of battle, and then reviewed the army. He chose the centre of the line as his post, where he was surrounded by his relations and connections, such as his brother Adrian who was at that time commanding the Latins, and other valiant gentlemen. The left wing was held by Nicephorus Caesar Melissenus, his sister's husband, and the leaders on the right wing were Castamonites and Taticius, whilst the Sauromatians, Uzas and Caratzas, commanded the allies. Then he chose six men as his own bodyguard and ordered them to attend to him and pay not the slightest attention to anyone else, these six were the two sons of Romanus Diogenes, Nicolas Mavrocatacalon who had had a long and varied military career, Johannaces, Nabites, the prefect of the Varangians, and lastly a certain Gules, a family retainer. But the Scythians too had arranged a plan of battle, for the science of warfare and of ordering troops is inbred in them; they set ambuscades and connected their ranks in close-ordered array, and built towers, as it were, of their covered wagons, and advanced against the Emperor in squadrons, and hurled missiles from afar. The Emperor adapted his army to meet these squadrons, and forbade the hoplites to move forward or to break the covering formed by their shields, until the Scythians had come quite close. Then when they judged the intervening space between the two armies to be no more than a bridle's length, they were to advance against the foe in a body. Whilst the Emperor was making these preparations the Scythians appeared in the distance travelling with their covered wagons, wives and children. When the battle commenced, it raged from morning till evening and the slaughter on either side was tremendous. And Leo, Diogenes' son, riding too recklessly against the Scythians, and allowing himself to be drawn closer than was wise to the wagons, received a mortal wound and fell. And Adrian, the Emperor's brother, who had been entrusted with command over the Latins, seeing that the Scythians' onset was proving irresistible, gave his horse his head and charged right up to the wagons and after fighting magnificently returned with only seven comrades, all the rest had been either slain or captured by the Scythians.

The result of the battle was still hanging in the balance, and both armies were fighting with great spirit, when some Scythian chieftains were seen in the distance coming with thirty-six thousand men; the Romans who could not possibly stand against so many, then turned their backs to the enemy. The Emperor had advanced in front of his own army and stood sword in hand; with the other he held up as a standard the Pallium of the Mother of the Divine Word and was supported by only twenty brave-hearted companions, Nicephorus, Diogenes' son, was there together with Michael Ducas the Protostrator, and brother of the Empress, and the servants of his family. Then three Scythian foot-soldiers leapt at him, two snatched at his reins on either side, the third at his right leg. Immediately he cut one man's hand off, against the other he lifted his sword and with threatening voice made him fall back, whilst he struck at the helmet of the man holding his leg. But he only gave a rather light blow with his sword nor did he use his whole strength in making it for he was afraid that one of two things might happen if, as is often the case, a severe blow from his sword missed altogether, namely, that he would hit his own leg, or the horse on which he was riding, and in that case he would easily be taken by the enemy. So he quickly gave him a second blow but made the motions of his hand very cautiously, for in all his actions, words and motions reason was ever his guide, and he was never carried away by anger nor led astray by passion. The Scythian's helmet had fallen off at the first blow so the sword descended on his bare head, and without a sound he fell straight to the ground. Seeing the uncontrolled flight of the troops (for the lines had long since been broken up, as all fled promiscuously), the Protostrator said, "To what purpose, Emperor, are you trying to hold out here any longer? To what purpose are you risking your life and entirely neglecting your own safety?" to which the Emperor replied that he would rather they should die fighting bravely than seek safety in ignoble flight. The Protostrator retorted, "If you were one of the common herd, your remark would be praiseworthy, but as your death involves world-wide disaster, why not choose the better part? For if you save yourself, you can live to fight another day and conquer."

The Emperor seeing himself in instant danger, as the Scythians were attacking him persistently, abandoned all hope, and said, "Yes, it is time now for us to take thought for our safety with the help of God, but we must not pursue the same road as our fugitives for in that case the Scythians who are pursuing our men might fall in with us on their return, but," and he pointed to the Scythians standing in the van of their army, "we must ride down upon those men there as if we had been born to-day, and were doomed to die today, and then if by God's aid we get to the rear of the Scythians' lines, we shall find a different road." After saying this and encouraging the others, he was the first to dash like a firebrand upon the Scythians and struck at the first who encountered him, and the latter straightway rolled from his saddle. As the closed ranks of the Scythians were thus split up, he and his companions reached the country behind the Scythians. At any rate the Emperor managed to do this, but the Protostrator had the misfortune to fall on the ground for his horse slipped; but one of his attendants immediately gave him his own horse. When he caught up the Emperor he never moved more than a foot's breadth away from him again, for he was so intensely devoted to him. In the confusion resulting from one party fleeing and the other pursuing, a second lot of Scythians overtook the Emperor; he immediately turned round and hit down his assailant and killed not only him but several others as well, as those who were present assert. Another Scythian who had crept up from the back was on the point of hitting Nicephorus Diogenes, when the Emperor caught sight of him and called out: “Look behind you, Nicephorus !” So the latter turned round sharply and struck the Scythian in the face; and I have often heard the Emperor say that he had never seen anything so swift and skilful. He used also to say, “If I had not been carrying a standard that day, I should have killed more Scythians than there are hairs on my head,” and this was not bragging, for who ever pushed modesty to such an extreme as he did? But sometimes conversation and the nature of events forced him to speak out about his doings within the circle of his family and intimates, though it was only as the result of much urging on our part; but no one in the world ever heard the Emperor boast of his prowess in public. As a strong wind was blowing, and the Patzinaks were attacking him he could no longer hold the standard upright. Then a Scythian wielding a long spear in both hands struck him in the buttocks, and though he did not break the skin, he inflicted exquisite pain which lasted for many years. Overcome by these difficulties he furled the standard and hid it in a germander bush so that nobody should see it; and then he rode through the night and came safely to Goloë (and from this the townsmen used to say, "From Dristra to Goloe is a fine feat even for an unwounded man, Comnenus"). During the day he went on to Beroë and stayed there as he wished to ransom the captives.

CHAPTER FOUR

DURING THE FLIGHT of the defeated troops that day Palaeologus was knocked off his horse and lost it; while standing helpless and well aware of his dangerous situation he gazed about in case he could see his horse anywhere, when suddenly he saw Leo, the Bishop of Chalcedon, of whom we have written above. This man was dressed in priestly garb and was offering him his horse; Palaeologus mounted it and continued his flight; but he never saw the holy man again. This priest had really a very frank and open nature, and the right character for a priest of superior rank, but he was somewhat simpleminded and occasionally displayed more zeal than knowledge, and he had no accurate acquaintance with the sacred canons. For these reasons disaster befell him, as has been already related, and he lost his bishopric; Paleologus, however, always adhered to him because of his preeminent goodness. So whether it was by reason of his fervent belief in this man that Palxologus was granted this heavenly vision, or whether some other mysterious design of Providence was manifested in this priest, I am unable to say. With the Patzinaks pursuing him, Palaeologus ran into marshy, thickly-shaded place and there fell in with about hundred and fifty Roman soldiers. As the Scythians enircled them and they saw their case was desperate for they could not fight against so many, they waited upon Palaeologus' decision for they knew his bravery and indomitable disposition of old. He advised them to rush headlong at the Scythians, taking absolutely no thought for their own safety, and thus, I fancy, purchasing it. "But first," he said, "we must confirm this plan by oath, and then if we are all of one opinion no one must fail to take part in the onset against the Scythians, but each must regard the general safety and danger as his own." Thereupon Palaeologus made a wild dash at the foe, and struck the first man he met, who straightway fell to the ground dazed. But the rest were half-hearted in their attack, and some of them were killed and others returned to the covered glade as if to their nest, and saved their lives by hiding in it. Whilst Palaeologus was making for a certain height he was again pursued by the Patzinaks and his horse was wounded and fell; he himself, however, escaped to the neighbouring mountain. Then he sought for the road to safety, which under the circumstances it was not easy for him to find, and so he wandered about for eleven days, when he fell in with a soldier's widow, who gave him shelter for several days, and then her sons, who had escaped with their lives from the battle, pointed out to him the road to safety. This is the story of Palaeologus' adventures.

Now the chieftains of the Scythians were minded to put the prisoners they held to death, but the majority of the people absolutely refused to allow this, as they wished to sell them for a price. And as this proposal gained the day, the Emperor was acquainted of it by letters from Melissenus who, although he was a prisoner, had done a great deal to persuade the Scythians to adopt this course. The Emperor, who was still in Beroë, at once sent to the capital for the requisite amount of money, and then redeemed the captives.

CHAPTER FIVE

AT THAT TIME TATUS returned to the Ister with the Comans he had won over; directly they saw the amount of booty, and of captives, they said to the Scythian chieftains, "We have left our homes and travelled a long way to come to your assistance on the understanding that we should share your dangers and your victories. Therefore as we have done our best it would not be right to send us back empty-handed. For it was not by our choice that we arrived too late for the battle, nor can we in any way be blamed for that, for it was the fault of the Emperor who hurried on the battle. Therefore you must either divide all this booty equally with us, or instead of allies you will find us your enemies." The Scythians refused to do this. As the Comans would not accept their refusal, a violent struggle took place between them and the Scythians were thoroughly beaten, and only escaped with difficulty to the town called Ozolimne. And there they stayed for some time, hemmed in by the Comans and not daring to cross the lake. This lake which we now call "Ozolimne "is the largest in diameter and circumference of all the lakes ever mentioned by geographers and yields to none for size. It lies beyond the Hundred Hills and is fed by very large and beautiful rivers; on its southern half it can carry a number of large merchant-vessels which proves how deep the lake must be in that part. It is called "Ozolimne "not because it emits any bad or offensive effluvia, but because a Hunnish, army once lodged near it (this name "Huns "(Ounni) was converted into "Ouzi "in the local patois) and made their camp on its banks, and thus the lake was called Ouzolimne, with the vowel “u” added.

Now in the ancient historians, no mention is made of a Hunnish army ever having come there, but during the Emperor Alexius’ reign the whole nation congregated there from all quarters and gave the place its name. These probable facts about the lake are now mentioned by me for the first time in order to prove that owing to the Emperor’s many expeditions in many directions many places obtained their names either directly from him or from his enemies who collected there; and we note that much the same thing happened in the time of Alexander, King of Macedon. For both the Alexandria in Egypt, and the other in India were named after him, and we further know that Lysimachia was named after Lysimachus, one of his soldiers. Therefore it does not surprise me if the Emperor Alexius, emulating Alexander’s zeal, occasionally fitted new names to places either from the tribes who assembled there or whom he had summoned, or gave names of his own choosing to places as the result of his own exploits. Let these remarks about Ozolinme be thrown out once for all in the true spirit of history. Now when their provisions ran short, the Comans returned to their homes to get a new supply, and then move against the Scythians once more.

CHAPTER SIX

IN THE MEANTIME THE Emperor recuperated at Beroë and fitted out the captives he had redeemed and all his hoplites with arms. At that time, too, the Count of Flanders on his way back from Jerusalem visited the Emperor there, and took the customary Latin oath and also promised to send to his succour five hundred horsemen directly he reached home. Consequently the Emperor showed him great honour and then dismissed him to his own country. After wards the Emperor left Beroë with the troops he had amassed and entered Adrianople. The Scythians next came down the narrow valleys between Goloë and Diabolis and pitched their camp near the place called Marcella. Now the Emperor heard of the doings of the Comans and, as they were expected to return, he was alarmed because he foresaw danger from their coming. So he sent Synesius armed with Golden Bulls to the Scythians to treat with them and say that if they could be induced to make a treaty and give hostages, though he would not allow them to enter further into his territory, yet he would arrange for them to stay in the place they had taken and provide them liberally with all necessaries. For Alexius meditated using the Scythians against the Comans if the latter crossed the Ister again and tried to advance farther. But if the Scythians could not be persuaded, Synesius was to leave them and return. This Synesius accordingly went to the Scythians and after making an appropriate speech persuaded them to enter into a treaty with the Emperor; and he stayed there some time and courted their favour, thus removing every possible cause of offence. The Comans returned, fully prepared for war with the Scythians, but not finding them and learning that they had come over the passes, occupied Marcella and after arranging terms of peace with the Emperor, demanded permission to cross the passes and attack the Scythians. However, the Emperor refused, as he had already concluded peace with the Scythians, saying, "We have no need of auxiliaries at present ; take a satisfactory present and go home! "He treated the ambassadors courteously, gave them satisfactory presents and sent them home in peace. This emboldened the Scythians who promptly broke the treaty, reverted to their former cruelty and laid waste the neighbouring lands and cities. For as a rule all barbarians are unstable, and the observance of treaties is not natural to them. Becoming aware of this Synesius returned to the Emperor and himself informed him of the Scythians' ingratitude and violation of the treaty. They seized Philippopolis and this placed the Emperor in a difficulty as against their large numbers his forces were far too small to allow of his opening battle with them. But accustomed as he was to find a way out of difficulties and never in any crisis to feel at all despondent, he decided that he must endeavour to reduce their numbers by skirmishes and ambuscades. And so guessing at the places or towns which they were likely to enter in the morning, he anticipated their arrival the evening before; or if in the evening he heard that they would take possession of a certain place, he occupied that same place in the early morning. And as much as possible, he wore them down from a distance by skirmishes and ambuscades to prevent their gaining possession of the forts. Well, both parties, the Scythians and the Emperor, reached Cypsella. And now, as a mercenary force which he expected had not yet arrived, the Emperor felt very helpless for he knew how quickly the Scythians moved and saw that they were already hastening towards the Queen of Cities. As he had insufficient forces for meeting their immense host, and considering that ' what was not worse, was better,' as the saying is, he again resorted to negotiations for peace. Consequently he sent ambassadors to confer with them about peace, and the Scythians at once fell in with the Emperor's wishes. Before the truce was made, a man named Neantzes deserted to the Romans. Then Migidemus was sent to f etch in recruits from the adjacent regions; in a battle which occurred later at a place . . . this man's son whilst making a fierce dash against the Patzinaks was snared and captured by a Scythian woman and dragged into the circle of their wagons with an iron sickle. His head which they cut off the Emperor bought at his father's request. Overcome by this unforeseen disaster, the father beat his breast for three days and nights with a sling-stone and then died. The interval of peace with the Scythians did not last long, but like 'dogs they returned to their vomit' ; they then removed from Cypsella and occupied Taurocomus, where they wintered and ravaged the neighbouring village-towns.

CHAPTER SEVEN

ON THE RETURN OF spring they came down from there to Chariopohs. The Emperor who was stationed at Bulgarophygum, wished to no longer delay but set apart a considerable section of the army, all picked men and amongst them too the young soldiers, called "Archontopouli," all with their beards scarcely grown, but irresistible in attack, and ordered them to fall upon the Scythians, who were standing on the tops of their wagons, from the rear.

This band of "Archontopouli "was first formed by Alexius. As the Roman Empire possessed no army owing to the carelessness of the preceding Emperors, he collected from all sides the sons of soldiers who had fallen in the field, and trained them in the use of arms and for war and called them "Archontopouli," as though they were the sons of "Archontes" ; in order that by their name they should be reminded of their parents' nobility and bravery, and therefore aim at impetuous valour and prove themselves very brave when circumstances demanded daring and strength. Such then was the band of "Archontopouli," and roughly speaking they numbered about two thousand; it was much the same as the 'Sacred Band' of the Spartans in former days. In obedience to orders, then, these newly-recruited "Archontopouli "marched to the attack. But some of the Scythians lying in ambush in a hollow below the hill, watched their advance; and when they saw them falling upon the wagons, they rushed out upon them with irresistible impetuosity. And during the close engagement which followed about three hundred of the "Archontopouli "fell fighting desperately. For some time the Emperor grieved deeply for them, shedding bitter tears and calling each by name as if they were absent. After this victory over their opponents the Patzinaks passed through Chariopolis and turned to Apros, devastating as they went. The Emperor then had recourse again to his former plan of action, and forestalled their entry into Apros ; for, as I have remarked more than once, he had not sufficient troops to risk a battle with his enemies. Thereupon, as he knew they set out on foraging expeditions at daybreak, he sent for Taticius (he has often been mentioned in this history) and bade him take the most courageous of the youths and picked men from his own bodyguard and all the Latins and keep watch during the night for the Scythians' expedition at dawn, so that when he supposed that the foraging party was at a good distance from their camp, he could ride down upon them at full speed. Taticius carried out these orders, killed about four hundred and took a large number captive. And what followed? The horsemen sent by the Count of Flanders, about five hundred picked men, arrived and brought as a present to the Emperor one hundred and fifty selected horses: moreover they sold him all the horses they did not require for their own use. The Emperor welcomed them very graciously and returned hearty thanks. Next he received a message from the East saying that Apelchasem, the governor of Nima (whom the Persians usually call a 'satrap,' and the Turks, who now imitate the Persians, an 'ameer'), was all but starting on an expedition against Nicomedia, so he sent those horsemen to protect that district.

CHAPTER EIGHT

AT THIS SAME TIME Tzachas who was assured of the Emperor's manifold troubles in the West and of his continuous warfare with the Patzinaks, thought that, as the opportunity offered, he ought to acquire a fleet. And chancing upon a certain Smyrniote, he entrusted the building of pirate vessels to him for he was experienced in this work. After he had built many of these at Smyrna, as well as forty covered trawlers he embarked experienced men on them, sailed for Clazomenae and took the town immediately. Thence he sailed to Phoma and took that too at first assault. From that town he sent letters to the Curator Alopus, the administrator of Mitylene, threatening him with dire punishment unless he left the town very quickly; he told him also that he wished him well and had for that reason warned him of the terrible future that awaited him if he did not depart. Alopus was thoroughly scared by Tzachas' threats, so embarked on a vessel by night and made for the capital. On hearing of his flight, Tzachas did not delay but sailed straightway to Mitylene and took it without any difficulty. The Emperor was informed about Tzachas, and immediately dispatched a large force by boat to fortify Methymna which is situated on the northern promontory of this island and had not gone over to Tzachas. However Tzachas thought Methymna was beneath consideration, but sailed direct to Chios and took that also at first assault. On receipt of this news the Emperor sent an adequate fleet with plenty of soldiers against him under the leadership of Nicetas Castamonites. So he departed, engaged in battle with Tzachas and was quickly worsted, and Tzachas also carried off a number of his ships. When the Emperor was informed of what had happened to Castamonites he equipped a second fleet and appointed as 'Duke' of it, Constantine Dalassenus, a great fighter and related to him on his mother's side.

Directly he reached the shores of Chios he started the siege of the citadel, fighting with great energy as he was eager to take the town before Tzachas could arrive from Smyrna. So he hammered at the walls with a number of siege-engines and catapults and destroyed the connecting walls between two towers. When the Turks inside perceived this and also recognized that the Roman forces were hard to resist, they used the Roman tongue and implored the lord of all to have mercy. But the soldiers of Dalassenus and Opus could hardly be controlled in their eagerness to enter the city, although their leaders restrained them because they were afraid that if their men entered the town they would seize all the booty and money that Tzachas had stored there. So they said, "You have heard the Turks clearly proclaiming their allegiance to the Emperor, and you know they have surrendered to us, it would not be right therefore for you to go in and slaughter them mercilessly." When day was almost over and night was at hand the Turks built up another wall in place of the one destroyed, and on its outer side they suspended from it mattresses, hides and any handy garment, so that the impact of the missiles directed against it would be deadened by them and thus slightly diminished.

And Tzachas prepared the fleet he had with him, enlisted about 8,000 Turks and then set off on the road to Chios, while his fleet accompanied him along the coast. When he heard this, Dalassenus ordered the admirals to embark sufficient soldiers and Opus the general, and to put to sea and, if they fell in anywhere with their adversary's fleet, they were to engage them in battle. Tzachas soon left the land and embarked and directed his course straight to Chios, and about midnight Opus met him. (Now Tzachas had got a very long chain and linked all his vessels together so that neither those which wanted to turn back could get away nor those who wished to sail ahead break from their attachment.) When Opus saw this new arrangement of Tzachas' fleet, he was horror struck and did not even dare to approach it, but turned his helm about and made for Chios. But Tzachas pursued him systematically and did not slacken in rowing. When they approached Chios, Opus managed to anchor his ships first in the harbour of Chios (Dalassenus had before this gained control of it), while Tzachas sailed past this port I have mentioned and stationed his ships close under the wall of the citadel. It was the fourth day of the week. The next day he turned all his men ashore, numbered them and made a list of them.

Meanwhile Dalassenus had discovered a small town near the harbour, so levelled the first palisaded camp he had made and went down there and made a new trench of adequate width and settled his whole army in it. On the following day both armies arrayed themselves and went forth to battle. But the Roman army stood motionless, as Dalassenus had commanded them not to break the ranks. Then Tzachas egged on the larger part of his barbarian army to attack the Romans and bade a very few horsemen follo-A them up. At this the Latins took their long spears and rode out against them. But the barbarians did not aim their javelins at the Franks but at the horses and some they struck with their spears; thus they killed a great many, routed the others and drove them into their camp lines, but they in a mad rush ran out from them towards the ships. When the Romans saw the Franks in headlong flight, they were terrified and retreated a little and drew themselves up close to the wall of the little town. Thus the way was left open for the barbarians to go down to the coast and capture some of our ships. Seeing this the sailors loosed the cables, pushed off quickly from the shore, cast anchor, and waited to see what would happen. Dalassenus then ordered them to sail along the coasts to the western part of the island and when they reached Bolissus, to await his coming there ; now Bolissus is a small town standing on the headland of the island. But some Scythians found their way to Tzachas and acquainted him with Dalassenus' plan. Then he in the first place sent out fifty spies to let him know at once when Dalassenus' fleet was getting ready to put to sea, and in the second he sent to Dalassenus under pretence of wishing to discuss terms of peace with him-but really, I believe, because having regard to Dalassenus' brave and adventurous spirit, he despaired of victory. The latter promised Tzachas to come to the edge of his camp on the morrow, when they could exchange views and hear whatever either had to say. The barbarians agreed to this, and so in the morning the two leaders met. Tzachas opened the conversation, addressing the other by name, and said, "I must tell you that I am the young man who many years ago overran Asia and though fighting bravely was trapped through my want of experience and captured by the famous Cabalicas Alexander. By him I was carried captive and handed over to the Emperor Nicephorus Botaniates, who at once bestowed on me the rank of 'Protonobilissimus ' and rich gifts, and I in return became his vassal. But ever since Alexius Comnenus assumed the reins of government, all my privileges have been annulled. And I have come here now in order to explain to you the reasons of my hostility. Let the Emperor be told of them and, if he wishes the enmity which has arisen to be brought to an end, then let him restore to me in full all the privileges due to me of which I have been deprived. And if you think favourably of a marriage between our children, let a form of betrothal be drawn up in writing as is customary among you and also among us barbarians. Then if all these conditions I have mentioned have been fulfilled, I will restore to the Emperor through you all the islands which I have overrun and taken from the Roman power and, after completing a truce with him, I will return to my own country." Dalassenus looked upon all this as empty talk as he knew well the crafty nature of the Turks, and therefore put off indefinitely the fulfilment of his demands, at the same time he told him plainly the opinion he entertained of him saying, "You will never hand over the islands to me, as you say, nor can I without consulting the Emperor agree to your demands upon him and upon myself. But since the Grand Duke, John, the Emperor's brother-in-law, accompanied by the whole fleet and numerous land forces, is on the point of arrival, let him hear your terms, and then, if he acts as mediator, I can assure you that your truce with the Emperor will be arranged."

This Duke John had been dispatched to Epidamnus with a strong army by the Emperor, partly to guard Dyrrachium, and partly to carry on war with the Dalmatians. For the chief called Bodinus was a great warrior and full of rascality and would not remain within his own frontiers but made daily incursions on the nearest large Dalmatian villages and annexed them to his own property. Duke John had spent eleven years at Dyrrachium and rescued many forts from the hands of Bolcanus and had also sent many Dalmatians captive to the Emperor, and at last he had engaged in a violent contest with Bodinus and captured him. Now the Emperor had found out from many things that this Duke John was exceedingly brave, skilled in warfare and never disposed to disregard even the slightest of his orders, and as he required a man of this kind to act against Tzachas, be sent for him from Dyrrachium, and dispatched him with a quantity of naval and land forces against Tzachas, after appointing him ‘ Great Duke’ of the fleet. How many battles he waged with him and how many dangers he incurred before he proved himself victor, this history will tell later on. As Dalassenus was expecting him, he shewed Tzachas in his conference with him that he wished to postpone everything till the Duke’s arrival. But Tzachas seemed to reply in the Homeric words, “It is already night ; it is well to obey the voice of night,” and he promised to send a large supply of provisions at daybreak. However it was all trickery and deceit, and Dalassenus was right in his supposition. For towards morning Tzachas went secretly to the shore of Chios, and, as there was a favourable wind,he sailed for Smyrnain order to collect more troops and then return to Chios. But Dalassenus proved himself a match for Tzachas' devices. For he embarked with his troops in the ships that were at hand, and went to Bolissus ; there he refitted the ships, prepared more siege-engines, gave his soldiers a rest and collected some more and then returned to the place whence he had started. Then he dashed into a fierce conflict with the barbarians, pulled down the walls and subjugated the town, whilst Tzachas was still dwelling in Smyrna. Afterwards as the sea was calm, he sailed with the whole fleet straight to Mitylene.

CHAPTER NINE

AFTER THUS DISPOSING OF the war with Tzachas, the Emperor heard that the Scythians were again aiming at Rusium and had pitched their camp near Polybotum, so he left Constantinople, just as he was, and took possession of Rusium. There accompanied him too the deserter Neantzes who was secretly hatching a horrible design against him, and in his escort were also Cantzus and Catranes, lovers of war and ardently devoted to the Emperor. Seeing a large detachment of the Scythians in the distance, he joined battle with them. Many of the Romans fell in the battle, and others were taken alive and put to death by the Scythians, while a goodly number reached Rusiurn in safety. But this was only a battle with the Scythian foragers. The Emperor was heartened by the arrival of the so-caued Maniacatx Latins and determined to fight in close combat on the day following with the Scythians. Since there happened to be only a short distance between the two armies, he did not venture to sound the war-trumpet as he wished to spring the battle upon the enemy. Therefore he sent for Constantine, who was in charge of the royal falcons, and ordered him to take a kettledrum in the evening and walk about in the army beating it all through the night, and tell the soldiers that they were to get ready, as with the dawn the Emperor intended without giving any signal to engage the Scythians in battle. The Scythians moved from Polybotum to a place called Hades which they occupied, and pitched their camp in it. Thus from the evening before the Emperor was making his preparations, and when day broke he distributed the troops and drawing them up in phalanxes proceeded against the enemy. But before the armies met and whilst each company was being drawn up into position, Neantzes ascended a hill close by in order to spy out the Scythian army, as he said, and bring the Emperor word of their disposition, but he did exactly the opposite. For in their own language he advised the Scythians to place their wagons in rows, and not to be at all afraid of the Emperor as he was another man as the result of his former defeat and disposed to flee because of his scarcity of troops and allies. After saying this he descended the hill to the Emperor. But a semi-barbarian who knew the Scythian language understood what Neantzes had said to the Scythians and came and reported it all to the Emperor. Neantzes was notified of this and demanded the proof ; whereupon the semi-barbarian boldly stepped forward and gave the proof. On the spot Neantzes drew his sword and cut off the man's head in the presence of the Emperor and the troops on either side. I imagine that Neantzes while wishing to exculpate himself from the suspicion of treachery, only brought more suspicion upon himself by slaying the informer. For why did he not wait for the investigation? However it seems as if in his desire to still in anticipation the tongue which would disclose his treachery, he ventured upon a most reckless deed, which was worthy of his barbaric soul, but just as suspicious as it was daring. The Emperor did not immediately proceed against the barbarian nor punish him as he deserved but he restrained himself for the moment, though boiling with rage and indignation, so as not to scare away his prey in advance and spread dismay among his men. But he cherished and dissembled his anger against Neantzes, as from this happening as well as from other signs he had already divined the man's treachery. The issue of the battle stood on a razor's edge, and for this reason the Emperor restrained his boiling wrath for a while, for he was perplexed how to act for the best in the immediate present. Shortly Neantzes approached the Emperor and dismounting from his horse, asked him for another, and the Emperor at once gave him one of the picked horses with a royal saddle-cloth. Neantzes mounted it and when the armies began to move to the encounter made a pretence of riding against the Scythians but turned the point of his spear backwards against our men, and went over to his countrymen and gave them much information about the Emperor's army. They followed his suggestion and engaged in a fierce battle with the Emperor whose army was utterly routed. On seeing the lines all broken and the men scattered in flight the Emperor was perturbed but decided not to endanger himself senselessly, and therefore turned his horse's head and rode to a stream flowing close to Rusium. Here he drew rein and with a few chiefs continued the fight as far as possible against his pursuers, making sorties against them and killing many and occasionally getting wounded himself. When George, called Pyrrhus, reached the river from another direction in his flight, the Emperor upbraided him and called him to his side. Noticing the headlong recklessness of the Scythians, and how their numbers increased hourly, for other parties kept coming to their assistance, he left George there with the rest and bade them keep up a faint resistance to them until he himself returned. Then he quickly wheeled round his horse, crossed the river and rode into Rusium; there he collected the fugitive soldiers he found, and all the natives of military age and even the peasants themselves, with their carts, and ordered them to come out with all haste and take their stand along the river-bank. This was done more quickly than one can tell and after arranging them in files he crossed the river again and rode back to George, and this in spite of suffering so from quartan fever that his teeth were chattering with cold. The whole Scythian army had now been gathered together, but when they saw the twofold army and the Emperor's great exertions, and remembered his love of danger and his unwavering spirit in victory or defeat, they felt they could not sustain his attack and consequently remained quiet and did not hazard an engagement with him. The Emperor, partly because he was distressed by his chill and partly because the scattered soldiery had not yet all returned, also stood still, only passing along the lines sometimes, riding at a slow pace and shewing them a bold front. Thus it came about that both arrnies remained stationary till the evening, and then when night fell, both returned to their own camps without having struck a blow. For they were afraid and not bold enough to fight. Gradually the men who had fled here, there and everywhere in the first battle re-assembled at Rusium, and the majority of them had not taken the slightest part in the battle. Further, Monastras, Uzas and Synesius who were brave followers of Ares, also arrived at Rusium, disabled too, after having traversed the district then called Asprum.

CHAPTER TEN

BUT THE EMPEROR, who was ill with a chill, as I have said, was obliged to retire to bed for a few days to recover. But even so he could not rest for thinking about what he ought to do on the morrow. As he was meditating on these things, Tatranes came to him. He was a Scythian who had frequently deserted to the Emperor and then gone back to his own people, each time he had been forgiven by the Emperor and in consequence of this forbearance he now bore a deep affection towards him and for the rest of his life he planned and worked for the Emperor with all his heart and soul. He came and said, "O Emperor, I have a presentiment that to-morrow the Scythians will surround the town and then commence a battle with us. You should therefore anticipate them and draw up your lines outside the walls at daybreak." The Emperor thanked him, took his advice and arranged to carry out this plan at sunrise. After giving this advice Tatranes went away and spoke as follows to the Scythian leaders, "Do not be puffed up with pride, because you have recently defeated the

Emperor, and when you begin a battle with us do not raise your hopes too high because our numbers are small. For the Emperor's might is invincible and a large mercenary army is expected at any minute. If you will not accept peace with him, the vultures will eat your corpses." This is what Tatranes; said to the Scythians. Now the Emperor was planning the capture of the numerous horses of the Scythians which were grazing in the plain, for the Scythians continued ravaging our territory both by day and by night, so he surnmoned Monastras, and Uzas and enjoined them to take some picked horsemen skirt round the rear of the Scythians and at dawn enter & plain and carry off all the horses and other cattle together with their herdsmen, and he exhorted them to be without fear. "For," said he, "as we shall be fighting the enemy in front, you will easily execute your task." And he was not disappointed, for his words soon became facts. As he was expecting the Scythians to attack he did not sleep at all nor even doze a little, but the whole night long he kept calling for soldiers, especially those who were proficient archers, and told them a great deal about the Scythians, thus stirring them up to battle, as it were, and giving them useful hints for the battle which he expected on the morrow, for instance, how to stretch the bow and direct their darts, also when to hold their horses back and when to let them go, and when to dismount even if necessary. This was his work in the night ; after which he slept for a short time. As day dawned, all the Scythians crossed the river and seemed eager to begin a battle, and thus the Emperor's conjecture was proved correct (he was wonderful in foreseeing what would happen, for from his almost daily battles he had gained wide experience); he at once mounted his horse, ordered the attack to be sounded, drew up his lines and himself took his stand before them. When he noticed that the Scythians were coming to the attack more recklessly than of late, he ordered the skilled archers to dismount and proceed on foot and to keep their bows bent continuously, the rest of the troops followed them and the Emperor held the centre of the army. The archers made a bold attack on the Scythians who, when the battle was well under way, became frightened either by the thick clouds of darts or by the sight of the close ranks of our army and the Emperor's spirited fighting ; and they turned back, anxious to cross the river in their flight to their wagons. But the Romans pursued them at full speed, some hit them in the back with their spears, while others hurled javelins. Many indeed were slain before they reached the edge of the river, still more, fleeing with all speed, fell into the torrent and were carried away and drowned. The ones who fought most bravely of all that day were the Emperor's household retainers, for they were all in the prime of life. As for the Emperor he was clearly the champion of the day, and being proclaimed victor be returned to his camp.

CHAPTER ELEVEN

AFTER TAKING THREE DAYS' rest there he moved on to Tzouroulus. He contemplated remaining there for some time, and therefore had an entrenched camp made on the eastern side of the town large enough for the troops he had with him and stored the imperial tent and all the baggage inside it. Then the Scythians in their turn advanced on Tzouroulus, but on hearing that the Emperor had already taken possession of the town, they crossed the river running through the plain somewhere near this town (the local name of which is Xerogypsos) and fixed their palisades between the river and the town. So they were outside and encircled this town, and the Emperor was cut off inside as if besieged. When night descended, 'all the gods; and warriors with horsehair plumes slept,' as Homer's muse says, 'but balmy sleep did not visit' Alexius; the whole night long he lay awake, revolving schemes for overcoming the Scythians' daring by craft. Seeing that Tzouroulus was a fortified town situated on a fairly steep hill and that the entire barbarian army was bivouacking down below in the plain, and that his forces were insufficient to allow of his attempting a pitched battle against their overwhelming numbers, he devised a most ingenious plan. He requisitioned the inhabitants' wagons and lifted off the bodies from the wheels and axle-trees, and then suspended the latter, for he had them hung out in order from the battlements on the outside of the walls and tied by ropes to the parapets. He no sooner thought of this than it was done. And within an hour there was a circle of wheels with their axle-trees hanging up, a regular row of than utter destruction), so he judged it wise to conciliate them; for it was he himself who had previously sent for them. Amongst a crowd of other captains in the Coman army, Togortac, Maniac and a few very valiant men stood out preeminent. The Emperor was afraid when he saw the multitude of approaching Comans, for knowing of old their easily-led nature, he feared that his one-time allies might become his foes and enemies, and inflict grievous harm on him. He thought it would be safer to take away the whole army and recross the river, but before doing so he determined to invite the chiefs of the Comans to a conference. They straightway came to him, Maniac himself too, though later than the others as at first he demurred. So Alexius ordered the cooks to spread a gorgeous banquet for them. When they had dined well he received them very graciously and presented them with various gifts, and then, as he was suspicious of their treacherous character, he asked them circles touching each other and fastened to one another by their axles. In the morning he armed himself and got the army ready and led out his soldiers from the gates and placed them in full view of the enemy. Now it happened that our troops were placed just on that side of the wall where the wheels were hanging, and the opposing army was straight opposite them. Then Alexius stood in the middle of the army and explained to the soldiers that, when the trumpet sounded the attack, they were to dismount and march forward slowly against the foe and by using mostly their arrows and javelins to provoke the Scythians to the attack; and as soon as they saw them drawn on and urging on their horses to the attack, they were to turn hastily and in fleeing wheel off a little to the right and left and thus open to the enemy a clear path for coming close up to the walls. And he had given orders to the men on the walls that when they saw the ranks dividing, they were to cut the ropes with their swords and let the wheels with the axles fall headlong down from above. All this was carried out according to the Emperor's orders. The Scythian horsemen raised their barbaric shout and hurled themselves in a body upon our lines who were marching slowly towards them, the Emperor alone being on horseback. Then our men according to Alexius' plan drew back step by step and, pretending to retreat, unexpectedly split into two parts as if opening a very wide entrance for the enemy into the town. Directly the Scythians had entered this mouth, as it were, of the two parts of our army, the wheels came whirring down. Each wheel rebounded at least a cubit's length from the wall, and through their rims springing back from the wall they seemed to be ejected from catapults and came hurtling down into the midst of the Scythian cavalry with tremendous impetus. Partly owing to their descent in unison caused by their natural weight, and partly because they gained further momentum from the sloping nature of the ground, they fell upon the barbarians with terrific force and crushed them on every side, mowing down, as it were, the legs of the horses. And no matter whether the wheels hit the fore- or the hind-legs of the horses, in either case they forced the horses to sink down on the side they had received the blow and consequently to throw their riders. So the Scythians fell one after another in great numbers, and our men charged them from both sides ; the battle pressed terribly on the Scythians from all sides, some were killed by the flying arrows, others wounded by spears, and most of the rest were forced into the river by the violent impact of the wheels and there drowned. The next day when Alexius saw the Scythian survivors preparing for battle again, and noticed that his own men were full of courage, he bade them get ready. He himself donned his armour and, after arranging the order of battle, descended to the slope. There he drew up his lines face to face with the Scythians and halted in order to join battle if possible. He himself held the centre of the line. A fierce engagement ensued and much to their surprise the Romans carried off the victory and then pursued the fleeing Scythians hotly. When the Emperor saw that they were pursuing them for a long distance, he was afraid that they might suddenly fall into an ambush and then, not only would the flight of the Scythians be arrested, but those who were fleeing would unite with the ambush and inflict a severe blow on the Roman army. The Emperor therefore kept riding up to his men and urging them to draw rein and breathe their horses. In this way the two armies parted that day, the Scythians fled and the brilliant victor returned joyfully to his camp. After this decisive defeat the Scythians pitched their tents between Bulgarophygum and little Nicaea. As winter had already overtaken them the Emperor decided that he ought to return to the capital in order to give himself and the larger part of his army some rest after their heavy labours. So he divided his forces and selected the bravest of the troops to remain on guard against the enemy. Over these he placed as commanders Joannaces and Nicolas Mavrocatacalon, of whom I have often spoken in this story; he ordered them to post an adequate number of soldiers as garrison in each town, and to requisition foot-soldiers from all the country together with wagons and the oxen which drew them. For with the return of spring he hoped to renew the war with the Scythians on a larger scale and therefore he made suitable provision and preparations beforehand. When he had carefully arranged everything, he travelled home to Byzantium.

BOOK EIGHT

War with the Scyths (1091), Victory at Levunium (29 April 1091), and Plots against the Emperor

CHAPTER ONE

THE EMPEROR WAS NOW informed that the Scythians had detached a division and sent it against Choerobacchi, and that their approach was imminent. As he was a man swift to act and ever proved himself ready in sudden crises-in spite of not having had a week's rest yet in his palace nor even taken a bath, nor shaken off the dust of battle - he at once assembled the troops appointed as garrison of the city and all the recruits there were, about 500 in number, and after seeing to their equipment all through the night, he marched out at dawn. On this occasion he made his expedition against the Scythians known, and to all his connections by blood or marriage and to the men of superior fortune who had enrolled themselves in the army (it was then Friday in Septuagesima week) he sent the following orders by his messengers: "I for my part am leaving because I have heard of the Scythians' rapid movement on Choerobacchi; you others, however, must march and join us during Quinquagesima week. As I do not wish to appear severe and inconsiderate, I grant you the days from this Septuagesima Friday to the

Monday in Quinquagesima week as a short breathing-space." Thereupon the Emperor marched straight to Choerobacchi, and on entrance closed the gates, and took charge of the keys himself. Then he stationed all those of his servants who were loyal on the battlements of the wall with strict injunctions not to lie down, but to keep a tireless watch all round the walls to prevent anybody's coming up there, stooping down and leaning over to communicate with the Scythians. At sunrise the Scythians, as expected, occupied and took up their stand on the ridge adjacent to the wall of Choerobacchi. About six thousand of them were afterwards set apart and dispersed for foraging and went as far as Decatum itself which is only some ten stades distant from the Queen of Cities ; it is from this fact, I imagine, that it got its name. The rest of the Scythians had remained where they were. The Emperor mounted by the wall to the parapets and carefully inspected the plains and hills to see whether perchance a second force was coming to join the Scythians, or whether they were meditating the planting of ambuscades to impede anyone who might possibly have the intention of attacking them. However, he noticed nothing of the kind but saw at the second hour of the day that they were not prepared for battle but had turned their attention to food and rest. He did not dare to engage them in a pitched battle, considering the large number they were, but was indignant at the thought that they might ravage the whole district and actually approach the very walls of the Queen of Cities, and that too when he had quitted the city for the purpose of driving them out of the county. Consequently he assembled the soldiers and wishing to test their feelings, said, “We must not let our courage flag by contemplating the number of Scythians, but put our trust in God and go to battle with them, and if only we are all of one mind, I am convinced we shall beat them utterly." But they all refused absolutely and dissented from his proposal. Then he aroused greater fear in them and awoke them to a sense of danger by saying: "If the foraging party returns and rejoins those who are here, our peril is clear and manifest. For they will either rush this fort and we shall be massacred, or maybe they will hold us of no account and march up to the walls of the capital and prevent us from re-entering the Queen-City by bivouacking before its gates. Consequently it behoves us to take the risk and not die like cowards. So I shall go out at once and whoever likes can follow me for I will lead the way and dash into the midst of the Scythians. As for you who cannot, or will not, do this, do not venture even outside the gates." With these words he immediately put on his armour and sallied out by the gate opposite the marsh. After skirting the walls and turning aside a little, he mounted the ridge from the back. For he had realized that his men would not follow him into a regular engagement with the Scythians. He was the first to seize a spear and push his way into the middle of the Scythians, and then he struck down the first man he encountered. And the soldiers, too, who were with him shewed themselves no less keen fighters, and the result was that the greater number of Scythians were killed and the rest taken prisoners. Then with his usual cunning he clothed his soldiers in the Scythians' garments and bade them mount the Scythian horses, whilst he entrusted their own horses and standards, and the heads of the Scythians that had been cut off to a few of the most reliable men and ordered them to get back inside the fort and await him. When he had completed these arrangements he marched down with the Scythian standards and his soldiers clad in the Scythians' dress to the river flowing past Choerobacchi, where he judged that the Scythians would pass on their return from foraging. And the foragers seeing the men standing there, and thinking they too were Scythians, lighted upon them unguardedly and were cut to pieces or taken prisoners.

CHAPTER TWO

WHEN EVENING HAD FALLEN (it was a Saturday) he returned with his captives (to Choerobacchi) and spent the next day quietly there. At daybreak on Monday he left the fort and divided his men into two parties, in front he placed the men carrying the standards of the Scythians, and behind them the Scythian captives each led by a countryman; the heads which had been cut off he had stuck on spears and carried aloft by yet other countrymen, and in this order he bade them journey. At a moderate distance behind these he followed with his soldiers and the usual Roman standards. Now Palaeologus, who was ardent in military enterprises, had started from Byzantium at dawn on Sexagesima Sunday before the others. As he was aware of the Scythians' rapidity in movement, he was not free from anxiety on his journey, so picked out a few of his accompanying retainers and ordered them to run some distance ahead and inspect the plains, valley and roads, all round, and in case any Scythians were to be seen, to return quickly and report to him. In this order then they travelled; when the scouts saw in the plain called Dimylia the men dressed in Scythian clothing, and the Scythian standards, they ran back and reported that the Scythians were close at hand. Whereupon he immediately stood to arms. On the heels of the first messenger came a second who affirmed that, at a good distance behind those who looked like Scythians, the Roman standards and soldiers advancing at a double could be seen. These newsbringers guessed a part of the truth indeed, but were also partly wrong. For the army marching in the rear was certainly Roman both in appearance and in reality and the Emperor was in command of it ; but the one in front equipped in Scythian fashion were all members of the Roman army, but dressed in Scythian garments. In the first place, the men dressed up in the way they were by the Emperor's command, managed as apparent Scythians utterly to deceive the real Scythians, as I have already described ; and in the second place, the Emperor made use of this Scythian get-up to cheat and trick our own men, in order that whoever met these our own soldiers first should be horror-struck, and think they had fallen into the hands of Scythians. This would be a soldier's joke quite free from danger, yet with a spice of fear in it; for before they were seriously alarmed, they would be reassured by seeing the Emperor behind. In this way the Emperor harmlessly scared those they met. All the men with Palaeologus were overcome with fear at what they saw, but he himself of far greater experience than they all, and knowing too how fertile in devices Alexius was, immediately understood that this was such a device, and therefore regained confidence himself, and urged the others to do so.

By this time, the whole crowd of his kinsmen and connections was rushing out from the capital, for they were hurrying, as they thought, to overtake the Emperor according to their agreement with him. For, as mentioned above, they agreed to meet him after Sexagesima Sunday in Quinquagesima week. However they did not succeed in leaving the city before the Emperor re-entered it in triumph. When they met him on arrival they would not have believed that the Emperor alone had gained trophies and achieved a victory so quickly, had they not seen the heads of the Scythians fixed on the spear-heads and many others, who had escaped the sword, with their hands bound behind their backs, being dragged and pushed along, one after the other, as prisoners. People were amazed at the swiftness of the campaign; but I heard a little tale about George Palaeologus (told me by some who were present), which was, that he complained bitterly and blamed himself for having been too late for the battle and not having been with the Emperor who had reaped so much glory by his unexpected victory over the barbarians. For he would have dearly liked to have had a share in that meed of fame. But with regard to the Emperor one could say that the words of the song in Deuteronomy were then visibly accomplished, namely, 'How should one chase a thousand and two put ten thousand to flight?' For at that juncture the Emperor faced the overwhelming mass of barbarians practically single-handed, and carried through that whole weighty war successfully right up to victory. And were one to enquire 'Who or what were his companions?' and then compare the Emperor's stratagems and his versatility, combined with his valour and daring with the barbarians' numbers and strength, he would only discover that the Emperor had achieved the victory alone.

CHAPTER THREE

IN SUCH MANNER DID God on that occasion grant the ruler an astounding victory. When the Byzantines saw him enter the city, they shouted with joy for they were astonished at the swiftness, the boldness and the cleverness of the undertaking and the immediate victory, they sang paeans, they leapt, and praised God for having given them such a saviour and benefactor. But Melissenus Nicephorus was annoyed at this and took it ill-such is human nature- and said, "This victory is a fruitless joy to us and a harmless grief to them." And indeed the Scythians, who were innumerable and dispersed all over the West, continued to ravage all the provinces and none of the disasters that had befallen them checked their unbridled audacity in the slightest. Now and again they would even seize small towns in the West, nor did they spare the villages in the neighbourhood of the Queen of Cities, for they even advanced to the one called Bathys Rhyax where stands the sanctuary sacred to the memory of Theodore, greatest of all martyrs. Every day a good many people used to go there to make intercession to the saint, and on Sundays the pious journeyed to the shrine in crowds and spent all day and night there lodging round it, or in the porch, or in the back chamber of the church. But the onward rush of the Scythians prevailed to such an extent that the people who wanted to go to the martyr's church did not even dare to open the gates of Byzantium because of the Scythians' frequent incursions. These indeed were the troubles which beset the Emperor on land in the West, and even at sea matters were far from calm for him, but on the contrary very disturbed as Tzachas had acquired another fleet and was sacking the coast towns. For these reasons, the Emperor was harassed and distressed, for he was beset by troubles on every side. And then news was brought to him that Tzachas had now collected a larger fleet from the maritime districts, and devastated the islands he had previously captured, and that he had further begun to consider an attack on the western provinces, and was sending envoys to the Scythians advising them to seize the Chersonese. The mercenary troops which had come to the Emperor's aid from the East, I mean the Turks, not even these did Tzachas allow to keep their treaty with the Emperor unbroken, but coaxed them with specious promises to desert the Emperor, and come over to him, as soon as he had seized the barley-crop. The Emperor heard this and felt that his affairs on land and sea were in a very parlous condition. And an exceptionally severe winter was blocking up all the roads to such a degree that even the doors of houses could not be opened, because of the weight of snow lying against them (it happened that there had been a very heavy fall, heavier than anyone had ever seen before). Under these circumstances the Emperor did what he could by letters to collect a mercenary army from all sides. But when the sun had reached the spring solstice and the threatening war from the clouds had ceased, and the wrath of the sea was abated, he decided, as his enemies were pressing him hard on either side, that the best course would be to go down to the coast; there he could easily resist his seafaring enemies, and at the same time conveniently fight against those who approached over land.

He immediately sent off the Caesar Melissenus Nicephorus with orders to occupy Enus with all possible despatch. He had previously signified to him by letters to enlist as many soldiers as possible, but not from the veterans (for those had already been distributed throughout the towns in the West to act as garrisons in the more important strongholds). He was partly to levy recruits from the Bulgarians and from the nomadic tribes (called Vlachs in popular parlance) and for the rest whatever horse- or foot-soldiers offered themselves from any country. He himself summoned from Nicomedia the five hundred Franks whom the Count of Flanders had sent, and leaving Byzantium with his kinsmen quickly reached Aenus. There he entered into a coracle, and was rowed past the town whilst he investigated the general lie of the river and its bed on either side and, when he had decided where it would be best to encamp his army, he returned. During the night he assembled the officers and explained to them the nature of the river and of the land on either side and said, "It would be well for you to cross to-morrow and carefully inspect the whole plain. And perhaps you will think the place which I will point out to you not unsuitable for pitching our camp." As they all agreed to this he was the first to cross the river at dawn, and then the whole army followed him. Then he inspected the banks of the river again with the officers, and also the surrounding plain, and shewed them the spot which pleased him. It was quite close to a small town, locally called Choereni, whose one side was flanked by the river, and the other by a swamp. Since the unanimous verdict of the soldiers was that this place was sufficiently protected, a trench was quickly dug and the whole army installed there. The Emperor returned to Aenus with a goodly body of light-armed troops, in order to repel the attacks of the Scythians who were advancing from that quarter.

CHAPTER FOUR

WHEN THE TROOPS ENTRENCHED at Choereni learnt of the advances of incredibly large Scythian armies, they sent word of this to the Emperor who was still at Aenus. He at once embarked in a coracle and sailing along the coast, entered the river at its mouth and effected a junction with his entire army, As he saw that his own forces were infinitely smaller than the Scythians he fell into great perplexity and fear, for as far as man could see, he had no one to help him. Yet he did not give way or shew weakness but was lost in a welter of reflections. Four days later he saw far off in quite a different direction an army of the Comans approaching, about forty thousand strong. Accordingly he reflected that if these made common cause with the Scythians, they would begin a terrible war against him (from which no other result could be expected

to give him an oath and hostages. They fulfilled his demands readily, and requested to be allowed to fight with the Patzinaks for three days; and if God should give them the victory they promised to divide all the booty that accrued to them into two parts and assign one half to the Emperor. He granted them permission to-pursue the Scythians, not only for three days, but for ten whole days in whatever way they liked, and gave them permission to keep the whole of the booty they took from them, if within that time God granted them the victory. However the Scythians and the Coman armies remained where they were for some time, while the Comans harassed the Scythian army by skirmishing. Before the expiration of three days Alexius summoned Antiochus (he was one of the nobles who surpassed most in energy), and ordered him to build a bridge. The bridge was quickly constructed by binding boats together with very long planks, then he called for the Protostrator

Michael Ducas, his brother-in-law, and the Great Domestic Adrian, his brother, and commanded them to stand at the river's edge, and not allow the infantry and cavalry to cross all together in a confused mass, but first to separate the infantry from the cavalry, and also the baggage waggon and the sumpter mules. When the infantry had crossed, through fear of the Scythian and Coman troops and their sly attacks, he had trenches drawn with all speed and lodged all the infantry within them; afterwards he ordered the horsemen to cross too, and he stood on the river's brink and watched them cross. Meanwhile Melissenus, acting on the written instructions he had previously received from the Emperor, collected forces from all sides; he had also requisitioned foot-soldiers from the neighbourhood and when these had loaded their own baggage and the necessary commisariat on ox-drawn wagons, he sent them off with all speed to the Emperor. When they had come within range of the human eye, the majority of those who saw them thought they were a detachment of Scythians advancing against the Emperor. One man even had the audacity to point them out with his finger to the Emperor, and insisted that they were Scythians. The latter believed what he said was true and was greatly dismayed as he could not prevail against so many. So in this difficulty he sent for Rodomerus (he was a noble of Bulgarian descent and related to the Empress, our mother, on his mother's side), and bade him go and spy out these newcomers. He quickly accomplished the Emperor's bidding, and returning told him they were men sent by Melissenus. Hereat the Emperor was overjoyed, and when they arrived shortly afterwards, he crossed the river with them, had the newly made camp slightly enlarged and then united these men to the rest of the army. The Comans at once took possession of the camp from which the Emperor had moved to cross the river with his whole army, and took up their position near there. On the following day the Emperor moved again intending to seize the ford lower down the river locally called Philocalus; but as he met a large body of Scythians he promptly attacked them, and a vigorous engagement ensued. Many were killed on either side during the fight, yet the Emperor gained the victory, and thoroughly worsted the Scythians. After the battle was concluded in this way, and the armies had retired to their respective encampments, the Roman army remained near the spot for the whole of the night. At sunrise on the morrow they moved on and occupied a place called Lebunium, which is a hill dominating a plain; up this hill the Emperor marched. But as there was not sufficient room on the hill itself for the whole of the army, he had a trench made at its foot and a camp, capable of containing the entire army, and lodged them there. At this moment the deserter Neantzes with a few

Scythians approached the Emperor again; when the Emperor saw him he reproached him with his former ingratitude and several other misdeeds, and had him and his companions arrested and cast into irons.

CHAPTER FIVE

SO MUCH THEN FOR the Emperor's doings. The Scythians, on their side, kept still in their position on the banks of the stream called 'Mavropotamos' and made secret overtures to the Comans, inviting their alliance; they likewise did not cease sending envoys to the Emperor to treat about peace. The latter had a fair idea of their double-dealings so gave them appropriate answers, as he wished to keep them in suspense until the arrival of the mercenary army which he expected from Rome. And as the Comans only received dubious promises from the Patzinaks, they did not at all go over to them, but sent the following communication to the Emperor in the evening: “For how long are we to postpone the battle? know therefore that we shall not wait any longer, but at sunrise we shall eat the flesh either of wolf or of lamb.” On hearing this the Emperor realized the keen spirit of the Comans, and was no longer for delaying the fight. He felt that the next day would be the solemn crisis of the war, and therefore promised the Comans to do battle with the Scythians on the morrow, and then he straightway summoned the generals and ‘ pentecontarchs ‘ and other officers and bade them proclaim throughout the whole camp that the battle was reserved for the morrow. But in spite of all these preparations, he still dreaded the countless hosts of Patzinaks and Comans, fearing the two armies might coalesce.

Whilst the Emperor was busy with these reflections, a band of hardy and war-loving mountaineers, numbering about 5,000 in all, deserted to the Emperor and offered him their services. Since the moment of battle could now no longer be postponed, the Emperor invoked the aid of God. At sunset he led the intercessory prayers for help to God, and conducted a brilliant torch-light procession, and sang appropriate hymns. Nor did he allow the army to sleep in peace, for he suggested to the more intelligent individuals that they should follow his example whereas he imposed it as an order upon the more clownish. And thus at that hour you could have seen the sun setting on the horizon, but the whole sky lit up, not as it were with the light of one sun, but as if ever so many more heavenly bodies were contributing their light. For one and all fixed lighted lamps or wax candles, whichever they had, to the tips of their spears. And verily the cries which were sent up by this army must have reached the orb of heaven, I think, or to speak quite truly, they were carried to the ears of our

Lord God Himself. From this circumstance, I fancy, one can deduce the Emperor's piety seeing that he thought it wrong to attack an enemy without asking God's help. For he did not place his confidence in men or horses, or military engines, but entrusted all to the Divine decision. These intercessions were continued till midnight; after which he allowed himself a little bodily rest and then leapt up from sleep. The light-troops he armed more strongly than usual, and some of them he supplied with cuirasses and helmets of silken material of an iron-colour, as he had not a sufficient supply of iron for all. At the first smile of dawn he same out of the gully in heavy armour, and bade them sound the attack. And beneath the hill called Lebunium (this place is . . .) he split up the army and drew up the infantry in troops. The Emperor himself stood in the fore-front breathing fierce wrath, whilst the right and left wings were commanded by George Palaeologus and Constantine

Dalassenus respectively. On the extreme right of the Comans stood Monastras with his men under arms. For directly they saw the Emperor drawing up his lines they too armed themselves and arranged their line of battle in their own fashion; to the left of them stood Uzas, and looking towards the west was Hubertopulos with the Franks. When the Emperor had thus fortified the army, so to speak, with the heavy-armed troops and encircled it with squadrons of horse, he ordered the trumpets to sound the attack again. The Romans in their dread of the countless Scythians and their horrible covered wagons which they used as walls, sent up one cry for mercy to the Lord of All and then, letting their steeds go, dashed at full speed into battle with the Scythians, the Emperor galloping in front of them all. The Roman line was crescent-shaped and at the same instant as if at a signal the whole army of the Comans rushed forward too, so a distinguished chieftain of the Scythians, foreseeing the issue of events, secured his safety in advance, and taking a few men with him went over to the Comans as they spoke the same language. For although these too were fighting fiercely against the Scythians, yet he felt more confidence in them than in the Romans, and approached them in the hope that they would act as mediators for him with the Emperor. The Emperor noticed his secession and grew alarmed lest more should go over and persuade the Comans to make common cause with the Scythians, and to turn their horses as well as their feelings against the Roman army. Consequently, as he was quick in perceiving what was expedient at a critical moment, he ordered the royal standard-bearer to carry the standard and post himself close to the Coman camp. By this time the Scythian array had been completely broken, and the two armies met in hand to hand fight, and then such slaughter of men was seen as nobody had ever witnessed before. For the

Scythians were being terribly massacred as if abandoned by the Divine Power, and their opponents who cut them down grew weary of the incessant, heavy mowing with their swords, and were growing faint and relaxing the pursuit. Then the Emperor rode right in among the foe, and confounded all the ranks striking down those who stood in his way, and even overaweing those further off by his shouting. When he saw that the sun was casting its rays vertically as it was about noon, he provided for his troops as follows. He sent for some men, and dispatched them to tell the countrymen to fill their waterskins with water, lade them on their own mules and drive them along to him. When neighbours and friends saw the countrymen doing this they, too, without receiving orders, did the same, and one with a pitcher, another with a skin, and another with whatever vessel he could lay hands on, brought water to refresh the soldiers who were delivering them from the dread hand of the Scythians; and the soldiers after drinking a little water resumed the battle. That day a new spectacle was seen, for a whole nation, not of ten thousand men only, but surpassing all number together with their wives and children was completely wiped out. It was the third day of the week, the twenty-ninth of April; hence the Byzantines made a little burlesque song, "just by one day the Scythians missed seeing the month of May." By the time that the sun was creeping to the West, and practically all the Scythians had fallen to the sword, and I repeat the children and the women too, and many also had been taken alive, the Emperor bade them sound the recall, and returned to his camp.

These doings might well seem a miracle, especially to a mind that reflected bow not so long ago the men who left Byzantium to fight the Scythians brought ropes and straps with which to bind the captive Scythians they meant to lead home, and then the tables were turned and they themselves became the prisoners and captives of the Scythians -this took place when we fought the Scythians near Dristra; on that occasion God broke the insolent spirit of the Romans. But later on, at the time I am now relating, when He saw them full of fear and devoid of all saving hope, as not being strong enough to prevail against such multitudes, He unexpectedly granted them victory, so that they bound and slew and captured the Scythians, and not only this (for such things often happen even in minor battles) but in one single day they wiped off the face of the earth a whole nation of myriads of men.

CHAPTER SIX

AFTER THE COMAN AND Roman troops had returned to their respective quarters, and in the early evening the Emperor was thinking of supper, the man called Synesius came in very angry and said to the Emperor : "What is this nonsense ? and what is this new arrangement ? Each soldier has thirty or more Scythian prisoners. The Comans in their masses axe quite close to us. Now if our soldiers fall asleep as most certainly they should do, dog-tired as they are, and the Scythians set each other free, take their daggers and kill them, what then? So give orders for most of them to be put to death at once!" But the Emperor gave him a severe look and replied, "Even though Scythians, yet they are men; and even though our foes, yet worthy of pity. And I really do not know what you are thinking about to talk such nonsense." On the other's insisting he dismissed him angrily. Then he had a proclamation made to the army that all arms should be taken from the Scythians and deposited in one place, and that the soldiers should carefully guard their prisoners. After issuing these orders, he spent the rest of the night free from anxiety.

But during the middle watch of the night, either by Divine guidance, or for some other unknown reason, certain it is that as if by one accord the soldiers killed nearly all of them. When the Emperor was told this in the early morning he at once suspected Synesius, and therefore had him called directly. After blaming him severely, he threatened him saying, "This is your work." In spite of the other's protestations that he knew nothing about it, he ordered him to be arrested and kept in chains, saying, "Thus you will learn what an evil mere chains are, and not to make decisions of this kind against men again." Perhaps he would have had him scourged too, had not the highest noblemen, the relations and connections of the Emperor, united in appealing to him on behalf of Synesius.

Most of the Comans were afraid that the Emperor was meditating some dreadful stroke against them by night, because they had taken all the booty, so they went away by night, taking the road leading to the Danube. To escape from the stench of the corpses, the Emperor marched away from his camp at daybreak, and reached another called 'Kala Dendra' about eighteen stades distant from Chcereni. On the march thither Melissenus met him. He had been unable to come in time for the battle, as he had been busy preparing that crowd of recruits to send to the Emperor. They naturally embraced and congratulated each other, and for the rest of the journey spoke about the events connected with the defeat of the Scythians. On arrival at Kala Dendra, the Emperor heard of the Comans' flight: thereupon he had all the goods which he had assigned to them according to their agreement loaded on mules, and sent them off after them, bidding the drivers make all speed to overtake them even beyond the Danube, if they could, and hand over to them what he sent. For throughout his life he considered it a sin not only to tell a falsehood, but even to appear to have done so, and he frequently would discourse at length to all about falseness. This is sufficient about the fugitives; as for all the other Comans who followed him, he saw to it that they feasted royally for the rest of the day. He judged it wiser not to give these soldiers the reward due to them on that day, but to let them first sleep off the effects of the wine they had drunk, so that when they had regained their clarity of mind, they would appreciate the gift. On the following day he assembled them all and gave them not only as much as he had promised beforehand, but a great deal more. Now when he wanted to dismiss them to their homes he reflected that they might wander about and turn to plundering on their way and inflict no little harm on the country-towns along the road, so he took hostages from them. They in their turn requested him to give them safe conduct, so he gave them Joannaces (a man of exceptional bravery and prudence) and entrusted him with the care and safe conveyance of the Comans as far as the Zygum.

Thus the Emperor's affairs prospered, thanks entirely to Divine providence. After he had fully settled everything he returned to Byzantium as a ' conquering hero ' in the course of the month of May.

I must now conclude my narrative of the Scythian wars although I have only related a few incidents out of a great number, and have only touched the Adriatic sea with the tip of my finger. But as for the Emperor's brilliant victories, the various defeats he inflicted on his enemies, his individual acts of bravery, the intervening events, and how he adapted himself to all circumstances, and by divers expedients resolved the difficulties that befell him-to relate all this explicitly not even a second Demosthenes would have had the power, nor the whole band of orators, nor even the whole Academy if it combined with the Stoa to celebrate the exploits of Alexius as a subject of prime importance.

CHAPTER SEVEN

ONLY A FEW DAYS had elapsed since the Emperor's return to the palace when Ariebes the Armenian and the Frank Hubertopoulos (two noblemen and devotees of Mars) were detected in a plot against the Emperor, in which they had involved a fair number of others. Witnesses came forward and the truth was openly stated. When the conspirators stood condemned, they were punished by confiscation of their property and banishment, as the Emperor remitted the penalty of death, which was prescribed by law.

The Emperor now heard a rumour of an invasion by the Comans, and learnt from another quarter that Bodinus and his Dalmatians had broken the truce and were contemplating an incursion into our territory;

he was divided in mind as to which adversary he should turn his attention first. He decided to proceed against the Dalmatians first, and to anticipate them in occupying, and, as far as practicable, in protecting the valleys lying between their confines and our own. Accordingly he convoked his council and imparted his ideas to them, and as they all approved he left the capital for the purpose of taking charge of affairs in the West. He soon reached Philippopolis where letters were handed to him from the archbishop of Bulgaria, who wrote about the Duke of Dyrrachium, John, the Sebastocrator's son, as he felt convinced the latter was hatching rebellion. For a whole day and night the Emperor was sunk in despondency, at one minute wanting to adjourn the investigation of the matter because of John's father, at another fearing lest report spoke true and that, as John was still a stripling, and at an age when he knew impulses are uncontrolled, he might start a rebellion and become the source of intolerable grief both to his father and uncle. Finally, he concluded that he must in some way contrive to frustrate his design. For he was exceedingly attached to the young man. He accordingly summoned the man who was then Aeteriarch[57] Argyrus Caratzas, who, though a Scythian, combined great prudence with a love of virtue and truth, and handed him two letters. The one addressed to John was conceived in the following terms: "Our Majesty being informed of the descent of the barbarians against us through the mountain passes, has travelled hither from the city of Constantine to secure the frontiers of the Roman Empire. Hence we naturally desire your presence that we may give you instructions with regard to the realm over which you rule. (I am also somewhat suspicious of Bolcanus, for he

57 or "Heteriarch" = the captain of the foreign guild

may be hatching some treacherous scheme against us.) Further, we wish you to give us a report on the state of Dalmatia and also to certify whether Bolcanus has observed the terms of the truce (for most unsatisfactory rumours about him are brought to us daily). We shall be better able to resist his machinations after we have received reliable information from you; then we intend to send you to Illyria after giving you the necessary directions in order that by attacking the enemy on both sides we may, with God's help, gain the victory." This was the tenor of his letter to John. The other addressed to the leading men in Dyrrachium, ran as follows : "As we were informed that Bolcanus was once again meditating treachery against us, we have issued from Byzantium partly to ensure the safety of the valleys, which lie in the debatable land between our country and the Dalmatians, and partly too to sift this matter of Bolcanus and the Dalmatians to the bottom. For this purpose we deemed it wise to summon hither your Duke, Our Majesty's dearly beloved nephew, and in his place we send the man who will hand you this letter, and whom we have created Duke. Therefore do ye receive him and yield him obedience in whatsoever he may command." When he handed these letter to Caratzas he enjoined him to deliver the one to John first. Then if John willingly obeyed the orders in it, be should send him forth in peace, and undertake the government of the district himself until such time as John returned. But if John proved recalcitrant or refused to obey, he was to assemble the leading men of Dyrrachium and read them the second letter with the object of gaining their help in arresting John.

CHAPTER EIGHT

DIRECTLY THE SEBASTOCRATOR WHO was in Constantinople got ear of this, he started off in great haste and reached Philippopolis in two days and nights. The Emperor was asleep so he crept noiselessly into the imperial tent and signifying with his hand to the attendants to keep quiet, he lay down on the second bed in his brother's tent, and fell asleep himself. When the Emperor woke up and quite unexpectedly beheld his brother, he kept quiet for some time and bade the persons present do the same. When in his turn the Sebastocrator awoke and saw his brother, the Emperor, awake, and the latter saw him, they arose and embraced each other. Afterwards the Emperor began to enquire what had brought him and why in the world he had come. To this the other replied, "For your sake," and the Emperor retorted, "You have tired yourself in vain by journeying such a distance so quickly." To this the Sebastocrator did not reply at the time, for he was lost in conjectures about the news which would be brought him by the messenger he had sent on ahead to

Dyrrachium. For the instant the rumours about his son had come to his ears, he scribbled two words to him, and ordered him to resort to the Emperor with all speed. He told him too that he himself was leaving Byzantium and hurrying to Philippopolis for the express purpose of confuting the statements made to the Emperor about him by putting before his brother, the Emperor, all likely considerations ; and concluded by saying he would await his arrival there. The Sebastocrator took leave of the Emperor and went to the tent assigned to him. And almost immediately the letter-carrier he had sent to John came running in saying he had returned and John was on the way. By this news the Sebastocrator was relieved of his suspicions and regained his former confidence, but was filled with anger against the persons who had been the first to denounce his son. Thus disturbed in mind he went to the Emperor and the latter looked at him and at once guessed the reason of his disturbance, yet asked him how he felt. And his brother answered, “Badly, and that because of you.” For he had not learnt entirely to control his anger when it howled around his heart, and was easily upset sometimes by a mere word. And he added a further remark saying, “I am not so much incensed against your Majesty as against this man” (pointing to Adrian) “who spreads calumnies.” To these words that gentle, sweet-tempered Emperor made no answer at all, for he knew how to assuage his brother’s boiling rage.

So they both sat down together with the Caesar Melissenus Nicephorus and a few more of their relations and talked privately to one another concerning the rumours current about John. But when the Sebastocrator observed that Melissenus and his own brother Adrian were indirectly calumniating his son, he was unable to restrain his wrath which was bubbling up again, and darting a fierce look at Adrian he threatened to pull off his beard and to teach him not to try to rob the Emperor of his relations by openly telling lies about them.

Upon this John arrived and was immediately conducted into the imperial tent and heard all the accusations made against him. However, he was not exactly subjected to a cross-examination, but the defendant stood at liberty while the Emperor said to him, “Out of consideration for your father who is also my brother, I cannot bear even to hear mentioned the accusations levelled against you. So go and be free from care as you were before.” All this was said inside the imperial tent, with no stranger present, only a few relations. Thus the whole affair which had either been falsely reported or perhaps really planned was hushed up. The Emperor then summoned his own brother, I mean the Sebastocrator Isaac, and his son John, and after a long conversation with them, concluded by saying to the Sebastocrator, "You go back in peace to the capital to give our mother all the news. As for him," he said, pointing to John, "I am sending him back again to Dyrrachium, as you see, to give his careful attention to the administration of his province." In this manner they parted, and the next day the one took the road to Byzantium and the other was sent to Dyrrachium.

CHAPTER NINE

UP TO THIS TIME the imperial throne was by no means safe. When Theodore Gabras was living in Constantinople, the Emperor who had remarked his violent and energetic nature, wished to remove him from the city and therefore appointed him Duke of

Trapezus[58], a town he had some time ago recaptured from the Turks. This man had come originally from Chaldaea and the upper parts, and gained glory as a soldier, for he surpassed others in wisdom and courage, and had practically never failed in any work he took in hand, but invariably got the better of his enemies; and finally after he had captured Trapezus and allotted it to himself, as if it were his special portion, he was irresistible. This man's son, Gregory, the Sebastocrator, Isaac Comnenus, affianced to one of his daughters, but as both the children were under marriageable age, matters only proceeded as far as a betrothal. After handing over his son Gregory to the Sebastocrator on condition that, when the children reached the legal age, the marriage should be celebrated, Gabras took leave of the Emperor and returned to his own country. Shortly afterwards his wife

58 Trebizond

paid the debt we all must pay, and he took to himself a second wife, a highborn woman of the Alani. Now it happened that the Sebastocrator's wife and the wife Gabras married, were the daughters of two sisters; when this became known, the betrothal of the two children was broken off as their marriage was forbidden both by the civil and the ecclesiastical laws. The Emperor, however, who knew the kind of soldier Gabras was, and the amount of disturbance he would be capable of creating, did not wish Gabras' son Gregory to return to his father when the betrothal was broken off, but desired to retain him in the capital for two reasons. The one was to hold him as a sort of hostage, and the second was to win Gabras' affection; with the idea that if the latter had been meditating any evil deed, he would now abstain. He intended to marry Gregory to one of my sisters; and for this reason kept postponing the boy's departure. But Gabras came up to the capital again, and as he had no inkling of the Emperor's intentions, he was planning to take his son back with him secretly. In the meantime he kept silent about his plans, although the Emperor did hint at and indirectly signify to him what he had in mind. But Gabras perhaps did not understand or owing to the late rupture of the other engagement he did not care; however it was, he asked the Emperor that his son should be allowed to return with him, and this demand the Emperor refused. Then Gabras pretended to be quite willing to let him stay and to leave all plans for the boy to the Emperor. After he had bidden the Emperor farewell, and was on the point of departure from Byzantium, he was hospitably entertained by the Sebastocrator close to the chapel built to the memory of the great martyr Phocas, in the very pretty suburb situated on the Propontis - this was because of their close connexion through marriage and their resultant intimacy. After a very lavish banquet there, the Sebastocrator returned to Byzantium and Gabras begged to be allowed to keep his son with him for the next day at least, and to this the other assented willingly. But when the next day came, and Gabras (whom I have mentioned so often) ought to have separated from his son, he asked the tutors to accompany him as far as Sosthenium, where he intended to pitch his camp. They agreed and went on with him; but when the time came for moving on from there he again asked the tutors the same thing, whether his son could not accompany him as far as Pharus; but they refused. Then he pleaded a father's affection, and his long absence, and by a string of similar pleas, he overcame their resolutions, and they let themselves be over-persuaded and accompanied him. When he reached Pharus, he revealed his hidden intention, for he seized the boy, embarked him on a merchant-vessel and entrusted himself and his son to the waves of the Euxine.

On receipt of this news the Emperor sent off swift ships after him with all possible expedition, and commanded the captains to hand Gabras the letters he gave them for him and to bring back the boy without loss of time with his father's consent, or if he refused, to inform him that the Emperor would thenceforth count him as an enemy. They departed and overtook Gabras beyond the town of Aeginus, near a town locally called Carambis. They handed him the Emperor's letter in which the Emperor stated that he hoped to marry the boy to one of my sisters, and after a long talk with him, they persuaded him to send his son back. On his return the Emperor only ratified the marriage-contract by the usual legal formalities and gave him into the charge of one of the Empress' attendants, the eunuch Michael, and as the lad lived in the palace he bestowed a great deal of care on him, tried to amend his manners and had him thoroughly trained in all military exercises.

But like most young men, he did not relish having to obey, and was vexed at not being treated, as he thought, with sufficient respect. In addition to this he disliked his tutor and began to consider how he could escape to his own father, when he ought rather to have been grateful for all the attention bestowed on him. He did not stop at merely meditating flight, but tried to put it into execution. Consequently he revealed his secret to a few; these were George, the son of Decanus, Eustathius Camytzes and the cupbearer Michael, generally called 'Pincema' by the imperial household. These were all warriors and among the Emperor's close intimates, one of them, Michael, went to the Emperor and acquainted him with the whole matter; but the latter could not believe it and refused to listen.

When (Gregory) Gabras began to insist and wanted to hurry on his flight, those loyal to the Emperor said "Unless you will guarantee your plot to us by an oath, we will not accompany you." As he assented to this, they showed him where the sacred "nail" was kept with which the lawless soldiers pierced my Saviour's side, and advised him to steal it and bring it out so that he could swear by Him who was pierced by it. Gabras listened to this advice, entered (the church) and secretly abstracted the sacred nail. Then one of the men who had already notified the Emperor of the conspiracy, came running in and said, "Look, here is Gabras, and the sacred nail is in his bosom." Thereupon Gabras was immediately brought in at the Emperor's bidding, and the nail was taken out of his bosom. On being questioned he admitted everything without hesitation, also revealed the names of his fellow-conspirators and the whole scheme. The Emperor found him guilty and sent him to the Duke of Philippopolis, George Mesopotamites, to keep him prisoner in the citadel. George, the son of Decanus, he dispatched with letters to Leo Nicerita who was at that time Duke of the districts round the Danube, ostensibly to help him in guarding the district, but really for Nicerita to keep him prisoner there. As for Eustathius, son of Camytzes, and the rest, he banished and imprisoned them.

CONTINUES IN VOLUME TWO

www.ingramcontent.com/pod-product-compliance
Lightning Source LLC
Chambersburg PA
CBHW020919310726
48980CB00011B/955/J

* 9 7 8 1 8 3 4 1 2 4 1 0 0 *